T0246611

RACHMANINOFF

For Michael and Pamela Hartnall

RACHMANINOFF

THE LAST OF THE GREAT ROMANTICS

MICHAEL SCOTT

The
History
Press

First published 2008
This paperback edition first published 2023

The History Press
97 St George's Place, Cheltenham,
Gloucestershire, GL50 3QB
www.thehistorypress.co.uk

British Library Cataloguing in Publication Data.
A catalogue record for this book is available from the British Library.

isbn 978 1 80399 345 4

Typesetting and origination by The History Press
Printed and bound in Great Britain by TJ Books Limited, Padstow, Cornwall.

FSC
www.fsc.org

MIX
Paper from
responsible sources
FSC® C013056

Trees for LYfe

Contents

Music, like poetry, is a passion and problem

Sergei Rachmaninoff

Acknowledgements

I should particularly like to thank many friends over the years who have generously helped me in countless different ways: Michael Aspinall of Naples who has given me the benefit of his erudition and knowledge; Gregor Benko of New York who has been unstinting in his efforts to secure information; the late Richard Bebb and his peerless collection of recordings and memorabilia; Jack Buckley; Peter G. Davis of *New York Magazine*; Nicholas Hamer of Mauritius for his unstinting generosity and exceptional patience; Michael and Pamela Hartnall; Stephen Hastings, Editor of *Musica*; the late Jack Henderson who went to Rachmaninoff recitals; the late Joel Honig; Francesco Izzo; the late Frank Johnson, Editor of *The Spectator*; Vivian Liff; Bert Luccarelli; Guthrie Luke, pupil of Alfred Cortot; Barrie Martyn, author of *Rachmaninoff: Composer, Pianist, Conductor*, and his wife Alice, who graciously invited me to their home before we had even met; Liz Measures; Andy Miller and Karen Christenfeld of Rome; Joel Pritkin who sent me photographs of Rachmaninoff's last Californian residence; the late Patric Schmidt of Opera Rara; Randolph Mickelson who entertained me at his homes in Venice and New York; Mary Tzambiras; John Ransley; my brother John and sister-in-law Coby who invited me to Riga; my sister Edith and brother-in-law Philip; Robert and Jill Slotover; Robert Tuggle, Archivist of the Metropolitan Opera, New York; the late Professor L.J. Wathen of Houston; Raymond A. White of the Library of Congress, Washington; and last, but not least, to Robert Dudley. I am also grateful to Christopher Feeney, Jim Crawley, Sophie Bradshaw and Kai Tabacek of The History Press.

I have transliterated Rachmaninoff the way he did himself, that is in the French style, as I have done with Chaliapin, Diaghileff, Baklanoff and Tchaikovsky. With other names I have preferred familiar spellings. Inevitably this has led to inconsistencies, but then English is irregular and systems are inapplicable.

Preface

Rachmaninoff was the last in the tradition of the great romantic composer pianists that had developed through the nineteenth century, from the days of Chopin and Liszt. By his time, the increasing complexity of music had led to a growth in the size and importance of the orchestra which demanded another new type of virtuoso: the conductor. Whereas before the revolution in Russia Rachmaninoff was well known as a conductor, after it, exiled in the west, he turned to the piano and to composing, and hardly ever conducted. Another, from our point of view today, more revealing respect in which he differed from his predecessors is that he lived into the age of recordings, and as well as his music we now also have records of him as a pianist and conductor. They have something interesting to tell us, not only about his own compositions, but they are hardly less illuminating for the light they throw on the interpretation of romantic music generally.

By the First World War, even in a society as reactionary as imperial Russia, his compositions reflected a musical style that had already become passé. His records shed light not only on his own compositions, but on the interpretation of romantic music generally. There is a paradox contained in the fact that although critics sniffed at his compositions, especially after he moved to

America and western Europe, the public continued to admire them inordinately. It is revealing that notwithstanding the Depression, the concerted works he played were almost always his own compositions.[1]

Today, more than sixty years have passed since his death and his music has become a part of the concert repertory; his reputation as a composer has been restored. In 1918 when he began his career as a piano virtuoso, aside from his own compositions, his repertory was of the narrowest kind. He played only a few token works from the classical period (often arrangements or paraphrases) and rarely played anything more modern than the works of Scriabin and Medtner. Looking over his concert programmes today, much in them may seem insubstantial or over-familiar. We might feel tempted to accuse him of cynicism – or of having his eye on the box-office. There was no need for him to adapt his playing, as every pianist must today, to the many divergent musical styles that are now available.

As soon as he touches the keys he immediately establishes his own personality, yet he does not obfuscate by imposing himself on the music; rather, he illuminates. His performance style comes in marked contrast to what we may expect, thinking of his music; his records will certainly surprise those who confuse romantic with self-indulgent. In 1927, Olga Samaroff, herself a distinguished pianist, wrote: 'Rachmaninoff seldom displays in my opinion the emotional warmth and sensuous colour so characteristic of his own creative muse.'[2] By then it was not his playing but the conception of what constituted the romantic style that had changed. Romantic music was fast going out of fashion, its style becoming decadent. For Rachmaninoff, the popular romantic classics were neither exhausted by the incessant replay that electric media has exposed them to, nor alienated by the introduction of a new, unsympathetic post-romantic style. Recordings of him conducting and playing the piano remind us how illogical it is to believe that a period so rich in the creation of great masterpieces did not know how to interpret its own music.

They reveal two telling aspects of his technique: his command of dynamics and his rhythmic control. In the last three-quarters of a century, just as amplification has gradually corrupted our appreciation of dynamics, so the overwhelming influence of Afro-American jazz has introduced a narrower, more literal sense of rhythm. His records remind us that virtuosity is not just a question of not playing any wrong notes but of playing the right ones in the right places.

> One no sooner reflects that perhaps the most fabulous aspects of his piano playing were his melodic eloquence and dramatic virtuosity, than one remembers the unique rhythmic bite in sustained, short or syncopated accentuation, or his way of orchestrating chords with special beauty through individual distributions of balances and blendings.[3] He use[d] the pedal dexterously in his production of light and shade ... he [did] not abuse this device; indeed he [wa]s often austere in the niceness with which by a perfection of timing, he released the sustaining pedal to avoid dissonance.[4]

In 1939 he recorded his First Piano Concerto. There can be no more fitting word for his playing in the cadenza towards the end of the first movement than Olympian. What is remarkable is his ability to organise it without the discipline of bar lines. Spontaneously he reconciles the details within his overall conception, yet he plays it without any sense of artifice or contrivance. The underlying rhythmic certainty dominating his conceptions cannot be notated, and in such a fashion he demonstrates what makes romantic music so effective. As time marches on through new musical territory, how grateful we are to possess his recordings. It has taken until the age of the CD, and of modern remastering techniques, for RCA to reissue them all in high fidelity. There are more of Rachmaninoff's recordings on sale today than have ever been available before, even during his lifetime.[5]

1

1873–1885

The Rachmaninoff family's aristocratic origins: Born twelve years after the emancipation of the serfs: Changed political circumstances enable him to become a musician: Secures place at St Petersburg Conservatory but fails examination: Cousin Siloti secures opportunity for him at Moscow Conservatory.

Sergei Rachmaninoff was born on 20 March 1873[1] at Semyonovo, one of his family's estates to the south of Lake Ilmen in the Staraya Russa region. 'It was near enough to ancient Novgorod to catch the echoes of its old bells',[2] or so he would like to remember years later when his childhood memories were particularly dear to him. By then, this world had long been swept away. Oscar von Riesemann paints a word picture of an estate like the Rachmaninoffs at the time of his birth:

> The manor-house was a low one or two storied wooden structure, built with logs from its own forests, whose sun-mottled gloom reached up to the garden gate; roomy verandas and balconies stretched around the whole front of the house, which was overgrown with Virginia creeper; behind lay stables and dog-kennels that housed yelping Borzoi puppies; in

front of the house was a lawn, round in shape – with a sun-
dial in the centre – and encircled by the drive; a garden with
gigantic oaks and lime trees, which cast shadows over a cro-
quet lawn, led into a closed thicket; a staff of devoted servants
who, under good treatment, showed an unrivalled eagerness
to serve, made house and yard lively.[3]

However, Riesemann's eloquence should not disguise the fact
that life in Russia in those days had another side to it, and that
the Rachmaninoffs were among the privileged minority. As
in France in the days of Louis XVI, or in the United Kingdom
at the time of the Industrial Revolution, the vast majority was
illiterate, many half-starved, and disease rampant.

According to a genealogy, 'Historical Information About
the Rachmaninoff Family',[4] it could be traced back to the days
of Mongolian domination in the Middle Ages. As photographs
taken in the last years of Rachmaninoff's life suggest, there is
something almost Mongolian-looking about his features – his
almond-shaped eyes with heavy bags under them, his pendulous
lips. Stefan IV, one of the rulers of Moldavia, had a daughter,
Elena, who married the eldest son and heir of Ivan III, the Grand
Duke of Moscow. Elena's brother accompanied her to Moscow
and it was his son, Vassily (nicknamed Rachmanin) from whose
line the composer's family may be traced. The name has its origins in an Old Russian word, 'rachmany', meaning hospitable,
generous, a spendthrift. As we shall see, Rachmaninoff's father
was all of these things.

In the eighteenth century, Gerasim Rachmaninoff, the
composer's great-great-grandfather, was a Guard's Officer
in one of the Romanoff family's many succession disputes.
When Elisabeth, Peter the Great's daughter, became Tsaritsa
he was rewarded with an estate in the district of Tambov at
Znameskoye. It lies in the steppes, one of the most fertile parts
of Russia, situated to the southeast of Moscow. The family
remained here for the next 150 years. Alexander Gerasimovich,

Rachmaninoff's great-grandfather, was a competent violinist and his wife was related to Nicolai Bakhmetev, a minor composer in the Imperial Chapel. Given how large Russia was and how poor communications were, families were obliged to make music for themselves in those days. Alexander's son, Arkady, joined the army but retired after duty in one of the many Russo-Turkish disputes. Arkady took piano lessons from John Field, the Irish virtuoso, but by the time Field came to Russia he was in the late stages of alcoholism and his powers were in obvious decline. Mikhail Glinka, the first important Russian composer, studied with Field and wrote of his playing, 'His fingers were like great drops of rain falling on the keys as pearls on velvet.'[5]

The only time Sergei met his grandfather was as a boy, but the memory of the occasion remained with him for more than half a century. 'I played my little tunes, consisting of four or five notes and he added a beautiful and most complicated accompaniment.'[6] Arkady played music at the homes of other members of the nobility and although he never pursued professional standards – as a member of the landowning class it was not necessary – a quantity of his waltzes, polkas and other salon compositions did get into print. He is the only other member of the Rachmaninoff family to merit even a footnote in history. Princess Golizin, in her memoirs,[7] recalls how as soon as he got up every morning he would go straight to the piano and let nothing distract him while he practised for four or five hours. His family was large (there were nine children) and the sons were all required to follow in their father's footsteps and join the army.

Vasily, Rachmaninoff's father, joined the Imperial Guards in 1857 at the age of 16. For the next couple of years he was sent off to the Caucasus to suppress a nationalist uprising by the Muslim leader, Imam Shamil. In 1862 he took part in the suppression of the Polish nationalists and thereafter spent his time in a typical fashion – drinking, gambling and making love. After nine years' military service he made a coup of his own by marrying Lyubov, the daughter and heiress of General Butakov, the head of the Araktcheyev Military College. Vassily quit the army to lead a princely life in the manner of his forebears. Like his father, Arkady, he too showed musical talent. His daughter Varvara recalls how 'he spent hours playing the piano, not the well-known pieces, but something – God knows what, and I would listen to him to the end'.[8] Years later in his recitals, Rachmaninoff would often programme a piece based on a theme he remembered his father playing, supposing it to have been written by him, *Polka de W.R.* (a French transliteration of his initials), but it was in fact the work of a prolific Austrian composer, Franz Behr, in the Johann Strauss mould.

Vasily Rachmaninoff's family consisted of three daughters (Elena, Sophia and Varvara) and three sons (Vladimir, Sergei and Arkady). Sergei was raised in the traditional manner by a nurse, and took lessons from private tutors. His mother introduced him to music and he was only 4 years old when she first sat him at the piano. Like members of his father's family, he showed an aptitude for music from an early age but it seems unlikely that his talent would ever have amounted to much without his mother. The part his mother played in securing his first piano teacher is recalled in a letter written years later to Rachmaninoff by Mlle Defert, his sisters' Swiss governess:

> You may recall how your mother enjoyed accompanying my singing. Do you remember how you stayed at home one day under the pretext of not feeling well, so I was obliged to stay with you? When we were alone you surprised me suggesting I sing a song your mother often accompanied me in. How astonished I was to hear your small hands play chords that may not have been complete but were without a single wrong note. You made me sing Schubert's 'Mädchenklage' three times. I told your mother that evening. The next day the news was sent your grandfather General Butakov and he ordered your father to go to St Petersburg and bring back a good piano teacher.[9]

As a result, Anna Ornatskaya, a young graduate of St Petersburg Conservatory, was engaged to give Sergei his first piano lessons.

Like his father, grandfather and great-grandfather, Rachmaninoff's social position precluded his making a career as a professional musician and it was ordained that he would join the *corps des pages* of the Guards. However, it did not take long before economic changes in Russia began to affect the Rachmaninoffs. From his father's youth his wealth had caused him to court pretty well every attractive woman he met, but that had not contributed to making him provident. In the first years of his marriage the income from his estates had proved more than enough to cope with, even with his profligacy; but soon there was no place left for the extravagant, often absentee, landlords of old Russia. The rapid progress of industrialisation in western Europe inevitably led to the collapse of feudal Russia: In 1861 the serfs were emancipated and for the landowners this necessitated a new and revolutionary husbanding of their resources.

By 1877, only five years after his wealthy father-in-law's death, Vassily had managed to squander his wife's entire inheritance. At first Lyubov's position had been little different from the heiresses of previous generations; so long as their husbands could manage their estates competently then they had to put up with their philandering. But Vassily became bankrupt and Lyubov was faced with the prospect of having to fend for herself. She had no mind to play the role of her namesake in Chekhov's play and sit back while the cherry orchard was taken from her. The furious rows resulting from the genteel poverty that the Rachmaninoffs were slipping into, led to Sergei's parents separating. Lyubov moved to St Petersburg with all of the children, where her mother, Sophie Butakova, joined her. Sergei who was only ten could not have understood much of what was going on; all he knew was that his father loved him very much. He thought him kind and generous, but his mother was aware of the importance of introducing orderliness into family life. Rachmaninoff remembers her years afterwards stating 'there should be a time for everything'.[10]

Soon after their arrival in Russia's capital, one of Vassily's married sisters, Maria Trubnikova, agreed to take Sergei into her family until Lyubov was settled. The Trubnikovs nicknamed him 'yasam' (myself); so independent was the little lad that when anyone in the family offered to help him he would brush them aside insisting 'yasam'. No sooner were they settled in St Petersburg than a diphtheria epidemic broke out. Three of the Rachmaninoff children contracted it, and although Sergei and his elder brother Vladimir both recovered, their sister Sophia died. Sergei's maternal grandmother helped to support the young Rachmaninoffs during these difficult years and it was she to whom the boy felt particularly close. Sergei enjoyed the summer vacations he spent with her at Borisovo, near the familiar landscape of Oneg, one of the family estates his father had been obliged to sell. He would wait impatiently for her to take him to church, where he would listen attentively to the music. Then, as soon as they were home again, he would go straight to the piano, and with his feet scarcely reaching the pedals, play through the chants he had heard. Although not conventionally religious, a preoccupation with Russian church music would remain an important influence on Rachmaninoff's compositions throughout his life.

It was during these summers that we first glimpse the composer. After dinner, the boy would improvise at the keyboard in front of his grandmother's guests, although he always claimed he was playing pieces by Beethoven, Mendelssohn and Chopin. After these impromptu recitals, he recalled, 'she never failed to reward me with twenty-five kopeks, and naturally, I was not loathe to exert my memory, for such a consideration meant a large sum to a lad of ten or eleven.'[11] His surviving elder sister, Elena, who was more than five years his senior, had a love of music which made for a common bond. She had a fine contralto voice with a natural individuality of timbre that foretold a great future. Sergei loved to accompany her. She would sing the latest fashionable song, like Tchaikovsky's 'None but the lonely heart'. Sometimes he was so deeply affected that he proved unable to finish, and she had to push him off the piano stool and accompany herself. In the autumn of 1885, when she was eighteen and had secured an engagement at the Bolshoi, Elena died suddenly. This was a traumatic event for the twelve-year-old Sergei.

The family's straitened circumstances made a place in the Guards impossible and Vladimir, Vassily's eldest son, had to go to an ordinary military academy. This, combined with the boy's obvious talent, made a career in music seem possible for Sergei. With the recommendation of Ornatskaya he gained a scholarship for the St Petersburg Conservatory. The fact that he had a perfect ear and could name almost every note in the most complicated of musical structures, persuaded his teachers that he had no need for basic theoretical training. Like many with exceptional talents, he did not fit easily into the conservatory regime and was allowed to go straight into harmony classes with older, more mature students. It was not until after failing his examinations that leading questions were asked him and his incompetence became obvious. At length, Karl Davydov, Principal of the Conservatory, complained to Lyubov, but she had no idea what to do. It was in 1885 that Lyubov's nephew, the young pianist Alexander Siloti, returned home after completing his studies to accept an engagement at the Moscow Conservatory. Having spent three years with Liszt and created a considerable sensation in concert, Lyubov begged Siloti to hear Sergei and give her his opinion of the boy's worth. Before doing so, however, Siloti happened to meet Davydov and asked him what he thought of Sergei. Davydov pulled a long face and replied that he could see no point in the boy continuing studying. It was with some difficulty that Lyubov finally managed to persuade Siloti to come to the Rachmaninoffs' apartment and hear his cousin play, but he was at once impressed. He told Lyubov that Sergei was very talented but that he needed stringent discipline. He recommended that she enrol him at the Moscow Conservatory and put him under the rigorous tutelage of Nicolai Zverev, his old teacher.

1885–1889

Rachmaninoff's most important piano teacher: Life at Zverev's:
Joins Moscow Conservatory, staff includes Arensky, Taneyev and his
cousin Siloti: Meets composers Rubinstein and Tchaikovsky: Begins to
compose: Sudden departure from Zverev's.

In 1885 Nicolai Zverev was fifty-three. He had studied piano
with two leading teachers, the Frenchman Alexandre Dubuque
and the Bavarian Adolf von Henselt, both of whom spent many
years in Russia. Dubuque, like Rachmaninoff's grandfather, had
lessons with Field and taught Alexander Villoing, who num-
bered among his pupils the Rubinstein brothers, the virtuoso
Anton, the pedagogue Nicolai and the composer Balakirev. At
the time of its composition Balakirev's 'Islamey' was rated the
ne plus ultra of virtuosity. Although Balakirev was not noted for
his modesty he is on record as stating: 'If I can play the piano at
all, it is entirely due to ten lessons I had with Dubuque'.[1] Henselt
rarely gave concerts and spent most of his time teaching. He told
the American pianist Bettina Walker, who studied with him in
his later years, 'I have never ceased wrestling and fighting with
the flesh.'[2] Walker was a devoted pupil yet she cannot forebear
from recalling how the soubriquet 'Henselt-kills'[3] stuck to

him. Like Henselt, Zverev was devoted to practice, but whereas Henselt did not need much coaxing to be persuaded to play, Zverev hardly ever touched the piano, even in front of his students. Rachmaninoff never heard him play. Older pupils, like Siloti, remembered 'a very elegant and musical pianist with an unusually beautiful tone',[4] especially the remarkable effect he created playing Beethoven's Moonlight Sonata.

In his affluent youth Zverev conceived his piano studies as no more than finishing lessons for a gentleman. However, like the Rachmaninoffs, his landowning family fell on hard times as was so often the way in the then rapidly changing Russia. At the age of thirty-five, less than a decade after the emancipation of the serfs, he was obliged to sell the family estate. It was then that he chanced to encounter Dubuque. When Zverev told Dubuque that the only living he could expect to find was that of a civil servant, Dubuque replied: 'Then you had better stay here and I'll get you piano lessons,'[5] and that he did. In only a few years Zverev became one of Moscow's leading teachers and by 1900 no less than twelve out of nineteen of the Moscow Conservatory's gold medallists had been his pupils, and many became professors. Zverev's career proves a Shavian axiom: 'If you can, do; if you can't, teach; if you can't teach, then teach teachers.'

At Dubuque's apartment Zverev met Tchaikovsky and the composer agreed to give him lessons in musical theory. As Tchaikovsky's diaries confirm, they soon became friends and he even dedicated a song to him: Distant Past (Op. 72 No. 17). In 1870 Nicolai Rubinstein, the founder of the Moscow Conservatory, appointed Zverev teacher of junior piano students. In the mornings, he would teach privately at home for two hours before departing for the Conservatory at ten o'clock. After a break for lunch he would resume teaching, but this time he would take a carriage round to the homes of the wealthy and fashionable giving lessons, sometimes until 10 p.m., and for more than appreciable sums. What he earned from his demanding labours was sufficient to satisfy his need for creature comforts, and it enabled him to accommodate a trio of the youngest and brightest conservatory scholarship boys in his home where they received tuition for free.

After hearing Sergei dispatch one of Reinecke's studies, Zverev immediately accepted him. At the time he had just lost one of his 'cubs', as he called them, and had room for another. Already studying with him were Matvei Pressman, three years older than Sergei, and Leonid Maximov, his contemporary. Pressman became director of the Conservatory at Rostov, while Maximov died in 1904 of typhoid. Zverev ran his students' lives in martinet fashion, supervising every minute of their time; his regime included a six day week for the whole year and they had no vacations. They shared a bedroom in which there was a piano. They would rise at six in the morning and take it in turns to start practising right away, irrespective of whether they had been out late with Zverev the previous night. If they had, they might play fistfuls of wrong notes. On such occasions Zverev, hung-over though he may have been, would storm in clad only in his night clothes and make cutting remarks and slap them hard. In such fashion he would literally afford them a taste of his famous loose-wrists technique.

Pressman discussed Zverev's method: 'An extremely valuable feature of his teaching was that he introduced us to music from the very beginning. To play unrhythmically, or without observing musical grammar and punctuation, was not tolerated and that, of course, is the whole basis of music, upon which it is not difficult to build even the biggest artistic structure.'[6] In later years Rachmaninoff remembered Zverev affectionately:

> He treated us as if we were his equals. Never, under any circumstances, did he let us want for anything. Our clothes were ordered from the most expensive tailor in town, the same who supplied his. There was no first night, no interesting or outstanding performance; no opera which we did not attend. We saw many performances given by famous theatre

stars. I had the good fortune to see great actors like Tommaso
Salvini, Ludwig Barnay and Eleonora Duse.[7]

During Sergei's first years of study, partly at the Conservatory
with Siloti and partly with Zverev, his progress was rapid. At
the beginning of his second year he won a Rubinstein scholarship, and thereafter appeared frequently at student concerts. As
the programmes show in 1885 he played Bach's English Suite in
A minor (BWV 817); he would play this at his last recital fifty-
eight years later. In 1886, he played Henselt's Study in D (Op. 5)
and in 1887, the second and third movement of Beethoven's
Sonata in E flat (Op. 31 No. 3). On other occasions he played
pieces by Moszkowski and Schulhoff, a pupil of Chopin. When
the boys were not at the conservatory, they would be at home
practising under the beady eye of Zverev's spinster sister, Anna
Sergeyevna, 'a rather disagreeable and spiteful person,'[8] as
Rachmaninoff described her. She would carry out her brother's
instructions and see that the boys were not late to start practic-
ing or early to finish. Although Zverev was not concerned with
the study of theory and harmony – these were of greater importance to composers than pianists – he did employ a teacher, Mme
Belopolskaya, who would play four-hand arrangements with
the boys in turn. Back then, before the existence of the radio
or record player, Zverev was concerned that his pupils should
acquire a complete musical background as well as become familiar with the new repertory being written, whether chamber
music, symphonic or orchestral works.

On Sunday mornings Zverev would give lessons to other
talented but poor students. Included amongst them was,
as Rachmaninoff recalled, 'a little cadet from the Moscow
Military College, who was about my own age, it was Alexander
Scriabin.'[9] On Sunday afternoons and evenings it was Zverev's
habit to keep open house at which the guest list would read like
a Russian musical who's who. It might include: Anton Arensky,
the composer and teacher at the Moscow Conservatory; Anton

Rubinstein; Siloti; Sergei Taneyev, another composer and teacher who was also the director of the Moscow Conservatory and his successor, the conductor Vasily Safonov; Tchaikovsky and his brother librettist Modest; the baritones Joachim Tartakov and Leonid Yakovlev. The boys would be called in to play a Mozart sonata, a piece of Mendelssohn's or a Cramer study. When they had finished Zverev would turn to his guests smiling and say "'See, that's the way to play the piano!'" His concern was that these events should advertise his pedagogic skill. 'He would not seem perturbed,' Pressman later recalled, 'that same morning, after hearing one of them play the same piece he had growled – "Is that the way to play the piano? No! Get out.""[10]

In January and February 1886, Rubinstein played his seven Historical Recitals at Moscow's Nobility Hall on successive Tuesday evenings, and repeated them on Wednesday mornings for non-paying student audiences. Zverev took his cubs to these performances. They were events of the first magnitude since critical opinion rated Rubinstein, after Liszt, the greatest pianist of the day. He presented a complete survey of works, beginning with the English virginalists Byrd and Bull, then Bach, Couperin and Scarlatti, continuing with Mozart, Beethoven and Chopin up to Liszt, and finishing with the Russian moderns. As a pianist, Rubinstein's catholicity was complete. In the variety and breadth of his musicianship he was a typical nineteenth-century figure and may be compared with Goethe: a great literary genius who had been deemed to know about everything from literature and the arts to philosophy and even science – it was still possible in those days. Certainly no pianist before Rubinstein, not even Liszt, attempted as comprehensive a repertory. An equivalent accomplishment today would be impossible, not only because most tastes do not care for Byrd and Bull on the piano, but because the century since Rubinstein has accumulated music of such widely divergent technical demands that no one pianist, no matter how virtuosic, could attempt to embrace so exhaustive a repertory with equal stylistic authority.

Rubinstein's playing had a mesmeric effect on the Zverev boys. Pressman never forgot him:

> He enthralled you by his power; he captivated you with the grace and elegance of his playing, with his tempestuous, fiery temperament and by his warmth and charm. His crescendo seemed to have no limits to the growth of the power of its sonority; his diminuendo would modulate to the merest pianissimo, yet it would still project surely even in the farthest reaches of the biggest hall. In his playing Rubinstein created, and created inimitably and with genius.[11]

Zverev gave a dinner party in honour of Rubinstein. Sergei remembered 'being chosen to lead the guest of honour in, by the coat-tails, for he was almost blind by then. Someone asked him Rubinstein about a young pianist [probably Eugen d'Albert] wanting to know how he liked his playing. Rubinstein thought for a moment and shrugged: "Oh, nowadays everybody plays well".'[12]

At one of Rubinstein's recitals, when he was playing Balakirev's 'Islamey', Sergei recalled:

> Something distracted him and he apparently forgot the composition entirely, but kept improvising in the style of the piece, then after a few minutes the remainder of the composition came back to him and he played it through to the end correctly. However this annoyed him so greatly that although he played the next piece on the programme [Tchaikovsky's Song without Words, Op. 2 No. 3] with the greatest exactitude, strange to say, it had not the wonderful charm of the interpretation of the piece in which his memory failed. Rubinstein was really incomparable, just because he was so full of human impulse and his playing very far removed from just mechanical perfection.[13]

This spontaneity and apparent lack of premeditation in Rubinstein's playing fits in with Rachmaninoff's account of another incident at another of these recitals when he repeated a passage in the third movement of Chopin's Sonata in B flat minor (Op. 35): 'Perhaps because he had not succeeded in the short crescendo at the close as he would have wished. I could have listened to this passage over and over again.'[14] It is not surprising that Rubinstein's playing of this piece should have left an indelible impression on Rachmaninoff and in later years he would often programme it in concerts he gave. Eduard Hanslick, the noted Viennese critic, has left a description of Rubinstein's playing: 'The mighty crescendo at the beginning of the trio in the Funeral March, and the gradual decrescendo after it, was a brilliant innovation of his own.'[15] As can be heard on Rachmaninoff's 1929 recording, he plays it in the same fashion.

Rachmaninoff's affection for Rubinstein's piano playing remained with him all his life, which may perhaps seem strange for although recorded evidence, as well as countless ear-witnesses, confirm that his playing was 'full of human impulse', no pianist rehearsed more assiduously or was more thoroughly prepared. Rachmaninoff's interpretations (though not his compositions) represent the epitome of what today could be called the classical style. As his records demonstrate that, 'His rubato consists of subtle adjustment of rhythmic detail, rather than the languishing mini-rallentando that tends to characterize the rubato of later pianists in Romantic music. As a result, his rubato does not hold up the flow.'[16] His playing has much of the rhythmic vitality and dynamic grandeur that so strongly impressed him in Rubinstein's. By the time Rachmaninoff's international career as a concert pianist began after the First World War, the growing population in the western world was becoming ever more prosperous. The popularity of the radio and the record player led to the increasing exposure of the standard repertory of classics and, inevitably, to the public's greater familiarity with it. This encouraged pianists – indeed, all performing musicians – to sacrifice spontaneity of execution to textual accuracy.

An interesting comparison may be made between recordings by Rachmaninoff and his contemporary Josef Hoffmann, the Polish pianist and Rubinstein's only private pupil. Hoffmann always spoke of Rachmaninoff as the greatest pianist of the day and so Rachmaninoff spoke of Hoffmann. Although Rachmaninoff left a considerable number of recordings, none is of a live performance. Hoffmann on the other hand made a much smaller selection of (often unrevealing) recordings, but a lot of live performances survive[17] and these show much of Rubinstein's spontaneity. Rachmaninoff is in the tradition of many great musicians – Chaliapin, Kreisler, Cortot and Callas – in that over the years his interpretations hardly change. Compare different recordings he made of the *Polka de W.R.* in 1919, 1921 and 1928, for example. Yet Hoffmann, as we hear in two live recordings of Chopin's Andante Spianato made only months apart,[18] could be interpretatively (though not technically) two different pianists. It is not difficult to believe that there is in Hoffmann's playing – in its exquisite finish and seeming weightlessness of tone, coruscating virtuosity and prodigious dynamic range – something of the temper of Rubinstein, as well as some of those wrong notes!

In the summer of 1886 Zverev took Sergei, with Maximov and Pressman, to the Crimea. He often went there in the summer, so as to give piano lessons to the children of the millionaire Tokmakov. He would rent a house nearby, 'but it was not to be a carefree vacation for his boys – that would not be consistent with his programme.'[19] With them went Nicolai Ladukhin, Professor of Harmony, who gave the boys a crash course 'in two and a half months, what would according to the conservatory curriculum, take two to three years to accomplish'.[20] This was Zverev's way of preparing them for the following year. They would quickly pass the theory and basic harmony examination and could soon begin more advanced work. The effect on Sergei was immediate. Pressman remembered how he began for the first time to compose:

> I remember how pensive and silent he grew, walking around, his head lowered, his eyes fixed on some distant point. This state lasted for several days. Finally, and somewhat mysteriously, choosing a moment when no one else was about, he beckoned me to the piano and began to play. 'Do you know what that was?' he asked. 'No' I replied 'I don't.' 'I composed it myself, and I dedicate it to you.'[21]

Unfortunately no trace of the piece, a study in F sharp, has survived.

Back in Moscow at the Conservatory, Tchaikovsky was present at the opening ceremony before the new term. He had been Professor of Theory and History until 1878, but by this time he was 46 and remained only in an advisory capacity. He had already composed many of his more famous works and it seems likely that most of the students present took more notice of him than he of them. Rachmaninoff already admired Tchaikovsky's music inordinately. Tchaikovsky's diary account of the event is cursory: 'Dedication service at the Conservatory. Reading of the report. Professor Nicolai Kashkin's speech on Liszt [who had died that summer] was endless.'[22] It was at this time that Sergei was first able to apply some of the fruits of his studies in theory and harmony when, in a gesture of respect and admiration, he produced a four-hand arrangement of Tchaikovsky's *Manfred* symphony, a work that had first been heard the previous spring. He and Pressman played it when Tchaikovsky came to one of Zverev's Sunday evenings. In the last movement there occurs a reference to the plainchant *Dies irae* and this, although Sergei was only 13 years old, was to become almost a signature tune. Tchaikovsky's diary, not a wordy document as we noted, mentions 'a supper at Patrikeyev's restaurant at which, with a number of others Zverev and his pupils had been present'.[23] On this occasion, as Tchaikovsky came in, the *salon de thé* ensemble got to its feet and struck up a waltz from one of his ballets. Rachmaninoff remembered him commenting: 'When I was young it was the dream of my life to think that some day my music would be so popular that I would be able to hear it played in restaurants. Now I am quite indifferent.'[24]

On Zverev's fifty-fifth birthday, 13 March 1887, his cubs had organised a surprise. After morning coffee they led him into the drawing room and played their birthday pieces. Sergei began with Tchaikovsky's Troika from *The Seasons* (Op. 37b), which he recorded three times and was still including in recitals more than half a century later. Pressman played The Snowdrop, also from *The Seasons*, and Maximov played a nocturne of Borodin's. 'Nothing could have given Zverev more pleasure,' Pressman remembered. 'At his formal birthday dinner that night Zverev boasted of the musical gifts he had received and made us sit down at the piano and show off to the guests. Everyone was pleased and Tchaikovsky kissed all of us.'[25] The stimulus offered by Tchaikovsky's music encouraged Sergei to start to compose. Three of his piano solos, Nocturnes, are dated between November 1887 and January 1888 and reveal a considerable advance, both musically and stylistically, on his earliest surviving piano solo, the Song Without Words. The latter was written as an exercise for Arensky's harmony class at the end of the 1886/87 academic year and years later Rachmaninoff wrote it out from memory for inclusion in Riesemann's *Rachmaninoff's Recollections*. Another piece of juvenilia, the Scherzo in D minor for orchestra, is dated 5–21 February 1888 although the date on this has been altered at some stage to 1887, 'which improbably places the work only two or three months after Rachmaninoff's initiation into the mysteries of orchestration'.[26]

Tchaikovsky's influence on Rachmaninoff's music is obvious enough but his two conservatory teachers – Arensky who taught him harmony, fugue and free composition, and Taneyev, from whom he learned counterpoint – were scarcely less important. Arensky, who was only a dozen years older than Rachmaninoff, wrote many compositions, many of them charming if slight, including a Suite for two pianos, a piece entitled Silhouettes and Variations on a Theme of Tchaikovsky, which Rachmaninoff would later conduct with the Moscow Philharmonic Orchestra.[27] Although a Rimsky-Korsakov pupil, that did not prevent his master dismissing him:[28] 'he will soon be forgotten,' he asserted. This may have been an oblique reference to Arensky's alcoholism which brought his career (and life) to an untimely premature conclusion, or maybe Rimsky was jealous because Arensky 'had fallen under Tchaikovsky's influence'.

Taneyev, five years older than Arensky, was at that time director of the Moscow Conservatory, where he had studied with Nicolai Rubinstein and Tchaikovsky. Rimsky-Korsakov described his music as 'mostly dry and laboured,'[29] although he admitted to finding an opera, *The Oresteia*, 'striking in its wealth of beauty and expressiveness'.[30] Unfortunately little of it is heard today, even on the fringes of the repertory. Taneyev and Rachmaninoff kept in regular contact and it was only months before Taneyev's death in 1915 that Rachmaninoff took his *All-Night Vigil* for him to look over before it was published. If Arensky's music reinforced the influence of Tchaikovsky on Rachmaninoff then it was Taneyev – the man – who had the more profound effect on him, as we shall see from the lengthy obituary Rachmaninoff wrote for *Russkiye Vedomositi*.

Immediately before the summer vacation in May 1888, an opportunity arose for Sergei. In the next year there was to be a division between general theory and special theory classes, the first was for interpreters and the second for creators. Tchaikovsky was on the examining board. Years later Rachmaninoff recalled what happened:

> At the last examination of the harmony class the pupils were separated and given two problems to be solved without the help of a piano. The first was to harmonize a melody in four

parts [I think the theme was Haydn's]. The second was to write a prelude of sixteen to thirty bars, in a given key and with a specified modulation, to include both pedal points on both the dominant and tonic. When all the candidates had turned in their work I alone was left; I had got entangled in a daring modulation and could find no satisfactory solution. At last, by five o'clock, I had finished, and handed my two pages to Arensky. When he glanced at them he did not frown, so this gave me some hope. On the following day the board was to hear us play our own work. When I had finished my turn, Arensky mentioned to Tchaikovsky that I had written some pieces in ternary form for his class, and perhaps he would like to hear them. Tchaikovsky intimated his assent so I sat down and played them; I knew them by heart. When I finished I saw Tchaikovsky go over to the examination record board and write something on it. It was not for another two weeks that Arensky told me what he had written; he was probably afraid I would become vain so he had tried to keep it a secret from me. The board had granted me a 'five plus' [top marks], and Tchaikovsky had added three more plus signs—above it, below it and to the side of it. So my fate as a composer was, as it were, officially sealed.[31]

As a reward Zverev permitted him for the first time, when he was fifteen, to visit the home of his relatives, the Satins. Natalia, the elder daughter of the Satins who Sergei would marry a decade later, remembered how condescending he was to her after she played through a piano reduction of one of Vanya's arias from Glinka's *A Life for the Tsar*. This was less, we may believe, a comment on her playing or his manners, than the effect of his rigorous experience with examples in front of him like Tchaikovsky.

He spent that summer at the Crimea again with Zverev, before returning to Moscow in September. That autumn he took part in student concerts at the Conservatory playing Bach's

Prelude and Fugue in C, Rubinstein's Study in F minor, Liszt's
Ballade in B minor and the first movement of Beethoven's
Sonata in D (Op. 28). It was at this time that the young Sergei
made his first attempt to write an opera, *Esmeralda*, the libretto
of which is based on Victor Hugo's novel *Notre Dame de Paris*.
Some fragments of the opera survive that are dated 17 October.
In Martyn's opinion, '[although] there is nothing musically significant in them, there is a surprising foretaste of maturity in
the theme associated with Frollo [bass], which unmistakably
looks ahead to the Prelude in G sharp minor [Op. 32 No. 12]
of 1910.'[32]

Cooped up in the confined surroundings of Zverev's with
Pressman and Maximov incessantly practising, Sergei found
it difficult to work creatively and finally plucked up sufficient
courage to ask Zverev for another piano and a room where he
could work alone and undisturbed. According to Riesemann,
'his pride, confusion and excitement somehow transformed a
calm conversation into a stormy argument and Zverev, losing
control, raised his hand against him. Sergei by then sixteen
would not tolerate such a gesture: "Don't dare hit me!" The
interview thereupon ended in a total breakdown of relations.'[33]
There was nothing so unusual in Zverev losing his temper and
after a few days he might have forgotten the incident, only this
time a whole month passed in which he never spoke to Sergei.
One day he curtly ordered Sergei to meet him after classes at the
Conservatory. They made their way to the home of the Satins,
where Zverev told them that he did not wish to leave Sergei to
fend for himself, but that it was impossible to continue living
with him. He had brought him to the Satins in the hope that
they would be prepared to take him in.

Another account of the severing of their relationship is rather
different, however. Some years later, after Zverev was dead,
Yury Sakhnovsky (with whom Sergei went to live in the autumn
of 1891 when he contracted malaria) told the critic Leonid
Sabaneyev that it was Sergei and not Zverev who brought their

relationship to an end because Zverev was homosexual. In Russia this was a punishable offence with a maximum penalty of a dozen years' hard labour. It is true that Zverev was unmarried, and appearing around Moscow with three boys in tow, as was his habit, would have been quite sufficient to incite rumours – even in a far more liberal society than Tsarist Russia. Not until after Zverev's death did Sergei feel able to express himself on the subject unambiguously.

The four years in which Sergei had been living with Zverev represented a most important period of his life, when he was growing to maturity. Whatever the reason for his leaving Zverev, it is not surprising that later he would come to show many of the same distinctive personality traits so characteristic of Zverev. Rachmaninoff's biographer Victor Seroff records:

> Those who knew him [sic] noted the resemblance to Zverev, the way they carried themselves and their marked ability to keep people at a distance despite their very warm and kind natures. The shyness and awkwardness that never left him, even after he became a famous musician. In his youth his face had not been that of a young man. It was old looking, with deep creases that lent an expression of disappointment, even disapproval.[34]

This impression is reinforced by conservatory contemporaries such as Nicolai Avierino, who spoke of his already formed personality even at the age of only seventeen. He was self-centred but not selfish, correct and well-adjusted, and never too familiar. If sometimes he gave an impression of hauteur, and even conceit, in reality, Avierino declared, 'this derived from shyness'.[35]

3

1889–1893

Moves in with the Satins: First summer at Ivanovka: Graduates from Moscow Conservatory: Finishes First Piano Concerto: Catches malaria: First appearance in public concert: Wins competition with one-act opera, Aleko: Introduces Prelude in C sharp minor.

Whichever tale is true to account for Sergei's sudden departure from Zverev's, he spent only a few days with his Conservatory colleague Mikhail Slonov before Varvara Satina, his father's sister, agreed to take him in. His mother also invited him to St Petersburg, where she lived, suggesting he might move back to the Conservatory there. Although he would have liked to study piano with Rubinstein, his problem was the presence of Rimsky-Korsakov on the board of staff, which even then to a lad of only sixteen, 'would have looked like a betrayal of Tchaikovsky and Taneyev'.[1] He may not yet have been able to articulate his musical instincts, but he already identified with Taneyev and the more rigorous counterpoint style of the Moscow school rather than the new freer folk-music style of the St Petersburg School.

There are usually considered to have been two groups in the composition of Russian music in the nineteenth century.

The first was led by Balakirev, and included Cui, Borodin, Moussorgsky and Rimsky-Korsakov. 'The Big Five', or 'The Mighty Handful' as they became known (a term first used in 1867 by critic Vladimir Stasov), were concerned to resist the influence of western Europe and to demonstrate their Russian quality. They were amateurs who not only had double careers (Balakirev was a railway clerk, Cui an officer in the army artillery school, Borodin, a Professor of Chemistry, Moussorgsky, a Lieutenant in the Guards and Rimsky-Korsakov a Naval officer) but resisted what they regarded as the old-fashioned academic style. However, it was not long before the youngest, Rimsky-Korsakov, became self-critical and discovered harmony, counterpoint and orchestration. In contrast to these was the second group, led by Tchaikovsky and Rubinstein, which had been influenced by music in western Europe, and with which Rachmaninoff became associated. In 1859 it was Rubinstein who founded the Russian Musical Society, in 1862 the St Petersburg Conservatory and in 1866 his brother Nicolai founded the Moscow Conservatory.

By this time Sergei must have found the freedom of life at the Satin's a welcome change from Zverev's. He was now sufficiently self-disciplined to be able to continue his Conservatory work unsupervised, and having a room of his own, he began a period of intense activity as a composer. In November 1889, he commenced a two piano version of a piano concerto in C minor, although abandoned it after fourteen pages. He usually began the composition of orchestral works at the piano. This was partly to do with the piano being his instrument, but in those days, with so much music being made at home, it would also have been more economically practical to have had a piano reduction published first. Before the invention of the record player, there was still a demand for two piano versions. By 1940, however, this can hardly have been the motive for completing his last new composition, Symphonic Dances (Op. 45), in an arrangement for two pianos nearly two months before the full orchestral version was published. By then, the habit must have become deeply ingrained.

Early in 1890 he wrote a two-movement string quartet, although chamber music never seems to have much interested him and the piece probably originated as an exercise for Arensky. It was performed the next year at a student concert, although arranged for string orchestra. Two songs are also dated from April and May of that year, although neither was published in his lifetime: 'At the Gates of the Holy Abode', to a poem by Lermontov, and 'I shall tell you nothing', to a poem by Fet whose many fashionable verses were set by other composers including Tchaikovsky. He also wrote an unaccompanied motet for mixed chorus in six parts, *Deus meus*, as a counterpoint set piece in two days under examination conditions. Years afterwards he dismissed it scornfully.[2] It was with this piece that he would make his first appearance as a conductor on 24 February the following year.

At the end of May 1890 he journeyed some 450km south-west of Moscow to spend the summer at Ivanovka, the Satins' estate. This was his first visit to what would become his Russian home, and he would return regularly until the Revolution, after which it was destroyed. Today the house has been restored and contains a Rachmaninoff museum. His four cousins included Natalia Satina, whom he later married, and Sophia Satina, six years his junior. Sophia outlived both of the Rachmaninoffs and their daughters and for more than thirty years after his death (she died in 1975) she remained an important source of bio-graphical information.[3] With its own farm, orchards, stable and studs and an English-style park cultivated by his aunt Varvara, it was a sizeable and well-organised estate where there were both family and guest houses. Like on so many Russian estates in those pre-revolutionary days, far from the then rapidly expand-ing urban world, the serfs who had lived there for centuries still felt bonded to the land. Situated far from the forest landscape that was familiar from his childhood, and the Crimea with its cliffs and beaches where he was taken by Zverev, it was not long before the landscape began to work a particular charm on him. 'It had none of the beauties of nature usually thought of – no mountains, precipices or winding shore,' he wrote years later. 'The steppe was a seemingly infinite sea of fields of wheat, rye and oats stretching in every direction to the horizon, wavering and shimmering like water in the balmy summer haze.'[4]

That year there was a large house party which was attended by the Satins as well as the Silotis, their relatives, and the Skalons. General Skalon had three young daughters, Natalya, Ludmilla and Vera. The first piece of music Rachmaninoff would write at Ivanovka was a romance in F minor for cello and piano, for the youngest, Vera. The daughters were all fond of music-making and in the long summer days they delighted in Sergei, encouraging him to play the piano and accompany them in songs. Each girl was soon vying with the other to capture his attention. One unaccredited tale (presumably told by Sophia Satina) in Sergei Bertensson and Jay Leyda's biography suggests that Vera's mother was 'horrified' to hear that her fifteen-year-old daughter and seventeen-year-old Sergei were seen 'sitting close together, and holding hands'. She soon put a stop to that.

During the next decade an appreciable correspondence would pass between him and the Skalon sisters. He wrote for them a waltz in a two part piano trio for six hands. The tune was Natalya's and he gave her the manuscript, dedicating it to her. In 1910, years after they had ceased communicating, he wrote asking that she return it so it could be destroyed. Perhaps he did so because he was worried that his wife, Natalia Satina, her cousin, might come across it and make too much of the dedication. It was never returned and years later in 1948, by which time they were all dead, it was published.

It was also during that summer that Tchaikovsky's publisher, Jürgenson, commissioned Siloti to make a four-hand reduction of *The Sleeping Beauty*, but he had a hand injury. Aware of Sergei's indigence (now that he had to fend for himself) Siloti passed the work over to him – this would be the first score Sergei ever earned money for. He also completed a setting of some other verses by Fet, 'In the Silent Night' (Op. 4 No. 3), which he would dedicate to Vera Skalon. His unrequited passion may account for its beauty, and it has remained one of his most popular songs ever since. Also dating from that summer is the theme that conductor Modeste Altschuler used in his orchestration of a melody by Rachmaninoff which was not published until after the composer's death.

Back at the Conservatory for the academic year 1890/91, Sergei found himself in the middle of a feud, between the new Director, Vasily Safonov, who had succeeded Taneyev, and Siloti, with whom he was studying the piano. Siloti announced that he would be leaving at the end of the year. This presented Sergei with a problem, but he decided not to risk a new teacher and to take his piano finals a year in advance. Safonov had no objections to this – he had heard of Sergei's creative gifts – but 'tried to persuade me I was not born to be a pianist,'[5] as Rachmaninoff later recalled. Although Sergei played the piano at student concerts he did so less frequently than Scriabin, a year his senior, or Josef Lhevinne, a year his junior. He was not then thought of as a pianist first and foremost. This opinion was confirmed by the cellist Mikhail Bukinik, who gave a brief account of some of the more outstanding students then at the Moscow Conservatory:

Lhevinne with his thick, curly hair; immaculate Scriabin, always modishly dressed and when it snows he wears galoshes; solitary Alexander Goldenweiser; Constantin Igumnov who looks more like a sexton; Nicolai Avierino with his droll sense of humour; business-like Altschuler; endearing Maximov, and then there is Sergei Rachmaninoff. Tall and gaunt, with a characteristic appearance, his face long and expressive, he smokes incessantly, speaks in a bass voice, and already seems adult. His successes in Arensky's free composition class are common knowledge, what an extraordinary sight reader he is, what a perfect ear he has, and his love of Tchaikovsky is contagious. Only as a pianist does he make less of an effect.[6]

In a letter to Natalya Skalon that October, Sergei wrote of finishing the first movement of a symphonic poem, *Manfred*, derived like Tchaikovsky's symphony from Byron's poem, although no trace of this has been discovered. In another letter, at the beginning of January, he tells how Arensky, to help keep the wolf from his door, had secured him a position at a music school, giving lessons to teachers of choral singing. But he recalls how awkward this made him feel. The students were twice his age and overly courteous, sitting down and standing up every time he did. Although he would do all the talking, he was conscious of not being able to explain precisely what he meant. His mind would wander and he would frequently find himself trying to think up ways of composing the second movement of the *Manfred* symphony. He could not endure having to give lessons, not even for the sake of five rubles. How demeaning it was, he moaned, to have to take on such menial work just to survive.

What he wanted was an opportunity to give his talent free rein. Goldenweiser recalls an occasion when:

his musical gifts surpassed any others I have ever met, bordering on the miraculous, like those of the youthful Mozart. The speed with which he could memorize new compositions: one day I remember Siloti telling him to learn Brahms's Variations and Fugue on a Theme of Handel; a difficult and very long work. Then days later he played it through with absolute accuracy.[7]

Sergei was at Taneyev's on another occasion when Glazounov came round to play his new Fifth Symphony through for the first time. While tea was being served, Taneyev asked Sergei to play something, whereupon he went over to the piano, and after quickly glancing through Glazounov's symphony, played it through from sight. The composer was amazed, demanding to know how he could possibly have done such a thing. Nowadays, when the musical style of the romantic repertory has become familiar if not hackneyed, this may not seem so remarkable, but in those days the effect it created was sensational. Another feat concerns Sergei and another student, who had composed the first movement of a symphony but did not know how to continue it. Sergei went through it and made a number of suggestions. When they met again after three years, Sergei immediately wanted to know what had happened to the symphony, and sitting down at the piano he played it through from memory.

Sergei spent Christmas of 1890 in St Petersburg with his mother. Perhaps at her insistence, he went to the barber's – the Skalon sisters had for long been pulling his leg over the length of his hair. He was given what we should now call a crew cut. Throughout the rest of his life, no matter what the fashion, he did not change it much – although some photographs suggest he seems to have forgotten to have it cut regularly. With the Skalons he went to the Maryinski to one of the first performances of Tchaikovsky's *The Queen of Spades*. On 12 January 1891, he began work on another piece written for two pianos, *Russian Rhapsody*, completing it within three days. Its first performance was planned five weeks later, when he was to have played it with Maximov. However, at the last minute Maximov was unable to take part: 'Zverev meanly refused to allow him',[8] Rachmaninoff recalled. It was postponed until the following October, when he played it with Lhevinne at a student concert. According to Goldenweiser, 'this concluded with a variation in octaves, passing from one pianist to the other, and at an ever increasing tempo, everyone waited to hear who would outplay whom, each had phenomenal wrists, but it was Rachmaninoff who won.'[9]

On 26 March he was writing to Natalya Skalon with news that he had started work on his First Piano Concerto. 'I'll probably finish it later in the spring, and orchestrate it during the summer,'[10] he told her. At the end of May he took his Conservatory finals. For the piano examination he played Beethoven's Sonata in C and *Waldstein* Sonata (Op. 53) and the first movement of Chopin's Sonata in B flat minor (Op. 35). Since it was impossible to undertake piano and fugue examinations at the same time, he had to sit the fugue paper separately the following day. After finishing the piano finals he was leaving the hall when he encountered Arensky and Safonov, who were discussing the fugue paper. Arensky told Sergei that he would not be free the next day so he had come to dictate him the theme. While he was copying it down Safonov, standing by, was whistling under his breath its correct fugal treatment. Whether he did so without thinking, because they had just been discussing it, Rachmaninoff could never be sure, but he was grateful for the prompting. He was the only one in the class to secure top marks.

At the end of term he made up his mind not to visit his mother again in St Petersburg; although she invited him he 'felt this was only to keep up appearances'.[11] On 29 May he travelled to Ivanovka with Siloti, but things had changed there from the previous year. They were now alone. The Satins were away at Saratov with their father on business, while the Skalons had gone to the Crimea. This was for the sake of Vera's health, or so they told him, but it seems likely that he may have been the reason. On the 31st he wrote to them mentioning that because Siloti was leaving the Conservatory, he was planning to finish early: 'I'll graduate in a year,'[12] he wrote. To do so would necessitate him undertaking a considerable amount of work including 'a symphony, a number of recitatives and an opera'.[13] However, on 14 June he had to put this on hold: Tchaikovsky had been mulling over the proofs of Sergei's four-hand transcription of *The Sleeping Beauty*, and sent Siloti a long list of complaints. It was apparent, he claimed, that it had not been made from the full score but from the two-piano version. Though it had not been carelessly done, it was without imagination and followed the original too slavishly. He insisted it needed a complete reworking – making superficial alterations and amendments would not do. Siloti helped Sergei to rework it. To judge from a letter Sergei wrote Natalya Skalon on 11 July, he accepted the criticism. 'Tchaikovsky swears at me quite terribly, but fairly and justly,'[14] he told her.

His transcription troubles interrupted the completion of his First Piano Concerto. He told Slonov: 'I could have finished it much sooner but after the first movement I idled a long while and didn't begin to write the rest until 3 July.' By the 6th he had completed the scoring. He went on: 'You may imagine what a job it was. I wrote from five in the morning until eight at night, and after finishing it I was so exhausted, still I am pleased with it. Although I cannot say that for my latest song ["Do you remember that evening?"], which I think has not turned out very successfully. Nevertheless, I definitely don't want to change it. For me changes are always unpleasant and distasteful.'[15] But in later years he would change many of his new works, generally if they were not at first successful, usually shortening and simplifying them. However, since complexity was a part of their style, meddling with them in such fashion did not inevitably improve them.

It is interesting tracing influences on this piano concerto. There is a resemblance to Tchaikovsky's and Arensky's concertos, but we might have expected something of Rubinstein's too; he had played the first movement of Rubinstein's fourth concerto in a student concert in February that year. Rubinstein's fourth and fifth concertos were then popular concert staples and live recordings survive of them both made by his pupil Hoffmann. More recently, Hoffmann's pupil, Shura Cherkassky, also recorded the fourth. Although the fifth was written in the same year as Tchaikovsky's first, Rubinstein's seems to be much older and has, Martyn states, almost Mendelssohnian lyricism.[16] Certainly there is little in common between either of them and the first version of Rachmaninoff's concerto. According to Vera Skalon,[17] Siloti had spent the summer of 1890 at Ivanovka endlessly practising the Grieg concerto. Its influence is obvious in the opening measures of Rachmaninoff's first concerto: a similar noisy fanfare and descending introductory passage for the soloist.

In August, feeling deserted without the Skalon sisters, he took the ten-hour drive to his grandmother's estate at Znamenskoye. From there on the 10th he informed Slonov that he was at work on the symphony, a part of his graduation exercise. He also worked on another piano piece for six hands that he had started the previous year, a Romance, a figure whose introduction is similar to one he would later use in the accompaniment at the piano entrance in the second movement of his Second Piano Concerto. Throughout that summer the weather was hot and sultry and he would take the opportunity of cooling off with a bathe in the river nearby. During September he returned to the apartment that he and Slonov rented in Moscow but he quickly fell ill with a high temperature. A physician diagnosed brain fever – what we would now probably call malaria. With the Satins still away on vacation there was no one to turn to, so Slonov arranged to have him looked after by Yuri Sakhnovsky. His father was wealthy and ran a racing establishment and Sergei was moved into an apartment in the family mansion. Seven years Sergei's senior, Sakhnovsky was a *bon viveur*: clever, brilliant and amusing. He could speak four languages fluently and was exceptionally good-looking – or had been, for at the age of 25 he already weighed more than 250lb. When the mood took him he could be lewd and obscene, yet in artistic circles he had a reputation as a poet. He was also a competent musician but coming from a wealthy family he had no need to earn a living. In later years he became an important music critic working successively for *Curier* (1901–03), *Russkaya Pravda* (1903–04) and *Russkoe Slovo* (1909–17). No one was more appreciative of Sergei's talent and it was Sakhnovsky who developed the young composer's appreciation of Wagner and 'The Five'.

At first Sergei's condition was alarming. For a time he was in a state of delirium, but he was strong and at length began to recover. For the next month and a half he remained seriously unwell, but by the end of October he was able to resume correspondence. Writing to Natalya Skalon on the 31st, weak and debilitated, he complained 'I wish I could get away from here but that would only be possible with health, leisure and money, and I have none.'[18] By 7 December he had his health back at least. 'I feel much better and am apparently quite recovered. I am in a good mood. Sometimes I walk because I can't afford to ride, sometimes simply from a desire to walk. I shall settle down soon and write a new piece. I am dedicating it to dear Professor Arensky. It will keep me busy until Christmas.'[19] By the 15th he had completed *Prince Rostislav*, a symphonic poem, dedicated to Arensky, which may have been part of his graduation exercise. Certainly other surviving compositions written that same year were: a fragment of an air for bass and piano with text by Lermontov, parts of two monologues from *Boris Godounov* and an unfinished quartet from *Poltava* by Pushkin. After Christmas, which he spent with the Skalons in St Petersburg, Sergei's father moved to Moscow and they met again after some years. Sakhnovsky was able to assist Vasily Rachmaninoff in finding work and father and son moved into an apartment that he owned.

On 30 January 1892 Sergei made his first public appearance at the Vostriakov Hall in a concert that he promoted and organised himself. He played the piano alongside David Krein on violin and Brandukov on cello. The programme began with his *Trio élégiaque*, a one-movement piece, the manuscript of which is dated 18–21 January, although Sophia Satina[20] maintains it was at least a year older. The rest of the programme consisted of: Chopin's Study in A flat (Op. 10 No. 10) and Study in C minor (Op. 10 No. 12), Tchaikovsky's Barcarolle (Op. 37bis No. 6) and Nocturne (Op. 10 No. 1), a Liszt study, Chopin's Scherzo in B minor and Rachmaninoff's own Prelude and *Oriental Dance* (Op. 2). The rest of his programme included a Tausig study, one of Liszt's Waltz-Impromptus, Godard's *En courant*, Tchaikovsky's Nocturne and Liszt's transcription of the waltz from Gounod's *Faust*. No review of the concert seems to have survived. On 18 February, he was lamenting to Natalya Skalon: 'I had difficulty even recovering my expenses.'[21]

After this he does not seem to have much cared to play concerts, whoever was promoting them, 'they are extremely, disagreeable, boring and time-consuming,'[22] he complained. However, on 17 March he did play the first movement of his First Piano Concerto, introducing it at a student concert with the Conservatory orchestra under Safonov. He was the ninth contributor to a substantial programme that began in the morning and finished that evening with Scriabin playing a movement of Liszt's First Piano Concerto. Bukinik, who was playing cello in the orchestra, describes the occasion:

> Safonov, who conducted, generally took it upon himself to change anything in order to make it play better, and most students, only too happy to have their compositions played, did not dare contradict him. But now it was Safonov who had the hard time. Sergei not only refused to accept any of Safonov's alterations but drew his attention to errors he made in tempi and nuance. Which may have displeased Safonov but he was intelligent enough to appreciate Sergei's talent.[23]

As his appreciation of Rachmaninoff's talent suggests, Safonov might well have proved an appropriate teacher for him. It was the first, and perhaps only,[24] time that Rachmaninoff would ever play any of the original version of his First Piano Concerto in public.

The most important work Sergei was to write for the finals of the free composition class was a one-act opera, *Aleko*. One-act

operas had become popular following the overwhelming success of Mascagni's *Cavalleria Rusticana* at the Costanzi, Rome,
in 1890. The same opera was introduced with equal success at
St Petersburg and Moscow the following year by an Italian company. Based on Pushkin's poem *The Gypsies*, the libretto of *Aleko*
is by Vladimir Nemirovich-Danchenko, the dramatist, stage-
director and co-founder of the Moscow Arts Theatre. The opera
is set in a gypsy encampment in Bessarabia. Aleko, a stranger,
has been living among the gypsies and is the lover of Zemfira,
but she has grown tired of him and fallen in love with one of
the younger members of her own tribe. Aleko comes upon
them together and pleads with Zemfira to return to him but she
mocks him. He becomes so jealous that he kills them both. The
gypsies then pick up their chattels and go off to another camp
leaving Aleko alone. Nemirovich-Danchenko cut Pushkin's
verses by approximately two-thirds and in the process, no doubt
with regard to the fact that he was writing a libretto for students,
reduced it to a series of stock scenes.

The story is a *crime passionnel* based on jealousy. Pushkin's
poem is much concerned with the gypsies – an anarchic group
not reliant on society's moral code. In Pushkin's day, under
the repressive regime of Nicholas I, freedom was a compel-
ling notion and gypsies had a special allure. They managed to
survive by keeping on the move, and their language and culture helped preserve their identity. During the nineteenth
century gypsy orchestras with their own instruments became
increasingly popular; they were part of the growth of a new
and original influence in western music. Composers like Liszt,
Johann Strauss, Brahms and Dvorak were much affected by
zigeunermusik. Sergei's own experience of it dates from his days
with Zverev who delighted in taking his cubs out to fashionable
restaurants where gypsy musicians would play *friska*s on their
cimbaloms. Pressman[25] tells of a party at Zverev's when, with
Sergei and Maximov, they heard a well-known gypsy singer,
Vera Zorina, accompanied in turn by Tchaikovsky, Taneyev,

Arensky and Siloti. In the autumn of 1891 Sergei came to know another gypsy singer, Nadezhda Alexandrovna, whom he met through Sakhnovsky and quickly developed a crush on. He would remain in her thrall for some years, dedicating a song to her, 'Oh Be Not Sad' (Op. 4 No. 8). Since he also dedicated his song 'Oh No, I Beg You, Do Not Go' (Op. 4 No. 1) to her sister, Anna Lodizhenskaya, wife of Peter Lodizhensky to whom he dedicated his *Gypsy Caprice* (Op. 12), it is difficult to say whether he was in love with either, neither or both. In Pushkin's day it was the gypsies that caused Aleko to run away with Zemfira, but by Rachmaninoff's time it was more common for things to be the other way round and many gypsies married into society.

Sergei had no sooner read through the libretto than he rushed back home to start work at once. He wrote to Natalya Skalon: 'it has been very well done; the subject is marvellous – however, I don't know how marvellous the music will be!' He found his father entertaining friends in the drawing room where the piano was, so was obliged to retire to his bedroom, doing his best to hide his frustration. Eventually his father came to find him and when he understood the situation immediately took his friends out so Sergei could start work. It took him less than three weeks, from 26 March to 13 April, to complete the opera. On that day he gave a progress report with two other students then graduating, Leo Conus and Nikita Morozov. Arensky stared incredulously as Sergei took the bound copy of the completed score out of his case. At the final examination, which was held before the board of the Conservatory faculty, *Aleko* earned Sergei top marks and he was awarded the Great Gold Medal. He was only the third student at the Moscow Conservatory to have earned it. As Bertensson and Leyda write, 'more rewards followed. Zverev came up to his former pupil, embraced him and with many good wishes took out his gold watch [and] gave it him. Sergei kept it for the rest of his life.'[26]

It did not take long for Zverev to make Sergei a friendly gesture. Hearing of the success of the opera, the publisher Gutheil,

anxious to secure Sergei on his list of artists, came to ask Zverev
for his help. Zverev was cautious, however, so he invited Sergei
to his house to meet Tchaikovsky and play him the opera; he
would be able to give Sergei the best advice on publishers. In
view of Sergei's obvious indebtedness to Tchaikovsky it was not
surprising that Tchaikovsky should have praised *Aleko* enthusiastically. 'You're fortunate. You were born under a lucky star.
I was a good deal older before I found a publisher, and even
then I didn't receive a kopek for my first composition. Indeed,
I thought I was lucky not to have to pay the publisher for the
privilege. As Gutheil not only offers you a fee, but asks you
to name your own, I suggest you go one better – insist that he
makes you the first offer!'[27] And so Sergei did. When Gutheil
paid him 500 rubles for *Aleko*, the two cello pieces (Op. 2) and
6 Songs (Op. 4) he was too astonished for words. On 31 May
at the graduation ceremony in the Hall of Nobility, the musical programme included the intermezzo from *Aleko*. A reviewer
in *Dnevnik Artista*, describes it as 'very powerfully written'.[28]
Present were Zverev, Scriabin, Altschuler, Pabst and Arensky.
Afterwards, as Avierino remembered, 'Zverev gave a supper
officially in honour of all us graduating, yet everyone sensed the
occasion was really his reconciliation with Sergei.'[29]

Thereafter for the vacation Sergei departed for Kostroma, to
stay with the Konovalovs and give their son Alexander piano
tuition. Whilst there, he corrected proofs of *Aleko*. On 7 June he
wrote to Slonov: 'My life is dull and monotonous. My mother
is here at the moment but she goes to St Petersburg on the
11th, then I shall be alone again. Of course, I'm not working as
planned, not practising at all. I've to sit at my desk the whole
time transcribing *Aleko* for piano. The cello pieces (Op. 2) are
due soon and I have to correct the second proofs, but they won't
be published before September.'[30] Three days later he was writing to Natalya Skalon, telling her that *Aleko* had been accepted
for performance at the Bolshoi the following Lent season.
Though he found the prospect of its production pleasant, it

would be good to see it and be able to check it for any inadvertent errors he may have made in setting the libretto, it would also be unpleasant for it was sure to fail. He was still complaining that the Konovalovs 'are nice people and take good care of me and there's no limit to their kindness, yet I am bored. I shall have to stay here at least until the middle of August.'[31]

By 2 August, he was writing to her again when his mood seems to have done an about-turn. 'I was born under a lucky star, as Tchaikovsky tells me – suddenly everyone loves me, passionately. Everyone invites me. Everyone asks me to stay at his place. After these lessons are done I have invitations to no fewer than five houses.'[32] In another letter from 13 October, back at the Satins' in Moscow, he reverts to type: 'I am in a disconsolate mood. I am afraid of becoming ill again. Now, when I've suddenly begun to be offered work I may have to give it all up because I have no coat.'[33] The Skalon sisters immediately sent him money enough to buy a coat, and their generosity changed his mood yet again. He wrote to Ludmila: 'The day before yesterday I told your sister I was not well and in a foul mood. Now, however, I feel wonderful, am well and in great spirits.'

Notwithstanding the censor having cleared publication of *Aleko* by 12 September, its first performance was postponed for a year until the following Lent. In the interim, Sergei was happy to accept fifty rubles for an engagement at the Moscow Electrical Exhibition on the 26th, where he played the first movement of Rubinstein's Fourth Concerto in D minor. His programme also included Chopin's *Berceuse*, the Gounod/Liszt Waltz from *Faust* and, for the first time, he played his Prelude in C sharp minor (Op. 3). The magazine *Artiste* noted: 'a prelude of his own aroused considerable enthusiasm'.[34] It did not take long for it to become his most famous work. First published by Gutheil the following year, it quickly advertised his name widely throughout the western world making it almost a household word. Despite this, he never earned royalties from it, for Russia did not then recognise international copyright law. As soon as he began his concert career clamorous audiences were forever entreating him to play it. As often as not he would give in, but his attitude to it was to remain ambiguous, increasingly so through the years.

Bukinik was equivocal about his playing at the Moscow Electrical Exhibition: 'One got the impression he had not mastered the instrument sufficiently, and only worked on it a little. His appearance was a failure in comparison with young Lhevinne's brilliant debut.'[35] Lhevinne had made his debut three years before, when he was fifteen, playing Beethoven's 'Emperor' Concerto conducted by Rubinstein. On 14 December, Sergei told Slonov how pleased he was when he read how Tchaikovsky had told a critic that with so much new talent around – Glazounov, Arensky and Rachmaninoff – he would soon be obliged to give up writing music. 'Hurrah. Thanks to the old man for not forgetting me,'[36] Sergei declared, though Tchaikovsky was then only fifty-two! That autumn he was again hard at work composing. He completed all five pieces for piano (Op. 3). As well as the prelude he included Elegy, Melody, Polichinelle and Serenade, dedicating them to Arensky. He first performed these altogether in recital at Kharkov on 28 December. The programme also included works by Chopin, Liszt, Schumann, Rubinstein and Pabst's Fantasy on Themes from *Eugene Onegin*.

To judge from the pessimistic, not to say lugubrious tone of a letter he wrote Natalya Skalon that winter, the continued postponement of the premiere of *Aleko* had its effect on him. 'My father lives a senseless life, my mother is gravely ill; my older brother accumulates debts that God alone knows how he will repay (at the present time there is little likelihood of my being able to help him), my younger brother is lazy and sure to have to spend another year at school; my grandmother is at the point of death.'[37] Nevertheless his grandmother lived another decade and his mother another thirty-five years. What happened to his elder brother is not certain, but the younger stayed in Russia, dying there three years after him. Fortunately for Sergei's peace of

mind, he was given a job by Taneyev. The Maryinsky was planning to produce Taneyev's three-act opera *Orestia*, so every day
Sergei came to relieve Taneyev of the chore of proofreading it.

Although *Aleko* had not yet been staged, dances from it
enjoyed a noteworthy success in Moscow that winter under
Safonov with the Conservatory orchestra. Hearing of this,
Sergei Siloti – another cousin and the brother of the pianist
– pressed Sergei to come to St Petersburg. He would, he promised, introduce him to the conductor at the Maryinsky, Eduard
Napravnik. Sergei went and although nothing came of the
meeting, he was invited to play through the dances from *Aleko*
at a soirée at the home of Evgenya Krivenko, wife of a court
dignitary. Among her guests was Vladimir Pogoshev, Chief of
the Chancery of Imperial Theatres, who was anxious to secure
Mme Krivenko's husband's patronage. After Sergei had finished
playing she congratulated him and turning to Pogoshev said
smilingly: 'You will produce this brilliant work, will you not?'

The premiere of *Aleko* took place on 27 April at the Bolshoi.
It was the first part of a substantial evening's entertainment
that also included Act IV scene I of Glinka's *A Life for the Tsar*,
Act III of his *Russlan and Ludmilla* and Act II of Tchaikovsky's
The Queen of Spades. During rehearsals, at which Sergei and
Tchaikovsky were present, Sergei was complaining under his
breath about conductor Altani's slow tempo in a particular
passage. Tchaikovsky asked why he didn't tell him himself. He
replied he was afraid to, whereupon Tchaikovsky, waiting for
a suitable pause, turned to Altani saying: 'I think that passage
might be taken a little faster.'

Of the first performance, the critic Kruglikov from *Artiste*
praised the opera and composer, although rather condescend-
ingly: 'As a talented young man of excellent taste, Rachmaninoff
may become a good composer of opera; he has a feeling for the
stage, a fortunate melodic flair and can write effectively for the
voice. As a student work it is beyond praise but, as an opera
designed for the Bolshoi, it leaves a great deal to be desired.'[38]

Tchaikovsky was much impressed and during the curtain calls at the end, every time Sergei came out to take a bow, he came to the front of his box, so that everyone could see him applauding vigorously. Afterwards he insisted that Vsevolozhky, Director of the Imperial Theatres, should come to hear it. He then asked Sergei whether he would let *Aleko* be performed the following season, as a curtain raiser before his own two-act opera *Iolanthe*. Sergei was overwhelmed: 'To be on the same poster as Tchaikovsky was about the biggest honour that could be paid me as composer – I would not have dared suggest such a thing.'[39]

Although in later years Rachmaninoff did not think much of *Aleko* – 'it is written in an old-fashioned Italian idiom[40] [what is now called the *verismo* style]' – it remains his most successful opera. Two reasons account for its continued neglect. Firstly, late nineteenth-century operas have not yet been subjected to the searchlight scrutiny of works of the *Bel Canto* era, principally for financial reasons since their large orchestras and choruses are costly. Secondly, these days operas are rarely translated and the comparative remoteness of Russian makes it difficult to find a cast sufficiently at ease with the language. However, the break-up of the Soviet Union and the large number of excellent Russian-speaking singers now living in the west make the prospect of revivals of *Aleko* more likely. Only recently the distinguished baritone Dmitri Hvorostovsky sang the air of *Aleko* memorably in a recital at Carnegie Hall.

4

1892–1897

*Fertile period, writes a considerable number of new compositions:
Lack of financial support obliges him to teach: Death of Zverev and
Tchaikovsky: Increased demand for new works encourages him to sign
contract with publisher Gutheil: Composes First Symphony, which
proves a disaster.*

In August 1892, after *Aleko* was finished but before its premiere,
Siloti approached Modest Tchaikovsky to see if he would provide Rachmaninoff with a libretto for another opera. Modest
suggested *Undine*, a fairy tale by Baron Friedrich de la Motte
Fouqué about a nymph transformed into a fountain. This
German story was affectionately known in Russia because of
Vassily Zhukovsky's verse translation. Tchaikovsky had been
attracted by it in 1869 in his more youthful days, but then failed
to persuade an opera house to stage it. Later he pillaged what
he could, using it in *Swan Lake*, another story with watery
allusions. After Modest looked at it again he thought it worth
trying to reawaken his brother's interest, but Tchaikovsky dismissed the idea: 'be content just to send it to Rachmaninoff,'[1]
he told him. Rachmaninoff seems to have become aware of the

brothers' exchange of letters to judge from one he wrote Modest on 13 May:

> At the end of the plot for *Undine* there is a date, 16 March, apparently that on which you completed it, but I did not receive it until the end of April. I like it, but one thing troubles me, it may not be possible to produce it; in a provincial theatre because of the large production it demands, and at Imperial Theatres because the director Vzevolozhsky doesn't care for the subject.

He suggested that Modest approach Vsevolozhsky first to see if he could get him to change his mind. There is no record that Modest ever did and on 14 October Rachmaninoff wrote again: 'I want to ask you to discontinue work on *Undine*. I am doubtful about it and at present having a great deal of travelling to do so I just can't find the time.'[2]

At the beginning of May 1893 Rachmaninoff went to Nizhni Novgorod to visit his grandmother, Sophia Butakova, who had not been able to come to Moscow for *Aleko*. Later that month, in company once again with Slonov, he journeyed to the estate of the wealthy merchant Lysikov at Lebedyan, in the province of Kharkov. Lysikov had a tower especially built in the grounds of the house for Rachmaninoff's use. That summer proved a fertile period. He finished some songs (Op. 4) and began another set (Op. 8). He composed a sacred concerto in three parts for unaccompanied mixed choir, *O Mother of God, Perpetually Praying*, as well as Fantasy Pictures for Two Pianos (Op. 5), two salon pieces for violin and piano (Op. 6) and *The Crag* – a fantasy for orchestra (Op. 7). The latter two were dedicated to Julius Conus and Rimsky-Korsakov respectively. The themes of *The Crag* are short, lacking opportunities for development. As a whole it is derivative of Tchaikovsky and while it is attractive musically, it sounds stylistically antiquated when compared with contemporary works like Strauss's *Tod und Verklärung* and *Til Eulenspiegel* or

Debussy's *Prélude à l'après-midi d'un faune*. Rachmaninoff introduces the score with some lines by Lermontov ('A golden cloud slept for her pleasure. All night long on the crag's breast.') but it was not Lermontov who inspired their use but Chekhov. In 1883, Chekhov had used the lines in a short story, *In Autumn*, and would do so again in the epigraph of his one-act play *On the High Road*. After Rachmaninoff came to know him, he presented him with a four-hand piano version of *The Crag* inscribing it: 'To dear and highly esteemed Anton Pavlovich Chekhov, author of *On the High Road* which, with the same epigraph, serves as a programme for this music: S. Rachmaninoff, 9 November 1898.'[3]

On 18 September, having returned from Kharkov back to Moscow, Rachmaninoff went to Taneyev's apartment to spend the evening in the company of a number of other musicians. He played through some pages of his new compositions including *The Crag*. Tchaikovsky, who was present, congratulated him: 'Well, what haven't you produced this summer – a symphonic poem, a concerto and a suite, and heaven knows what else while I wrote only a symphony!'[4] Since that symphony was the *Pathétique*, his sixth and last, certainly his most popular and usually accepted as the greatest in the Russian School, that hardly seems such a modest achievement. Taneyev and Leo Conus then played through their four-hand version of the symphony. Unfortunately, according to the composer Mikhail Ippolitov-Ivanov, who was also present: 'It was the first time Tchaikovsky had heard the reduction. He kept interrupting to change one detail or another, making innumerable complaints, eventually everyone became so nervous that the work quite failed to make an effect.'[5] Tchaikovsky then asked Rachmaninoff to play one of his new works, but he demurred – perhaps he was remembering Tchaikovsky's complaints over his reduction of *The Sleeping Beauty*. Instead he invited Tchaikovsky to a concert the following January when he would play his own music.

In Moscow that autumn, Rachmaninoff was living alone for the first time. Having little money he had been obliged to take

furnished rooms in a seedy apartment block called 'America'
– a prophetic name in view of his ultimate destination. But
nowhere could have been less like America as it was quite devoid
of the creature comforts that were to become familiar on the
other side of the Atlantic. After the gracious lifestyle he had
led that summer at the Lebedins', the stark simplicity of his
surroundings only served to depress him. 'I can't live schem-
ing counting every kopeck,' he complained to Slonov. 'I must
forget for the moment everything that disturbs and worries me.
I must find a way of adjusting myself to the situation, of cutting back my expenses. But what am I talking about? Cutting
my expenses further is next to impossible; I shall just have to
concoct something extraordinary.'[6] In fact, what he concocted
was ordinary, if not prosaic. He became a piano teacher at the
Maryinsky Academy for Girls where he was to remain for the
next five years.

He wrote to the Skalon sisters news of three deaths that followed in quick succession. First, Alexei Pleshcheyev, the poet
who translated into Russian the text that Rachmaninoff based
his 6 Songs (Op. 8) on. Then Zverev died on 30 September.
'We buried him yesterday. A great pity. Each year the old conservatory family shrinks and loses its "Mohicans". Meanwhile
the world has one fine person the less. No one expected such a
swift end. He himself sensed it only hours before it came.'[7] At
Zverev's funeral he met Tchaikovsky. When he told him how
he would shortly be conducting *Aleko* in Kiev, Tchaikovsky
exclaimed: 'So, now we are both famous composers, one off to
Kiev to conduct his opera and the other to St Petersburg to conduct his symphony.'[8] Rachmaninoff never forgot these words
since this was the last time they would meet.

Tchaikovsky died suddenly from cholera on 25 October.
Rachmaninoff no sooner heard the grim news than he determined to compose one of the relatively few pieces of chamber
music he would ever write, *Trio élégiaque* in D minor (Op. 9) for
piano, violin and cello, dedicating it 'To the Memory of a Great

Artist'. He paid tribute to Tchaikovsky, not only by using the same title Tchaikovsky had used for a trio he composed in 1881 following the unexpected death of Nicolai Rubinstein, but as Martyn writes: 'the close structural correspondence between them shows the extent to which he consciously copied his model'.[9] He began it quickly but soon became bogged down and was still working on it seven weeks later. At length, after finishing it, he told Natalya Skalon: 'It is a composition on the death of a great artist. How earnestly, intensely and painstakingly I have worked. However such things only go well for priests and pathologists!'[10]

The trio was first performed on 31 January 1894 in a concert devoted to his own works. Sergei played the piano, Julius Conus the violin and Brandukov the cello. Tanayev, in his diary, writes harshly: 'It may show talent, but it is formless, a pointless essay in modulations, without themes and endlessly repeating the same thing.'[11] Critical opinion now regards it as one of his more important early works, anticipating some of the typical characteristics of his later music, yet it did not enjoy anything like the success of Tchaikovsky's trio. As was his way through the years, he made various attempts at revision. An odd, uncharacteristic feature of the first edition is the introduction of a harmonium, which raised critical eyebrows when it was performed in London in 1898, according to *The Musical Times*. The same programme included his Fantasy Pictures (Op. 5) with Paul Pabst, two of his songs (Op. 4 and Op. 8) performed by the contralto Elizaveta Lavrovskaya to his accompaniment and his Prelude and *Oriental Dance* (Op. 2) with Brandukov. He brought the evening to a close with his 5 Fantasy Piano Pieces (Op. 3) dedicated to Arensky, and his 7 Salon Pieces for Piano (Op. 10) dedicated to Pabst. The title of the latter suggests the pieces may be slight but full of sentiment, yet they are quite without sentimentality. Years after in 1919 he recorded the Barcarolle for Edison and the Humoresque for Victor in 1921. In 1940, he would repeat the latter, but in a slightly touched-up version.

In April he produced 6 Piano Duets (Op. 11) which are of
slight musical value. He did not dedicate them, nor does he ever
seem to have played any of them. They are, as Martyn states,
'so lacking in originality as to defy recognition of its author
by anyone unacquainted with it. [They were] no doubt [writ-
ten] with an eye on potential sales among amateur pianists.'[12]
Notwithstanding the steady flow of works from his pen, the
only source of income he could rely on was to continue teaching. At the end of May, he left his Moscow apartment journeying
first to the Konovalovs at Kostroma. There he began another
symphonic poem, two episodes '*à la* Liszt',[13] based on Byron's
Don Juan. At the end of July after toiling over it for five weeks –
longer than either *Prince Rostislav* or *The Crag* had taken – he put
what he had written to one side. 'It was impossible to make up a
good programme, a good plan,'[14] he wrote to Slonov. Instead he
took up another orchestral work, *Gypsy Caprice* (Op. 12), which
had been on his mind some while and which he had originally
written as a piano duet two years earlier. 'There is a certain interest in the manner in which he sought to impose a unity in the
composition through economy of material and thematic trans-
formation, a technique that was to become a feature of much of
his later work.' Sergei never thought much of the piece, and this
does not seem to have been as result of his later condescension
towards his juvenile essays since he was still playing some of his
early 'Salon Pieces' (Op. 10) and the First Piano Concerto (albeit
a revised edition) in concerts just before his death. In August, he
went to the Satins' at Ivanovka where he played cards, smoked
endlessly and proofread *The Crag* for Jürgenson, another of
Russia's music publishers. When he returned to Moscow in the
autumn the Satins, having moved into a larger residence, did
something to ameliorate his economic problems by inviting him
to stay with them, and so he was at least able to leave 'America'.

At the beginning of January 1895 Rachmaninoff commenced
writing his First Symphony in D minor (Op. 13). Six months
later, on 17 July, he wrote to Slonov complaining how slow

his progress was, even though he was spending seven hours a day on it. At least in this respect it was markedly different from some of his previous compositions – even *Aleko* had taken only twenty-four days to complete. 'Maybe, if God permits, I shall finish everything soon, but it's very onerous,'[15] he told Slonov. Notwithstanding increasing his workload up to ten hours a day, it took until 2 September before it was anything like complete. He told Slonov, 'I am happy about the first three movements, though the first is not perfect, several things need changing.'[16] But when he wrote about it next, on the 15th, he seems to have been having second thoughts. This slowness was perhaps less a reflection on the failing of his creative powers than on the escalating demands of his compositions. He was beset by music publishers anxious to secure smaller-scale, less demanding, popular pieces from him. He had scarcely finished the symphony when, at Jürgenson's instigation, he wrote 6 Choruses for Women's or Children's Voices with Piano Accompaniment (Op. 15). The title, rather a mouthful, suggests a work more imposing than it was. Five of the choruses had originally been published in a magazine entitled *Reading for Children* at odd intervals during 1895. They would appear to have followed inevitably from his teaching experience at the Maryinsky Academy, although 'no child will ever be able to sing them,'[17] he later admitted. In fact, for a very long time no one seemed to want to. Their first public performance did not take place until 1973, the year of the centenary of his birth, when the Yurlov State Chorus sang them under Evgeny Svetlanov.

In the autumn of 1895 came Sergei's first opportunity to earn a little money. Impresario Henrik Langiewicz engaged him to accompany a violinist and play solos on a concert tour of Russia and Poland. He described the tour to Slonov:

> I played pretty well and had a great success but she – Contessa Teresina Tua Franchi-Verney della Valetta, of course – had an even greater success. She did not play particularly well, her technique is only so-so. It is with her eyes that she plays

most effectively on the public. As an artist she is not serious.
Although she's always charming to me, afraid I'm about to
scamper off.

At twenty-eight she was making a comeback after a six-year
absence following her marriage, from which she had acquired
the name above – she was born plain Maria Felicita. The first
Grove's Dictionary of Music, like Rachmaninoff, seems not to have
been much impressed with her. Grieg, on the other hand, was
inspired to dedicate his Third Violin Sonata (which Kreisler
and Rachmaninoff would later record in Germany in 1928) to
her after she had visited him at his Norway home. On tour the
Contessa and Rachmaninoff played Beethoven's *Kreutzer Sonata*
and various pieces by Schubert, Vieuxtemps, Wieniawski and
Sarasate. He also included a selection of his familiar solos by
Chopin, Liszt, Rubinstein, Arensky and Pabst. After twenty-
three concerts, and long before the three-month stint was up, he
did scamper back to Moscow, using the fact that his fee was not
being paid regularly as an excuse.

In his absence, news that he was composing a symphony had
reached the ears of Mitrofan Belayav, a wealthy timber merchant
and enthusiastic music-lover who, by magnificent bequests,
had contributed considerably to the improvement of Russian
music life.[18] He set up a Leipzig publishing firm, and inaugu-
rated The Glinka Prize, 'a yearly award for the best symphonic
or chamber music work.' He also sponsored Russian symphony
concerts '… [which] included only works written by Russians.'[19]
Belayev heard this news through Sakhnovsky and determined
to have Rachmaninoff premiere the new symphony at one
of his St Petersburg concerts. In fact, Belayev already knew
Rachmaninoff from 1893 when he had invited the composer to
his St Petersburg house. Rachmaninoff describes the occasion:

Belayev asked me to play for them (his guests included
Lyadov and Rimsky-Korsakov). I had just written my

Fantasy Pictures (Op. 5). They put Felix Blumenfeld at the other piano with the score, for he could sight-read perfectly. I played it from memory at the first piano. Everyone, including Lyadov and Rimsky-Korsakov listened attentively and seemed to like it. At the end they all praised me and Rimsky-Korsakov said. 'It's perfect but, at the end when the chant "Christ is Risen" is heard, it would be better I think just to state it first alone, and only the second time with the bells.' But I was silly in those days and in love with my own work, so I shrugged my shoulders and asked 'Why? It sounds very good the way it is.' And I didn't change it.[20]

It was on 20 January 1896, at one of Belayev's concerts, that *The Crag* had its first St Petersburg performance conducted by Glazounov. Afterwards, Cui complained that 'the whole composition shows that he is more concerned about sound than music'.[21] This did not prevent Belayev, who was determined to secure the best young composers on his roster of artists, from commissioning a piano transcription of Glazounov's Sixth Symphony from Rachmaninoff for 200 rubles. Belayev had already signed up Taneyev and Scriabin and was out to secure Rachmaninoff, a fact of which the publisher Gutheil, who quickly upped his advance to 500 rubles for his forthcoming symphony, seems to have been well aware. On 22 March, Rachmaninoff visited Taneyev's apartment in Moscow. Taneyev noted in his journal: 'he is writing a quartet. We discussed quartet style and especially Mozart's Quartet in C [K. 465].'[22] But, perhaps because Rachmaninoff seems not to have had much sympathy for chamber music, he never finished it. Two movements were completed but they were not performed until after the Second World War by the Beethoven Quartet in Moscow. The music was not published until 1947.

At Taneyev's apartment Sabaneyev tells of what might be called a ring cycle of Wagner soirées. At that time, sixteen years since the Master's death, his music was entering its golden age.

Each session lasted six hours and extended over a period of days, during which a flush of young pianists came and went including Igumnov, Goldenweiser, Catoire, Scriabin, Conus and Pomerantzev. Wagner's genius may have been greater than his pretensions, but even among those who admired his music inordinately his lack of humour could be his Achilles heel, providing a source of amusement. On occasions like these, although humour may not have been Rachmaninoff's strongest suit, Sabaneyev relates 'how he just sat in the corner in a rocking chair, leafing quickly through the pages of one of Wagner's scores to see how much more music there was. He would chuckle "a thousand pages more", then an hour later, "still another eight and hundred and eighty!"'[23] On other occasions, again at Taneyev's, Rachmaninoff took part in a series of improvisations with Arensky and Glazounov: 'Each was commenced by its author to which the others then contributed in turn,' someone copied them down and eventually they were published in a biography of Taneyev which appeared long after his death in 1925.

In October, he completed a dozen new songs (Op. 14). Several are outstanding including 'Spring Waters' (No. 11), with text by Tyutchev. This is one of his finest and quickly succeeded in earning him a reputation. Like so many Russian songs, it was only infrequently sung in the West until recently. Only after the break-up of the Soviet Union was it easy to engage top-ranking Russian-speaking singers. When Rachmaninoff's songs were new, in the days before translations were frowned upon, the famous Irish tenor John McCormack made a recording in his own beautiful, and beautifully enunciated, English translation of Pushkin's text: 'O cease thy singing maiden fair' (Op. 4 No. 4). It vies with a version in the original by the tenor Ivan Kozlovsky as the finest recorded interpretation. It is a great pity that Caruso, who sang 'Spring Waters' (in French) on several occasions, did not record it. The last pieces Rachmaninoff wrote before leaving for the St Petersburg premiere of his First

Symphony were *Moments Musicaux* (Op. 16) for piano. As it transpired, they would also be the last pieces he would write for quite some time. 'In them,' Martyn states, 'his piano writing rises to new heights of virtuosity, he finds his own style more distinctly than ever before. They provide incontestable evidence that almost all of what we now think of as the *echt* features of Rachmaninoff's mature style had crystallized before his Second Piano Concerto.'[24]

During the First Symphony's gestatory period when Rachmaninoff first brought the score to Taneyev, Taneyev had been unimpressed: 'The melodies are flabby and colourless; there is nothing that can be done with them.'[25] As a result, Rachmaninoff did make some changes in the orchestration while at Ivanovka in the summer of 1896. Although critical to his face, Taneyev went out of his way to reassure Belayev that 'Rachmaninoff has made alterations to his symphony, but not as yet incorporated them in the score. I sincerely trust the committee [Rimsky-Korsakov, Lyadov and Glazounov] do not regard too severely a certain harmonic pretentiousness in this work. He is a talented young man with rich musical gifts and will find his way more quickly if he hears his works performed. Shortcomings in them are generally characteristic of young composers.'[26] After a protracted exchange of letters, in which Taneyev again sought to reassure Belayev (who could not help recalling the disagreeably conceited impression the young composer had made with his riposte to Rimsky-Korsakov), the symphony's performance was finally scheduled.

Even at the rehearsals the reception of the new symphony was inauspicious. Rimsky-Korsakov told him frankly: 'I do not find this music at all agreeable.'[27] On the day of the first performance, 15 March 1897, Rachmaninoff had become so apprehensive that he did not dare to enter the concert hall, preferring to listen outside on the steps of the fire escape. What he heard completely demoralised him: 'the audience reception was hostile; it was the most agonizing hour of my life!'[28] Afterwards, he rushed out and took a tram downtown and 'drove up and down the endless streets, through wind and mist'.[29] It was not for some time that he mustered sufficient courage to go to the party that Belayev had arranged in his honour. As he recalls, 'all my hopes, all belief in myself, had been destroyed; abject misery had taken the place of my former arrogance.'[30] Cui's appraisal, in *St Petersburg News*, is most often quoted: 'If there's a conservatory in hell, and one of its talented pupils were required to write a programme for a symphony based on *The Seven Plagues of Egypt*, and he composed something resembling Rachmaninoff's, then he would have succeeded brilliantly delighting the inmates of hell.'[31] He goes on in the same vein accusing Rachmaninoff – of all composers – of modernism! By this time Cui was sixty-two, and scarcely a musical progressive. Some of his antipathy would have been generated by the traditional internecine hostility between the composers of St Petersburg and Moscow. St Petersburg was the capital of Imperial Russia, its most international city, and it was there that 'The Five', the group of nationalist composers, were ensconced. By 1897, however, Borodin and Moussorgsky were dead, Balakirev had become misanthropic and nobody took Cui seriously, so it might have been more accurately styled, with only Rimsky-Korsakov still living, 'The One'.

The symphony's premiere was an event that would always cause Rachmaninoff traumatic recollections. When we hear it today its musical style scarcely sounds advanced: its failure must have had something to do with the instrumental writing taxing the resources of the players or the technique of its conductor, Glazounov, or maybe both. Critic and musicologist Alexander Ossovsky states: 'The conducting lacked any definite clear conception. Rhythmic vitality, so essential in the works of Rachmaninoff, withered, everything found in the music – dynamic shadings, gradations of tempi, expressive nuances, just did not exist. The slothful character of the conductor completed the picture.'[32] Another conductor and teacher, Alexander

Khessin, wrote much the same: 'It was insufficiently rehearsed, the orchestra was ragged, stability in tempi lacking, errors in the orchestral parts remained uncorrected, but the main thing that wrecked the performance was the lifeless, superficial, bland, matter-of-fact playing, there was no animation, energy or brilliance in it.'[33] In Glazounov's defence, it should be pointed out that the programme not only included the first performance of Rachmaninoff's symphony, but also two other world premieres: a posthumously put together symphonic poem by Tchaikovsky, *Fatum*, and Artzibashev's *Valse-Fantasie*. Glazounov may have been no more than a routine conductor, yet the evidence of a recording he made in 1929 of his ballet suite, *The Seasons*, does not suggest he could have been solely responsible for generating such a reception.

After the performance Rachmaninoff returned home and spent the days moping. By 6 May, however, when he wrote a two-page letter to Zatayevich, the composer and folk song collector, he seems to have worked some improvement in his mood and makes an attempt to come to terms with himself.

I am indifferent to my failure and am not discouraged by the abuse of newspaper critics, but I am very sorry the symphony, which I loved – and still do, should have so dissatisfied me after I had heard the first rehearsal. If it is claimed it is badly orchestrated, I reply that good music can always be recognized even through the orchestration – in any case I don't consider it bad. I consider it was badly performed. I am very much surprised that anyone as talented as Glazounov should conduct so badly. I am not speaking of his conducting technique – that is hardly to be expected of him. I am speaking of his musicianship. He doesn't feel anything; it is as if he didn't understand it. I assume, even if I do not assert, his performance was the cause of the symphony's failure. If the public were familiar with the work then they would blame the conductor, but as it is they blame the composer.[34]

However, by 1933 he had changed his mind. He told Riesemann: 'its fate was not undeserved. It is true that the performance was beneath contempt and the work in parts almost unrecognizable yet, apart from this, its deficiencies were revealed to me with a dreadful distinctness even during the first rehearsal.'[35]

What precisely happened to the complete orchestral score of the symphony is not known. It is strange that when he left Russia in 1918, assuming he kept it up until then, he did not take it with him. Instead he took Rimsky-Korsakov's *Le Coq d'or,* which he had never even conducted. Sophia Satina told Martyn that he gave it to her locked up in a desk and she took charge of it. In 1921, when Sophia emigrated, it must have remained behind in her apartment with other autographs of his. Since these eventually found their way to the Glinka museum it is surprising that the symphony never showed up. Martyn speculates that it was stolen. In view of Rachmaninoff's known antipathy towards it – only months before he left Russia he told Asafiev, 'I haven't let anyone see it and in my will I shall make sure no one does'[36] – it seems more probable that it was never in Satina's desk and that he had already destroyed it. It was not until 1945 that the original band parts were found in the Belayev Archive in the Leningrad Conservatory, from which a complete orchestral score was made. It was performed for the second time on 17 October 1948 at the Moscow Conservatory, conducted by Alexander Gauk.

5

1897–1902

*Fallow years: Visits Tolstoy on two occasions: Takes up conduct-
ing: Joins Mamontov's opera company: Meets Chaliapin: Makes
his London debut: Dahl and hypnosis: Resumes career as composer:
Premiere of Second Piano Concerto.*

Rachmaninoff's first fallow period as a composer came between
the calamitous reception of his First Symphony in March 1897,
and the composition of his Second Piano Concerto, begun in
the second half of 1900. The blow his ego suffered was severe,
and he could not adjust to it easily. Someone older and more
mature might have just shrugged his shoulders – he was not the
first composer to have to endure a failure. 'But he was young,
with a very passionate nature, easily carried away, sentimental,
spoiled by early success, flattery and fame, and with none of the
strength of will and equilibrium which he later developed.'[1] At
first he sought to forget his problems by involving himself in the
undisciplined and chaotic lifestyle of friends like Sakhnovsky
and Slonov, who were noted for the amount of hard liquor they
consumed. This might account for his rapid mood-change: three
weeks after the symphony's failure he started work on another,
but managed less than a page, signing himself off as follows:

'sketches for a new symphony which, by the look of things, won't amount to much.'[2]

Princess Lieven, a friend of his aunt Varvara Satina, suggested he seek counsel from an acquaintance of hers, the great Tolstoy. After learning of Rachmaninoff's problems Tolstoy was unsympathetic: 'Young man do you imagine everything in my life has gone smoothly. Do you suppose I have never had any troubles, never lost confidence in myself? Do you really think faith is always equally strong? All of us have difficult moments; but that is life. Hold your head up high and keep to your anointed path.'[3] Not surprisingly, Rachmaninoff did not care for such a homily. Later when he met Chekhov and told him, he was chagrined when Chekhov sought to excuse Tolstoy: 'He was probably just suffering from stomachache, not feeling himself,'[4] Chekhov smiled. Another later occasion tells how he and the young bass Feodor Chaliapin received an invitation to visit Tolstoy, who was then in Moscow. For the occasion they took with them one of Rachmaninoff's songs, Fate (Op. 21 No. 1), which contained words by Apukhtin. Its first measures are imitative of the opening bars of Beethoven's Fifth Symphony. Chaliapin describes the occasion: 'Rachmaninoff accompanied me and we did our best to present the work as well as possible, but we could not have pleased Tolstoy. He said nothing and then asked. "What kind of music is most necessary – classical or popular music?"'[5] Rachmaninoff's memory, perhaps because of Tolstoy's attitude at their first meeting, presents the great man as being in a peevish mood. 'We performed my song Fate. When we finished the enthusiastic applause was hushed, everyone was silent. Tolstoy sat in an armchair looking morose and surly. For the next hour I avoided him, but he suddenly came up to me declaring excitedly: "I must speak to you, I must tell you how I disliked it."'[6]

During the spring of 1897, Rachmaninoff was suffering from pains in his back, arms and legs, and was diagnosed with neurasthenia (these days it is likely to be called psychosomatic). Accepting medical advice, at the end of May, with the Skalon sisters, he departed for their country estate, where he was advised 'not to work strenuously at the piano and not compose anything'.[7] Apart from finishing a commission that Belayev had given him (transcribing Glazounov's symphony) he had nothing to fill the time. He may have felt there was no future composing, but he still had to do something. There was no chance of conservatory work, or of being invited to play the piano at a Russian Music Society concert; both positions were dependent on Safonov's recommendation, and Safonov's hostility to Siloti included his relatives. The only thing he could turn to was his limited experience of conducting. In 1895, he conducted a performance of his own *Gypsy Capriccio* at a concert with the violinist Tua, as well as a couple of performances of *Aleko* in Kiev. The more he thought about it the more he realised this was his only option, even though 'he admitted he had but a hazy idea of the technique of conducting. At that time, there were as yet no conducting classes at the Conservatory nor could he have learned much from the conductors he heard.'[8]

The history of reputable conductors goes back only to the beginning of the last quarter of the nineteenth century; even by the end of it they were not the exalted figures they have since become. At this time the population of western Europe, stimulated by industrialisation, was beginning to grow at a faster rate than it had ever done previously, and was shifting from the countryside to the towns. As economic prosperity grew, so did the number of concerts and performances of opera. Orchestral compositions in the late Romantic age were becoming larger and more complex, and the repertory began to include an increasing number of revivals of works from the past. These factors contributed to the greater need for conductors and their increased authority. Their ultimate seal of approval came after 1925 with the advertisement that electric recording provided. They then came to step into the composers' shoes and it became not Mozart's but Beecham's *Zauberflöte*, not Beethoven's but Toscanini's *Fidelio*, not Wagner's but Furtwängler's *Ring* cycle.

After Rachmaninoff's return to Moscow that September, Slonov suggested he should conduct opera for the company of the millionaire impresario Savva Mamontov. In those days, millionaires in Russia like the timber merchant Belayev and the railway magnate Mamontov were members of the artistic community; today billionaires in Russia seem to prefer football to opera. Mamontov had purchased an estate at Abramtsevo, some 50km to the north of Moscow. Just as the newly rich textile barons in England had revived the gothic style to suit their palatial abodes, Mamontov sought to recreate a Russian arcadia with mock old-fashioned buildings including an onion-domed, traditionally-styled church (where he is buried) and a specially-built bathhouse and children's playhouse designed like the hut of Baba Yaga, a fairy-tale figure. Since he made his fortune during the railway mania, he was concerned to ensure that Russia's rapidly developing industry would not destroy its cultural heritage. He started a school of folk art to teach peasants traditional methods. One piece of folk art that he was responsible for making and popularising survived the revolution; the *matryoshka* (nest of dolls) has become familiar in the west. Ironically, it was copied from a Japanese original.

Mamontov's principal preoccupation was the Private Opera, which he founded. At first, he concentrated on spectacular productions of modern Russian works, mostly in Nizhni Novgorod. Abroad foreign painters of repute had been lured into designing for the opera, but not by impresarios, more often by singers. The famous Italian contralto, Giulia Ravogli, who reintroduced Gluck's *Orfeo* at Covent Garden in 1890 in its first nineteenth-century performance, wore costumes specially designed for her by Burne-Jones. Mamontov secured the services of a number of reputable Russian painters including Ilya Repin, Constantin Korovin, Valentin Serov and Mikhail Vrubel (husband of soprano Zabela-Vrubel), to whom Rachmaninoff would dedicate his song Twilight (Op. 21 No. 3). In 1895, Mamontov brought his Private Opera to Moscow where, to compete with the Bolshoi, he introduced new Russian operas and enticed the bass Chaliapin. What he needed, he decided, was to have his performances conducted by a musician of an equal competence, so he was encouraged to engage Rachmaninoff.

Rachmaninoff's engagement was to have begun with Glinka's *A Life for the Tsar*. Although he studied the opera thoroughly, the first dress rehearsal ground to a halt when he failed to give the singers their cues. 'In my ignorance and innocence I had imagined that a singer who walks on to the stage to sing an opera is bound to know it as well as the conductor. Why should I give him a cue? I had no idea of the astonishing lack of musical understanding that characterizes most singers, who know nothing of an opera except their own part.'[9] This sounds disingenuous for singers, unlike the orchestra players, or the conductor, have to accomplish a trio of activities; they have to sing, learn the text and act – or at any rate, as Noël Coward put it, 'be careful not to fall over the furniture'. At the first performance of *A Life for the Tsar* Rachmaninoff left the podium to the resident conductor, the Italian expatriate Eugenio Esposito, and took the opportunity to watch him at work. As he says: 'The experience I gathered enabled me to rehearse Saint-Saëns's *Samson et Dalilah* [with which he made his debut on 12 October 1897 at the Hermitage Theatre] without difficulty and without a hitch.'[10]

A critic was quick to notice a particular feature of his conducting: 'his chief merit is that he has been able to charge the sound of the orchestra.' This ability is part of a great conductor's genius. We can hear it in recordings Rachmaninoff would later make conducting his own symphonic poem, *The Isle of the Dead,* and his Third Symphony (both with the Philadelphia Orchestra).[11] They confirm how important the sound of music always was to him. It was a part of what he would so much admire, not only in the conducting of others, like Stokowski, Mitropoulos and Mengelberg, but in the then characteristic playing of orchestras, like the Philadelphia, Vienna Philharmonic

and the Concertgebouw. As recordings confirm, the relationship between orchestra players and conductors is different today.
Although the population has more than doubled in the last fifty
years, the world has also become a smaller place as a result of new
media: broadcasts, recordings, CDs, television, video, etc. As
such, a unanimity of style becomes inevitable. It is not that the
greatest conductors have lost their individuality, but the sound
quality of leading American and western European orchestras
has become virtually synonymous, and it often takes a degree
of concentration to be able to differentiate easily between them.
The only orchestras that are still exceptional are from Russia,
and were until recently locked away behind the iron curtain.
They retained players who acquired their style and technique
locally, as well as Russian instruments that were sufficiently old-
fashioned to give their performances an individual character, as
one still notices in orchestras such as that of the Kirov.

In the course of that season at Mamontov's Private Opera,
Rachmaninoff conducted: Alexander Dargomizhsky's *Rusalka*;
Alexei Verstovsky's *Askold's Tomb*, *Carmen*, *Orfeo*; Alexander
Serov's *Rogneda* and Act II of *The Power of Evil*; Thomas's *Mignon*
and Rimsky-Korsakov's *May Night*. The critic Lipayev wrote in
Russkaya Muzykalnaya Gazeta: 'He leads the orchestra a hundred
times better than Esposito. If I were manager I would not bother
giving Russian opera with the untalented Esposito if I had as
splendid a musician as Rachmaninoff. We need conductors like
him, with solid education and great talent.'[12] Maybe Lipayev
was unaware of the jealousy his review caused, but Esposito certainly noticed. He cut Rachmaninoff's duties, leaving him only
leftovers: the Sunday matinées for children, and two operas with
Chaliapin in leading roles, *May Night* and *Rusalka*.[13]

On 22 November, Rachmaninoff wrote a letter to Ludmila
Skalon giving a detailed account of the company backstage:

> Chaos truly reigns. Nobody knows what is going to happen
> the day after tomorrow, tomorrow, or even today. We cannot

rely on the singers; in our large company of thirty about twenty-five should be dismissed as incompetent. There is almost nothing worth performing – the repertory is huge, but everything is so badly and sloppily produced [with the exception of *Khovanshchina*], ninety-five per cent should be shelved or completely restudied. The trouble is that our chief executives are not very bright musically. It is too bad that we are supervised, not by one, but by ten of them, and everyone wants something different. The worst is Mamontov himself, he is so indecisive and yields to everyone in turn. For example, having got him interested in Schumann's *Manfred*, I gave orders for its production but scarcely five minutes had passed before Korovin, the set designer, who understands nothing about music, had talked him out of it. I'll try and persuade him again. If only Chaliapin would agree to the spoken dialogue, he would be a magnificent Manfred. As for *Rogneda* and *The Snow Maiden* being turned over to me; I am trying to persuade Mamontov not to produce them. They are already splendid productions at the Bolshoi, and we have neither time nor means to mount either even tolerably. Still, I am employed here and hope to be able to endure it until the end of the season, though except for the money, the time spent will have benefited me but little. I want the total attention and compliance of the musicians, which as a second conductor I will never get. One of the players, in the presence, no less, of the rest of the orchestra and a full house, slapped Esposito full in the face for something he was alleged to have said – and Esposito continues to conduct! What if that should happen to me?'[14]

Rachmaninoff left the Private Opera before the season had ended – a season's conducting proved enough to regenerate his interest in composition. It is unclear when the final severance took place, for he remained a member of Mamontov's company throughout that summer and continued to prepare Chaliapin his roles the following season: Boris Godounov and Salieri in Rimsky-Korsakov's *Mozart and Salieri*.

At the end of May, Rachmaninoff departed for the Putyatino retreat of the wealthy diva Tatiana Lyubatovich along with Chaliapin, Mamontov, the painters Korovin and Serov, and other members of the Private Opera. At the time, he had entered into correspondence with Modest Tchaikovsky on the subject of an opera based on Shakespeare's *Richard II*, but the prospect of a leisurely summer caused him to put it to one side. Not until the end of July did he write again to Modest about *Richard II*. One theory has it that he did so because he knew Chaliapin was looking for a role to vie with Boris Godounov, but this is unlikely for Chaliapin had not yet sung the role of Boris and there was little in common between the two characters. Pushkin's Boris is a strong ruler devoured by ambition who meets his end in suitably tragic style – appropriate stuff for Chaliapin. Shakespeare's Richard is almost the opposite – vain and effete, he is murdered after being dethroned. If Rachmaninoff was concerned to find Chaliapin a fitting drama of Shakespeare's, we may wonder why neither he nor Modest thought of *Macbeth*. At all events, the next time Rachmaninoff wrote, at the end of August, he is taken up with another idea of Modest's: *Francesca da Rimini*, based on Canto V of Dante's *Inferno*, which he would eventually set, but not until 1906.

In his autobiography Chaliapin acknowledges his debt to Rachmaninoff: 'He taught me something about the fundamentals of music and harmony, striving to complete my education. Boris Godounov appealed to me to such an extent that, not content with learning my role, I sang the whole of the opera, all the parts, male and female and I began to study other works in their entirety, even operas I was already familiar with.'[15] In *Rachmaninoff's Recollections* Riesemann has him spend a paragraph on Chaliapin:

> I count it among the most important and finest artistic experiences I have ever known. I can hardly think of another artist

who has given me such deep and purely artistic enjoyment. To accompany him when he sang, to admire the facility of his musical conception, the quickness and naturalness with which he responded to musical and artistic stimuli and assimilated and transformed them in his own inimitable way – these experiences rank without doubt amongst the greatest artistic joys of my life.[16]

During that summer we catch a glimpse of Rachmaninoff chez Lyubatovich after Chaliapin married the Italian ballerina Lola Tornaghi. The ceremony took place on 27 July and the entire company of the Private Opera continued celebrating long into the summer night. Chaliapin remembers the occasion:

> There were none of the things usually considered indispensable at a wedding; no richly decked table laden with all kinds of foods, no eloquent toasts. Around six in the morning, an infernal racket erupted outside our bedroom window – a large group of friends led by Mamontov himself performed a concert with kitchen dishes, stove lids, buckets and tin-whistles. They banged pieces of metal and blew their whistles, this chaos was conducted by Rachmaninoff.[17]

Later that summer after another bout of neurasthenia, Rachmaninoff's doctor advised him to go to the Crimea to recuperate, a trip that he financed through recitals with Chaliapin. After one such recital, Chekhov came backstage and, notwithstanding Chaliapin's presence, went straight across and introduced himself to Rachmaninoff. 'I have been looking at you, young man. You have a wonderful face – you will be a great man!' We can understand the effect this greeting had on him – 'Until I die I shall recall those words with pride and joy.'[18] The remainder of 1898 he spent homeless, dividing his time between the Satin estate at Ivanovka with another trip to Putyatino, in between time spending a week in Moscow to be

able to earn enough from music lessons to afford the incessant
to-ings and fro-ings.

That autumn Siloti, who had been abroad giving concerts
in western Europe and the United States, programmed his
cousin's Prelude in C sharp minor. Its effect was tumultuous
and had audiences everywhere clamouring. Publishers rushed
to print editions with titles varying from the apocalyptic ('The
Day of Judgment') to the inaccurate ('The Moscow Waltz'). It
was so attractive to publishers because it was not in copyright,
but Siloti knew of Rachmaninoff's indigence, and was embar-
rassed. Since it was too late to shut the stable door, he did at
least secure an engagement for Rachmaninoff to appear himself as conductor and pianist with the Philharmonic Society in
London the following April. By the time he arrived, the prelude had made him famous and had joined the ranks of what
was then the most popular music: Mozart's *Rondo alla turca*,
Beethoven's *Für Elise*, Chopin's revolutionary study, Liszt's
Liebestraum, Rubinstein's *Melody in F* and Paderewski's *Minuet*.
He had no difficulty securing an audience; the Queen's Hall
was packed to the eaves. His London debut, and first performance outside Imperial Russia, took place on the 19th. He
conducted his symphonic poem *The Crag*, Yaroslavna's aria
from *Prince Igor* (sung by mezzo-soprano Christianne Andray)
and then played his Elegy in E flat minor and the Prelude. *The
Times*, although not much impressed with *The Crag*, thought
'his orchestration, in a word [sic.], is superb and original, and as
a conductor the Russian musician showed to great advantage.
His command was supreme; his method quietness idealized. As
a pianist, he plays like a conductor [as we shall see later, a sage
observation]. Rachmaninoff can certainly claim a success on
his first visit to England.'[19]

He was immediately invited to return and it was suggested
he play his First Piano Concerto. He promised to come again
but would, he said, bring a second concerto with him. This is
not the first time we hear of it. Nearly three years before he

told Alexander Zatayevich, a composer and folk song collector whom he met on tour with violinist Tua in 1895, that he was thinking of composing a new piano concerto. Goldenweiser had also heard of it and wanted to perform it at one of Belayev's St Petersburg concerts, so he wrote to him to ask his permission. On 18 June, Rachmaninoff replied equivocally: 'I don't yet have a concerto and because all my intensive work on it has got nowhere, I want to ask your permission to give you a final answer in August.'[20]

At the beginning of May, Rachmaninoff travelled to Krasnenkoye in the province of Voronezh to spend the summer months with the Kreutzer family. It was here that he received news that *Aleko* would be performed at the Tavrichesky Theatre in St Petersburg to commemorate the centenary of Pushkin's birth on 27 May, and that Chaliapin was to sing the title role. Although memories of the failure of his symphony made him a little apprehensive, he immediately rushed off to St Petersburgh. No sooner had it started than he could relax; it was a complete triumph. Chaliapin swept all before him. Not everything that spring was consoling, though – Vera Skalon was married that year. It was probably Rachmaninoff's financial position that caused nothing to come of their friendship, since Vera destroyed more than a hundred of his letters, and according to her sister Natalya, 'right up until her early death in 1909 he had a special place in her heart'.[21] As was the way with Rachmaninoff, he was disinclined to give expression to his intimate feelings. Many of his works, although he was always cautious admitting it, reflected his mood. The song 'Night', which he composed at the time, has Daniel Rathaus's fittingly mournful lyrics:

> My heart is saddened by daily cares,
> And ardour of desire is dead in my breast.
> A mocking fate has long since closed,
> All paths to happiness...

At the end of 1899, the Satins urged Rachmaninoff to visit a
neurologist living nearby, Nicolai Dahl, who might be able to
help him. Dahl was a cultured man who had become interested
in the then fashionable power of hypnosis; today he would probably be described as a psychoanalyst. As an amateur composer
himself, he immediately agreed to see Rachmaninoff without
charge when he learned of his problem and his inability to finish
his concerto. For three months, until April, Rachmaninoff paid
him daily visits. With Dahl he gradually began to sort through
his problems and look at life more positively. At these sessions,
in a darkened room, he was persuaded to relax completely so
that he would sleep undisturbed and wake refreshed. Not only
did this restore his health but, more importantly, it refreshed
his appetite for composition. 'Dahl would repeat day after day,
while I lay asleep,' Rachmaninoff told Riesemann: '"you will
begin to write your concerto. You will begin to work with great
facility. The concerto will be of an excellent quality."'[22]

To speed his recuperation he left for the Crimea at the end
of April, in company with Chaliapin. There he met a troupe of
actors from the Moscow Arts Theatre, who had gone there to
be with Chekhov who was ailing from tuberculosis. There too
he met the composer Vassily Kallinikov, who would die of the
same disease the following year. Perhaps, on the principle that no
matter how badly off you are yourself, there are always others in
worse circumstances, Rachmaninoff became preoccupied with
Kallinikov. In the afternoon he would go to Kallinkov's lodg-
ings and play him works of Glazounov, Taneyev and Arensky.
What particularly disturbed him was the fact that Kallinikov
had completed a number of compositions, including two symphonies, but had never been able to secure their publication. He
wrote to the publisher Jürgenson, and to Kallinikov's great joy
Jürgenson not only bought both symphonies and some songs
but paid for them in advance. On 10 May, Rachmaninoff wrote
to Slonov that he may not be doing much work himself but at
least he was doing something!

It was that May that Chaliapin was offered his first international engagement: to sing the title-role in Boito's *Mefistofele* at La Scala in Milan the following March. Caruso would be Faust and the opera would be conducted by Toscanini. Not taking it very seriously, Chaliapin, who had not yet sung outside Russia or in any language but Russian, asked a sum that was far in excess of any bass's fee until that time: 15,000 francs a performance. To his surprise, La Scala at once agreed, but this made him apprehensive. He determined to learn Italian at once, and what better place to study Italian than Italy. He asked Chekhov to come too, the weather would be perfect, but Chekhov declined; for him the journey would be too arduous. He then asked Rachmaninoff. He would pay and Rachmaninoff could teach him Mefistofele. At the end of June, Rachmaninoff arrived at the villa Chaliapin was renting at Varazze, a resort on the Italian Riviera, only to find Chaliapin was not there yet. 'He is preoccupied with, in all probability, the lady problem,'[23] Rachmaninoff conjectured in a letter to Morozov. At length Chaliapin arrived and determinedly adopted a serious mien. Chaliapin recalls 'how modestly we lived, gave up smoking, retired to bed early, and rose early. I found work under such conditions a delight, as with my other operas, I thoroughly studied it, learning not only my own role, but all the other parts too.'[24] But for all Chaliapin's discipline and abstemiousness, he was in company with his new wife, whereas Rachmaninoff was lonely, 'without family or some substitute, life was hard'.[25] The heat irritated him, making him even more moody and taciturn than normal.

But perhaps the main reason for his wanting to leave was that, at last, he felt able to resume composing. In July, he returned to St Petersburg. That summer he visited the Kreutzers again and wrote a new piece that so appealed to his hosts that they sang it through on several occasions. It was a cantata entitled *Pantaley the Healer*, with text by Alexis Tolstoy. 'Pantaley is a kind of rustic deity who practises herbal medicine and shakes his knobbly

stick at poisonous herbs and collects wholesome ones. The poet
appeals to him to help those maimed in heart, soul and mind.'[26]
Its attraction to the composer was obvious. During that autumn
he finished the second and third movements of his Second Piano
Concerto. It was arranged that he should play these at a concert for the Ladies' Charity Prison Committee in Moscow on
2 December, with Siloti making his debut as conductor. The
concert was arranged by Princess Lieven and Varvara Satina.
Although he caught an infection a few days beforehand, it
did not prevent his appearance. As Lipayev wrote: 'this work
contains, much poetry, beauty, warmth, rich orchestration,
healthy and buoyant creative power, Rachmaninoff's talent is
evident throughout.'[27]

    With this behind him he felt ready to assault new citadels
again. However, to do so he needed financial aid to tide him
over during the next three years so that he could compose
free of worries about where the rent was to come from. Siloti
agreed to advance him a sum; he had married the daughter of
the wealthy art collector Pavel Tretyakov (a Moscow museum
still today carries his name). By the end of April 1901, he had
completed a four-movement suite for two pianos, dedicating it
to Goldenweiser, and the first movement of the Second Piano
Concerto, dedicating it to Nicolai Dahl. On 27 October, all
three movements of the concerto were premiered in Moscow,
and again conducted by Siloti. It began its international progress with Siloti playing it at Leipzig in January 1902 with the
Gewandhaus orchestra under Nikisch. Performances rapidly
followed and it soon came to rank as one of the last great popular romantic piano concertos, in succession to those of Chopin,
Liszt, Schumann, Grieg and Tchaikovsky.

6

1902–1906

Composes five new works in five months: Marries Natalia Satina:
Travels to Vienna for first time: Conducts at the Bolshoi: Elder
daughter Irina born: Composes Francesco da Rimini and The Miserly
Knight: Relationship with Chaliapin: Conducts Rimsky-Korsakov
opera, comes to know and admire him: Political events of 1905 make
conducting impossible.

On 26 March 1902, five months after the premiere of the Second
Piano Concerto, Rachmaninoff and Siloti changed places in a
performance of the same concerto in Moscow – Siloti played
while Rachmaninoff conducted. Flushed with the success
generated by his ability to compose once again and freed from
financial worries, Rachmaninoff was able to repay the loan
from Siloti in full within a year of receiving the last instal-
ment. During that time he wrote five new works: the Cello
Sonata (Op. 19), which he dedicated to Brandukov; the cantata
Spring (Op. 20) for baritone, chorus and orchestra; eleven of
the 12 Songs (Op. 21), which includes one of his most famous
songs, Lilacs, which he later transcribed for piano; Variations on
a Theme of Chopin (Op. 22) and 10 Preludes (Op. 23), which he
dedicated to Siloti.

That winter, he became engaged to his first cousin, Natalia
Satina. She had also studied piano with Zverev and later graduated from Igumnov's class at the Conservatory. 'The news came
like a bomb exploding' as their cousin Anna Trubnikova remembers.[1] The family all knew of the many obstacles there were
– family, civil and clerical – yet somehow or other they were all
surmounted. In the first place, Sergei did not attend church regularly and did not go to confession. Rachmaninoff's aunt on his
father's side, came to the rescue and got an acquaintance, Father
Valentin Amphiteatrov, of the Cathedral of the Archangel
Mikhail at the Kremlin, to promise to help them. The biggest
problem was securing the Tsar's permission. It was decided to
delay obtaining this until the day of the ceremony 'for had the
Tsar refused then no priest would agree to marry them', but the
Tsar did not raise any objections. Sergei and Natalia were mar-
ried on 29 April 1902, a wet spring day, at an army chapel outside
Moscow that was not under the jurisdiction of the Orthodox
Synod. The young couple's honeymoon progress took them via
Vienna, Lucerne, Venice and Bayreuth. In Vienna he presented
Safonov's letter of introduction to the distinguished piano
teacher Theodor Leschetizky, and in Bayreuth they went to per-
formances of the *Ring* cycle, *Der Fliegende Höllander* and *Parsifal*
– Siloti had given them tickets as a wedding present.

    Whatever his newfound marital felicitations, Rachmaninoff
did not appear to have got much pleasure out of visiting any
of these cities, to judge from a letter he wrote to his friend
Morozov: 'For a whole month every day, no matter how interesting – city, cathedral, art gallery, dungeons in the Doge's
palazzo – finally grew confused, insipid even boring.'[2] Music
was on his mind. When they reached Lucerne, he rented a piano,
'quite cheap,' he told Morozov, 'and not bad'. By this time he
had begun work on *Spring* (Op. 20) for Chaliapin, and a number
of songs (Op. 21). Whereas the previous year he had been quick
to go abroad with Chaliapin, now he was married and after his
summer customarily spent at Ivanovka (where he completed

Spring and began a set of variations on a Chopin prelude) he was only too happy to rent an apartment on Strasnetzy Boulevard. 'I plan to be back in Moscow not later than the first of October,' he assured Morozov.[3]

At the beginning of February 1903, he gave a concert introducing some of his new pieces for Princess Lieven's Ladies' Charity Prison Committee in Moscow. Critic Engel in *Russkiye Vedomosti* was not unduly enthusiastic about them. The programme included three of his ten new preludes (Op. 23), which Engel liked well enough, but he thought the Chopin Variations (Op. 22), which were based on Chopin's Prelude in C minor (Op. 28 No. 2), were 'not always worthy of the beautiful theme that inspired them'.[4] Strangely, although Rachmaninoff came to include twelve out of twenty-four preludes in later recitals, he never included the one upon which the variations are based. During the rest of that year he also found time to play concerts in St Petersburg and elsewhere in Russia. He travelled to Vienna to make his debut with the Philharmonic on 27 December [N.S.] playing his Second Piano Concerto, although he nearly didn't since Safonov had been engaged as conductor. On Taneyev's wise counsel, he decided to accept the handsome fee and not get involved in the feud between Siloti and Safonov.

In the spring of 1903, his *Trio élégiaque* was revived by the Moscow Trio, nearly a decade after Tchaikovsky's death. Even then Sergei had started a practice in which he persisted, ever more so with the passage of time, of scorning many of his early and not immediately successful works. He happened to meet the pianist David Schorr in the street, who invited him to the performance, but he brusquely refused: 'Why do you insist on playing a work I don't care for?'[5] he demanded. However, later that day Schorr received a note from him saying that his wife would attend. She must have liked it for when the Moscow Trio repeated it at a special Tchaikovsky memorial concert he was present and even came around afterwards to tell the players: 'You made me love it. Now I'll have to play it!'[6] That spring, he interrupted his work schedule to appear in concerts at Vienna and Prague playing his second concerto, with Safonov conducting on both occasions. On 14 May a daughter, Irina, was born to the Rachmaninoffs and the family left for Ivanovka. That summer was not a period of great creative activity because the baby was a constant diversion. Much of their time was taken up with mundane matters, as he told Morozov, 'of course, the question of my being able to work was in other hands.'[7]

During the summer he did find time to start work on a new opera – not *Francesca da Rimini* for which he had completed a duet for Paulo and Francesca three years earlier – but *The Miserly Knight*. The libretto is almost a word-for-word setting of one of Pushkin's quartets of 'little tragedies'. All were adapted for the lyric stage, and each illustrates a deadly sin. Dargomizhsky set 'The Stone Guest' (lust), a reworking of the Don Juan legend; Rimsky-Korsakov set 'Mozart and Salieri' (envy) and Cui, 'A Feast in the Time of the Plague' (gluttony). Chaliapin had appeared in a double-bill of the Rimsky-Korsakov and Cui operas at the Bolshoi in November 1901 and, as Rachmaninoff tells us, 'he it was who inspired me to write *The Miserly Knight*.'[8] The sin presented here is avarice and the principals are all men. The first scene shows Albert, son of the miserly knight and a spendthrift, lamenting his poverty. He tries to get a loan from a usurer who suggests that a good way of securing it would be by poisoning his father. The second scene consists of a long monologue in which the miserly knight is extolling his treasure. In the next scene, Albert goes to the Duke lamenting how mean his father had become. The Duke summons them to his presence and, in the final scene, Solomon-like he prepares to pass judgement. Before he can do so, however, the miser rounds on his son challenging him to a duel, and the son accepts. The Duke, horrified, banishes the son and is about to pass sentence on the father when the miser falls dead, clasping the keys to his treasure. So, perpetrator and victim of avarice both receive their just deserts.

In the spring of 1904, Telyakovsky, Director of Imperial Theatres in St Petersburg and Moscow, signed a contract with Rachmaninoff to conduct at the Bolshoi. Telyakovsky was a retired colonel from the Horse Guards and much mirth was made at his expense: 'a man in charge of horses is now in charge of actors!'[9] But he was perceptive and shrewd and it did not take him long to become well-suited to the work. He also persuaded Chaliapin to leave Mamontov and join the Bolshoi. Chaliapin describes the imperial theatres at that time:

> Nowhere in the world, except perhaps in France under Louis XIV or during the Empire, was the theatre so pampered and caressed. Having worked for them and travelled all over the world, I have never found any stage with which they could be compared. The beauty of their productions of drama, opera and ballet inspired many great musicians, and it is common knowledge that they produced not only exceptional compos-ers, but great and serious dramatists.[10]

This judgement appears in Chaliapin's *Pages from My Life*, pub-lished in 1927, five years after he finally left Russia. Photographic evidence seems to substantiate it. Seroff, another émigré, despite asserting that the orchestra was outstanding and the chorus and ballet 'the best in the world', gave a candid opinion of the back-stage organisation: 'For a long time Muscovites had regarded members of the theatre company as just another branch of the civil service working in a bureaucratic institution, they judged them not by their artistic merits but whether or not they took bribes.'[11]

That Rachmaninoff should join the Bolshoi had first been suggested eighteen months previously. An agreement was finally reached that he would conduct six operas for five months each year, leaving the rest of his time free to compose. As he himself stated: 'When I feel like writing music, I have to concentrate on that – I cannot touch the piano. When I am conducting I can neither compose nor play concerts. Other musicians may be more fortunate in this respect, but I have to concentrate to such a degree on any one thing I am doing that it does not allow me to take up anything else.'[12] Most of those at the Bolshoi were engaged annually, so having his contract arranged in such fashion created a precedent and inevitably caused resentment. Composer Ippolotov-Ivanov and critic Lypayev were quick to express disapproval. They claimed Rachmaninoff wanted to have it both ways – to be creator and performer at the same time, and so he did. Though he did not complete the orchestration of *The Miserly Knight* until June 1905, the vocal score was finished by February 1904 and in March he was writing to Modest Tchaikovsky asking for a revision of the libretto for *Francesca da Rimini*. It was his plan that both should be ready for performance at the Bolshoi by the following season.

He made his debut at the Bolshoi on 3 September 1904, conducting Dargomizhsky's *Rusalka*. In his first season he made fifty appearances. At once he created a precedent by introducing a practice that he had seen in Bayreuth and which was already familiar in western Europe. He moved the conductor back from his time-honoured, seated position immediately behind the prompt box (situated, so to speak, at the singer's feet, with the orchestra players straggling around him) to his present standing position with the whole performance under his direct surveillance. This was one of Wagner's innovations, occasioned by the increasing size and importance of the orchestra. For Rachmaninoff it proved an adroit move psychologically; he regarded strict discipline as an essential part of a successful career as a conductor. In Glinka's *A Life for the Tsar*, his fourth opera that season, desiring that one of the dances in the Polish scene be played pianissimo, he insisted on the male dancers removing their clangourous spurs. At first they refused, but since the stage-manager did not have sufficient authority to insist on this, there followed a heated exchange and Rachmaninoff eventually got his way. Notwithstanding the presence of Chaliapin in the cast, and two other highly-reputed singers (the soprano Antonina Nezhdanova and contralto Evgenia Zbrujeva) the critic Kruglikov hailed Rachmaninoff 'hero of the evening'.[13]

The rest of his repertory that season included three of Tchaikovsky's operas (*Eugene Onegin*, *The Oprichnik* and *The Queen of Spades*), Borodin's *Prince Igor*, and Moussorgsky's *Boris Godounov*. Chaliapin performed the part of Boris, occasionally Galitzky in *Prince Igor*, the Miller in *Rusalka*, and on the occasion of the 100th performance of *The Queen of Spades*, he played Tomsky and the small role of Pluto. In a charity gala he appeared as Varlaam in the Inn scene from *Boris Godounov*, Onegin in Act I of Tchaikovsky's *Eugene Onegin* (for the only time in his career) and Aleko in the last performance of it that Rachmaninoff would ever conduct.

In January 1905, Rachmaninoff received 500 rubles in the first Glinka Awards founded in the will of Belayev, who had recently died. His Second Piano Concerto shared first prize with a trio by Arensky and a symphony by Scriabin. On the 8th his cantata *Spring* was performed in St Petersburg with Chaliapin. With the opera season over, Rachmaninoff conducted a number of concerts: two charity events at the Bolshoi, one of the all-Russian programmes organised by Arkady and Mariya Kerzin (founders of the Circle of Lovers of Russian Music) and a couple for the Philharmonic Society. At the first of these, on 14 March, the programme commenced with Tchaikovsky's Fifth Symphony. The composer Nicolai Medtner had not forgotten the occasion more than a quarter of a century later:

It is sad that such a performance can only be remembered. Before Rachmaninoff conducted it, we heard this symphony mainly from Nikisch and his imitators, for he rescued it from a fiasco at the hands of the composer. Nikisch's brilliant interpretation, his distinctive style of expression, his sentimental slowing of the tempi became, as it were, the law for

Tchaikovsky style. Suddenly, from Rachmaninoff's first beat, all this imitative tradition fell away and we heard it once again as if for the first time. Particularly effective was the shattering impetuosity of the finale, an antidote to the pathos of Nikisch that had always impaired this movement.'[14]

Goldenweiser also makes a comparison between Rachmaninoff and Nikisch: 'Nikisch was as graceful and theatrical in his manner as Rachmaninoff was close and miserly – as though he were simply counting off the bars – yet his power over orchestra and audience was absolutely irresistible.'[15] The rest of his concert programmes that season included works by Wagner, Grieg, Borodin, Balakirev, Glazounov, Moussorgsky, Glinka, Beethoven and Tchaikovsky.

It was at the beginning of February 1905, the year of the first revolution in Russia, that Rachmaninoff – along with Chaliapin, Gretchaninov, Rimsky-Korsakov, Siloti and Taneyev – put his name to an appeal for freedom, so repressive had the imperial regime become. During the summer he returned to Ivanovka to work on the orchestration of *Francesca da Rimini*. On 26 March 1904, he had written to the librettist Modest Tchaikovsky urging him to dispense with the first two scenes, including the one with the Cardinal, to rewrite sixteen lines in the second and to lengthen the love duet. However, for whatever reason Modest seems only to have produced what Rachmaninoff later called 'a very few banal lines'.[16] Although he found some worth in *The Miserly Knight*, in 1933 Rachmaninoff wrote to Riesemann lamenting that:

The libretto supplied by Modest Tchaikovsky [for *Francesca da Rimini*] was poor. I composed it suffering agonies over its inadequacy. When I came upon a situation that was ideal dramatically and called for a suitable musical response – for instance, when Malatesta comes upon Paulo and Francesca embracing, there would be nothing to set. In spite of a

lengthy correspondence with urgent requests I could not persuade Modest to add more than a few verses.[17]

In July, he wrote to Morozov describing his daily regime in
Ivanovka. He worked from half past nine to half past three after
which he would play tennis. He began scoring *Francesca da Rimini*
on 9 June and in a month had completed the prologue, epilogue
and the first scene. By 6 July there was only the orchestration of
the second scene to complete. He calculated that he would need
about another ten days to finish a total of about forty pages. He
was conscious how time was flying. He had been told that the
opera's premiere was announced for October, but in fact it was
postponed until January the following year. On 17 August the
Rachmaninoffs returned to Moscow. The 1905/06 season at the
Bolshoi opened on the 30th with *A Life for the Tsar* and during
September he conducted *Eugene Onegin*, *The Queen of Spades* and
Rusalka. On the 27th, he introduced Rimsky-Korsakov's *Pan
Voyevoda* at its world premiere. Although Rachmaninoff found
'the music rather poor, the instrumentation was quite stupendous. In his work room Rimsky had many music stands and
would move from one to the other filling in the instrumental
parts, without writing a full score, so marvellous was his ear.'[18]

   In later years in America he admitted with regret, as a
member of the Moscow School, the hostility he had once shown
Rimsky-Korsakov:

   His mastery of the technique of composition, especially
   his skill in instrumentation and his sensitive control of tone
   colour could not but fill me with sincere admiration. To this
   day [1933] my appreciation of his music has not reached its
   limits. My association with him taught me a lot. I had more
   than one occasion to verify his incredibly fine ear for orchestral detail. After the last rehearsal for *Pan Voyevoda*, in the
   fortune-telling scene there is a fortissimo dominant chord
   played by the whole orchestra. During the performance

however I noted the tuba player was silent, so I checked his part and there was nothing in it. I asked Rimsky whether accidentally the copyist had left his part out: "No." he replied. "One would not hear it, and I hate writing superfluous notes!" He then asked, "But why are the drums playing?" "Probably the directions say so," I replied. "No," he insisted, "they give only the triangle." When I called the musician he produced the part with the drums indicated. Rimsky then asked to look at the full score and, of course, there was nothing written for drums – the triangle was to play alone. This proof of the sensitivity of his ear convinced me that the tuba player would have been inaudible.[19]

In a letter to Rimsky-Korsakov on 17 September, he wrote telling him how grateful he was for coming to the rehearsals and indicating the errors. Rimsky-Korsakov recalled in his memoirs how he liked 'the talented Rachmaninoff. The opera proved to have been well rehearsed, orchestra and chorus went splendidly, I was pleased with the way it sounded both the vocal parts and the orchestral parts.'[20]

Whether because *Pan Voyevoda* was not a masterpiece, or because of a printers' strike which made it impossible for the opera to get much media attention, it survived only six performances that season, the last taking place on 9 November. It was during October that news of the defeat of the Russian Navy by the Japanese in the war in the far East forced the Tsar to grant a constitution. Pressured by the Bolshevik and Menshevik groups, the Imperial government reluctantly accepted measures of reform. However, these had scarcely any effect on the vast majority of Russians, for the police and army remained as ruthlessly repressive as ever. Far from assuaging the wrath of the revolutionaries during November and December, the situation became increasingly tense. A general strike spread rapidly throughout Moscow; soon there was no water or electricity, nor postal and telegraphic services. Everything ground to a halt.

Muscovites were obliged to stand in seemingly endless queues taking turns to draw water from the few wells still functioning. After five in the afternoon, when the sun set, the streets were patrolled by police, pickets and pick-pockets – in the dark one could hardly tell one from the other, indeed, perhaps they were all the same. At first theatres remained open, but they were soon playing to empty houses and so were obliged to close. As a result, orchestra players, stage-hands and other theatre employees, *faute de mieux*, found they had joined the strike. These circumstances were hardly conducive to a conductor like Rachmaninoff, a member of the old landowning aristocracy. Locked away in his own world we cannot expect him to have had much sympathy for the vast majority of his countrymen then living in squalid conditions. His own limited experience of life, if it taught him anything, persuaded him not to give way to every indulgence. We see this in his attitude to orchestral musicians who had a tendency to slip outside for a smoke when they were not playing during a performance. Notwithstanding the fact that he was himself a heavy smoker, he nearly caused a revolution to break out there and then by threatening them with dismissal if they left their seats.

In spite of the background of political strife, Rachmaninoff kept busy. He took part in three Kerzin concerts. On 30 October, he conducted Rimsky-Korsakov's *Antar*, Balakirev's *Tamara*, Liadov's Intermezzo in C and *Baba Yaga* and Glinka's *Night in Madrid*. On 26 November, Arensky's First Symphony in C minor, Glazounov's *Lyric Poem*, Tchaikovsky's *Voyevoda*, his own Second Piano Concerto played by Igumnov and Moussorgsky's Introduction and Gopak from *Sorochintsky Fair*. This was the first time he had conducted the latter, and after the First World War he would compose his own piano transcription of it. At the final concert, on 18 December, he conducted Rimsky-Korsakov's *Scheherazade*, Glazounov's *Spring* and Tchaikovsky's *Francesca da Rimini*. On 11 January 1906, when the disturbances were over for the time being, he conducted the premieres of his new operas, *The Miserly Knight* and *Francesca da Rimini,* at the Bolshoi. Critics shared his preference for the first. Engel thought:

> The most interesting scene in it is the Miser's Monologue. His talent shows throughout in harmonic detail and orchestral colour as well as in the supple precision of the musical declamation. Yet this opera is not for a large audience, this is, perhaps, a *Kabinetstuck* for those who can appreciate the subtle filigree work of its exquisite composition.[21]

The most important roles in both operas – the title-role in *The Miserly Knight* and Malatesta in *Francesca da Rimini* – were written with Chaliapin in mind, but he undertook neither. Chaliapin had known Rachmaninoff was composing them for some years. Goldenweiser and critic and musicologist Ossovsky both recall occasions when Chaliapin sight-read parts of *The Miserly Knight*, and included Malatesta's monologue from the second scene in one of Siloti's concerts in St Petersburg the following year. Yet for all the close friendship of Chaliapin and Rachmaninoff – both of them were then at the Bolshoi – Chaliapin never undertook either role, although he continued to programme Aleko's air at recitals until the very end of his career. Rachmaninoff later told Riesemann: 'One day Chaliapin surprised me saying that my vocal writing was faulty. I contradicted him, I was not aware of it. This was followed by a heated argument, and since then my operas have not been mentioned by either of us.'[22]

It is apparent, notwithstanding Rachmaninoff's remarkable lyrical gifts that he does not compose for the voice sympathetically. It was Wagner who realised that, no matter how complex and brilliant the orchestration, singers must still be *primus inter pares,* for they have to sing the words clearly, and so make the melodrama. As Rimsky-Korsakov shrewdly observed:

> Rachmaninoff's main attention is the orchestra, the vocal part is, as it were, adapted to it; as a whole, the almost unvaryingly

thick texture of the orchestra overwhelms the voice. This results in a relationship the opposite of Dargomizhsky's *The Stone Guest*, where the role of the orchestra is reduced to a minimum, as a straightforward support for the vocal part. Whereas Dargomizhsky's orchestra, without the vocal part, has no importance in itself for Rachmaninoff the reverse applies, the orchestra absorbs all the artistic interest, so the ear misses the melody which the vocal writing lacks.[23]

Even Tchaikovsky's operas, for all their lyricism, have never rivalled the popularity of his ballet suites. The business of knowing how to put the singers first is what distinguishes the Italian school. We hear this even in the works of *verismo* composers which, notwithstanding increased orchestral resources, still show how to write expressively and effectively for singers having the example of their predecessors to follow.

Although not as unequivocally lyrical as Rachmaninoff, Rimsky-Korsakov shows how to write music that is perfectly scored for the orchestra – 'The Song of the Indian Guest' from *Sadko* and 'The Hymn to the Sun' from *Le Coq d'or* are good examples – and does so in a way that does not present the singer with any unfitting competition. Paradoxically, this explains why Rachmaninoff's songs, when piano-accompanied, are often so masterly, and why as Goldenweiser reports, although Chaliapin did not sing either work on stage, he made a considerable effect sight-reading the music of the Knight and Lanciotto Malatesta with Rachmaninoff himself at the piano. The trouble with *The Miserly Knight* also affects *Francesca da Rimini*. Rachmaninoff first tried talking Nezhdanova, one of Russia's leading lyric sopranos, into singing the role of Francesca but her voice could never have stood up to the orchestral competition. She must have realised this as soon as she looked at the score. She cried off, using the excuse that she had to sing Mozart's *Queen of the Night*, a short but exceedingly taxing role rising to repeated high Fs. By this time Rachmaninoff seems to have realised the difficulties the part involved. He wrote to the soprano, Nadezhda Salina, who eventually created Francesca, almost desperately: 'I've written the devil only knows what, which nobody can sing; for one it's too low, for another too high. I'll give you all the phrasing, everything you want – just try and sing it!'[24]

Only two months after these operas had been performed the first time, to judge from his correspondence, he got taken up with the idea of writing another opera based on Flaubert's *Salammbo*. He seems to have worked it all out in his mind, so lengthy are some of his letters. In his search for a librettist he tried to interest Mikhail Slonov (a teacher of singing who wrote a libretto for another of Rachmaninoff's operas which he never completed), Mikhail Svobodin (a journalist who tried his hand at poetry) and even Modest Tchaikovsky. He did not succeed. But then as quickly as he got taken up with the idea he dropped it; after a letter to Slonov on 24 May we hear no more of it.

Towards the end of the 1905/06 season, Rachmaninoff told Telyakovsky[25] that it was doubtful whether he would conduct at the Bolshoi the following season. He would, he said, probably be undertaking an American tour. Telyakovsky endeavoured to get him to return, even offering him the post of musical director. Rachmaninoff then listed the circumstances that made such a proposition unacceptable to him: all the political events the previous year had had a most unfortunate effect on the orchestral players; discipline, once so good, was deteriorating. Working with such an ensemble and getting a proper response to a conductor's demands was virtually impossible. Most of the time the players were not concerned with art but with all sorts of intrigues generated by envy and malice. If the harmful and improper elements were not eliminated, he insisted, it would soon become uncontrollable. Telyakovsky replied that he could not just fire musicians who had served a lifetime when they had only a year or two before retiring with pensions. Rachmaninoff maintained that was not his business, but if Telyakovsky was concerned to have an orchestra equal to the demands of the Bolshoi then he had no alternative.

In May 1906, he left for a vacation in Italy with his wife and daughter. That he had not definitely decided to leave the Bolshoi is apparent from a letter he wrote Morozov from Florence on 27 April. He lists the various financial details of contracts offered to him for the following season.[26] As conductor at the Bolshoi his fee would be 8,000 rubles for five months' work beginning on 1 September. For ten symphony concerts with the Philharmonic Society he would receive 4,500 rubles, and for three concerts with the Kerzins, a further 900 rubles. There was also some possibility of his being offered a contract in America, but he wondered what kind of fee he should ask for: 'It seems nothing will work out with America. I think they want to squeeze me down to the smallest sum. At any rate I've sent them an ultimatum with a month's deadline. But if I don't go to America and have given up my Moscow contracts then what am I to live on?'[27] In the event, he did not go to America until the following season, did not return to the Bolshoi, but did accept the concerts.

At the beginning of June the Rachmaninoffs went from Florence to Marina di Pisa to rent a villa where they were joined by his cousin Anna Trubnikova. She draws a telling picture of life in the sultry heat of an Italian summer:

Venetian blinds remained lowered over the windows and doors. Streets were empty. Whenever the temperature dropped a little, the first to appear on the street were a couple of itinerant musicians. A young man poorly dressed with silk hat and cane, and a young woman in a brightly coloured dress. With them a tiny donkey with very long ears pulled an upright pianola on wheels, and a cot with a baby was attached to it. The young man sang popular ballads and the woman cranked the piano. Our favourite number was a simple but quite tuneful polka. Many years later, when I

heard Rachmaninoff's Italian Polka, I knew where he had
first heard it.[28]

The heat in Italy did not seem to agree with the Rachmaninoffs.
At the beginning of July, as a result of the illness of his wife
and child, he was telling Morozov that he could not remember a summer as bad as this one.[29] He must have been too much
preoccupied with plans and problems to remember three years
earlier when, as well as his wife and child, he had been complaining how unwell he was. At the end of July, the Rachmaninoffs
returned to Russia and were soon back again at Ivanovka,
restored to health.

On 2 August he wrote to Mariya Kerzin, of The Circle of
Lovers of Russian Music, about some song lyrics she had
selected for him to set. 'What could be taken I have taken, but
it's only a little. In your selection all the words demand the
minor key.' Then, rather atypically bearing in mind his naturally mournful disposition, he asked: 'Would it not be possible
to find a few verses slightly more major in key?'[30] By the time
he completed his 15 Songs (Op. 26), which were dedicated to
the Kerzins, five had modulated into the major! On the 29th, he
wrote to Morozov saying that Jürgenson had warned him that
one of the concert series he was to conduct the following season
was not likely to take place. 'There's only one way out,' he told
Morozov, 'to compose and go abroad for the winter. We have
decided we could manage to live, for example, in Leipzig or
Dresden. We can pay with the trifles I'm now busy with.'[31] Freed
of his Russian commitments Rachmaninoff left Moscow for
Dresden, where he could work on new compositions unham-
pered by concert engagements.

1906–1909

Moves to Dresden to be able to compose undistracted: Completes Second Symphony, First Piano Sonata and symphonic poem The Isle of the Dead: *Diaghileff engages him to take part in first Saisons Russes in Paris: Remeets Scriabin: Younger daughter Tatiana is born: As his international reputation grows, he appears at an increasing number of concerts outside Russia.*

The two principal reasons why Rachmaninoff chose Dresden to move to in the autumn of 1906 were that he had been deeply affected by a performance of *Meistersinger* conducted by Ernst von Schuch that he had heard on a brief visit two years previously, and that Leipzig, with its Gewandhaus Orchestra and conductor Artur Nikisch, was only an hour's train journey away.

On 9 November he wrote to Morozov:

The villa on Sidonienstrasse is charming. No apartment has pleased me as much. The house is surrounded by a garden. There are six rooms, three below, all facing the sun. The bedrooms are upstairs, downstairs is my study and the dining room. I can live like a real lord – it rents for only 2,200 marks. Some things, however, are less agreeable. The people are

often unsympathetic, sometimes downright rude. Living here
is very expensive – don't believe it's cheap. Meat, just to make
soup, costs a mark. A pound of ham, two. A chicken or duck,
three. I went looking for a goose but, you won't believe it, it
cost seven marks! Six candles come to seventy-five pfennigs, a
bottle of milk, twenty-two.

Still, these vulgar preoccupations were not what he had come to
Dresden for.

I've been to a performance of Richard Strauss's *Salome*, and
was delighted with it. Most of all the orchestration, of course,
but many things in the music I liked. Strauss is undoubtedly a
very talented man; his instrumentation is quite extraordinary.
As I sat listening I could not help worrying how an opera of
mine might sound. I should feel as if I were being undressed
before an audience; Strauss certainly knows how to dress up.[1]

His exposure to *Salome* seems only to have temporarily cooled
his desire to write any more operas.

In Leipzig he attended one of Nikisch's conductor-classes,
but did not find it a particularly worthwhile experience: 'All
three students should have been strung up,'[2] he complained to
Morozov. The same afternoon he was taken to the publisher
'Breitkopf's plant and saw the whole process of printing music'.[3]
That evening he heard the Gewandhaus orchestra conducted by
Nikisch play Brahms's first symphony and Tchaikovsky's sixth.
'In the full sense of the word it was conducting of genius; it
would be impossible to surpass.'[4]

During the two and a half years he spent based in Dresden,
he completed three new works: his second symphony, the First
Piano Sonata and his symphonic poem, *The Isle of the Dead*.
The symphony seems to have had its origins in 1902. Siloti
had programmed it in his concert series to be conducted by
Rachmaninoff as long ago as 1903, but it was still unfinished

when he arrived in Dresden. He wrote to Morozov on 11 February 1907, 'a month ago, or more, I really did finish the symphony, to this must be added the phrase "in draft". I shall not announce it to the world until I have completed the final writing.'[5] He then goes on to lament how tired he had become of it and that it was not until Siloti wanted to know what had happened to it that he agreed to conduct its St Petersburg premiere the following year. Of his three symphonies it has proved the most successful. As Martyn says, 'the glory of it is that it is not only a moving masterpiece of natural flowing lyricism but, for those who bother to investigate, intellectually satisfying as well in its organic growth.'[6] In 1945, the critic Kuznetsov called it the Russian Lyric Symphony, 'so direct and sincere are its themes and so naturally and spontaneously do they develop.'[7]

He wrote to Morozov again detailing his daily work schedule and complaining about the headaches he was suffering from, the result he supposed of poor lighting. He would compose three and a half hours in the morning then after lunch go out for an hour's walk before practising a recital he was to play in Paris. He felt obliged to accept the latter for economic reasons, although he was under pressure to complete his compositions:

> I've finished nothing – nothing is yet in final shape. The symphony, which I've already written you about, only its draft is complete, to trim it I still need another few days. The sonata, I shall need two weeks to complete. I am only fully satisfied with my third work, *Monna Vanna*. This is my whole consolation. Otherwise I'd be completely crushed.[8]

Although he claimed to be only fully satisfied with 'Monna Vanna', this is the only one of these works he never did complete. The play, by the Belgian dramatist Maurice Maeterlinck, enjoyed a hugely successful production in St Petersburg in 1906 with the actress Vera Komissarzhevskaya. After going to a performance Rachmaninoff determined to turn it into an opera.

From Dresden on 3 November he wrote to Sonov asking him to prepare in blank verse about six pages from the play to see if he could make a suitable setting.

At Dresden he found time to go to the opera, where he saw *Tristan* and *Meistersinger*. He also went to several oratorios including Beethoven's *Missa Solemnis*, Handel's *Samson*, Bach's *Mass in B minor* and Mendelssohn's *St Paul*. 'All works of genius,' he reflected. 'They may write well today, but they wrote even better then. I went to an operetta of Lehár's, *Die lustige Witwe*. It too is a work of genius. Absolutely wonderful!'[9] At the beginning of May he was again lamenting to Morozov how terribly behind he was:

> Yesterday I finished the second movement of my piano sonata. I played it to Riesemann but he didn't seem to like it – generally I've begun to notice that whatever I like no one else seems to! The sonata is certainly wild and interminable; I think it takes about forty-five minutes. Nobody will ever play it; it's too difficult, too long and more importantly, of dubious merit musically.'[10]

At the end of May 1907 he departed for Paris to take part in the first and hugely successful Saisons Russes, a series of cultural events organised in western Europe by the Russian impresario Serge Diaghileff. Diaghileff seems not to have much cared for Rachmaninoff's music: 'for me it was too emotional'[11] he said. On the 26th, Rachmaninoff appeared as composer and conductor of his cantata *Spring*, with Chaliapin, and played his Second Piano Concerto, conducted by Camille Chevillard. In Paris he met Scriabin again, who was living there. At another of Diaghileff's concerts, Nikisch conducted Scriabin's second symphony and his piano concerto, which Hoffmann played. Leading Russian musicians also present included Glazounov and Rimsky-Korsakov. The latter had only reluctantly been cajoled into coming: 'If I must, I must, as the parrot said when the cat pulled him out of the cage.' Scriabin was much taken up theorising. Rachmaninoff remembers the biggest effect he created was non-musical – walking about without a hat, 'for hygienic reasons',[12] so he claimed. He remembers a discussion with Scriabin and Rimsky-Korsakov one day while they were sitting in the Café de la Paix. One of Scriabin's discoveries concerned the relationship between musical sound, certain harmonies and keys, and the spectrum of the sun. 'To my astonishment,' Rachmaninoff recalls, 'Rimsky-Korsakov agreed in principle with Scriabin about the connection between musical keys and colour.'[13] He then explained the whole of *Le Coq d'or,* although at the time he had only finished the first act. He said, '"I will now tackle the third." I wondered, why not the second?'[14] There was certainly something peculiarly heady in the air.

Rachmaninoff returned to Moscow from Paris. Here, he played one of his new Dresden works, his Piano Sonata, to a group of friends including Catoire, Leo Conus, Medtner and Igumnov. According to Igumnov, he told him his inspiration had been Goethe's *Faust* – the first movement represents Faust, the second Gretchen, and the third Mephistopheles and the flight to the Brocken. Martyn notes it is the same programme Liszt uses in his *Faust* symphony, a work that Rachmaninoff knew and studied. Igumnov immediately wanted to include it in concert. Rachmaninoff agreed, so it was the only one of his more important piano solos which he did not play himself at the premiere. It was not until the following April, after several letters had passed between them in which Igumnov suggested a variety of amendments, that it was completed. Rachmaninoff did not stay long in Moscow, but travelled on to Ivanovka where he would spend the summer. On 21 June, Natalia gave birth to their younger daughter, Tatyana at Ivanovka.

Meanwhile, although busy with both his Second Symphony and First Piano Sonata, he was still taken up with the possibility of the opera *Monna Vanna*. He complained to Morozov how for just an act Slonov had sent him about a thousand lines,

while for *The Miserly Knight* there was less than half as much
for the entire opera. On the 27th, he wrote a letter to Slonov to
thank him for the libretto of Act II. This correspondence with
Slonov and Morozov over *Monna Vanna* continued for a while,
but at length he had to put the idea on ice. At the beginning
of August he was obliged to orchestrate his Second Symphony,
although he still seems not to have abandoned the idea of writing an opera for the following year he returned to it again. This
time he determined to put the horse before the cart, asking
Stanislavsky to secure rights from Maeterlinck, the author of
the play. By then, however, the publisher Heugel had already
disposed of them to the French composer Henri Février. In
January 1909, Février's *Monna Vanna* was premiered at the Paris
Opéra where the great singing actress Mary Garden appeared in
it in its first season. It became one of her staple roles, which she
undertook regularly in Chicago until 1928. It continued in the
Paris Opéra repertory until after the Second World War. In the
face of this, Rachmaninoff had to abandon *Monna Vanna* but he
kept the manuscript, or as much as he had written, for the rest
of his life. He considered other librettos from Turgenev's works
(*The Torrents of Spring*, *The Song of Love Triumphant* and *The Lull*)
and from Chekhov too, although he later states: 'Chekhov's
works do not lend themselves to a musical setting. To my great
regret I could not use his novel "The Black Monk"'.[15] Yet in
the summer of 1906 he did compose a song entitled 'Come, let
us rest' (Op. 26 No. 3), a setting of Sonya's final speech from
Uncle Vanya.

That autumn and winter Rachmaninoff spent travelling
around playing the piano and conducting concerts in Warsaw,
Berlin, St Petersburg, Frankfurt and Moscow. At a concert
in Moscow for the Philharmonic Society on 2 February, he
conducted his Second Symphony. He also played his Second
Concerto under Brandukov and accompanied Nezhdanova
in the air and 'How painful' from Rimsky-Korsakov's *The
Snow Maiden*, and some of his own songs. Engel praised him

in *Russkiye Vedomosti*: 'he is one of the most significant figures in the contemporary musical world, a worthy successor to Tchaikovsky, if not in the demonstration of talent (of which it is too early to speak), then certainly in his concentration, sincerity and subjective delicacy – successor, and not imitator, for he has already his own individuality.'[16] On the way back to Dresden he stopped off in Warsaw again on 14 March to conduct his Second Symphony, Moussorgsky's *Night on the Bald Mountain*, 'It Will Soon Be Midnight' from Tchaikovsky's *The Queen of Spades* with Yanina Korolevich, and Liadov's Scherzo in D. He also played his Suite for Two Pianos (Op. 17) with Alexander Michalowski.

In Dresden on 12 April he had to confess to Morozov that he had not been able to write very much:

> Soon it will be two months since I left Moscow and this is how my time has been spent: two weeks with flu, a week in Warsaw, a week with the young Satins visiting us here. The symphony has taken about ten days, with a thousand silly errors. Only the other night did I finish the sonata, tomorrow I send it to the printer.[17]

He was also considering reworking his First Piano Concerto but it would take another decade before he got round to it. He returned to London to appear on 26 May at the Queen's Hall playing his Second Piano Concerto for the first time, with Koussevitzky. *The Times* was revealingly appreciative:

> The direct expression of the work, the extraordinary precision and exactitude of Rachmaninoff's playing, and even the strict economy of movement of arms and hands which he exercises, all contributed to the impression of completeness of performance. The slow movement was played by soloist and orchestra with deep feeling, and the brilliant effect of the finale could scarcely have been surpassed, and yet freedom from extravagance of any kind was its most remarkable feature.[18]

Back in Ivanovka during the summer he corrected proofs of his piano sonata and worked on a four-hand transcription of his Second Symphony before returning once more to Dresden. Unable to attend the tenth anniversary celebrations of the establishment of the Moscow Arts Theatre, he sent a salutation to Stanislavsky in the form of a Musical Letter for Chaliapin to sing:

> Very dear Constantin Sergeyvitch, I congratulate you sincerely, with all my heart! For the last ten years you have moved forward, forward, and forward, and somewhere on this road you found 'The Blue Bird'! It is your greatest victory. I must tell you how sorry I am that I am not in Moscow; that I'm not able with all the others, to honour you, to applaud you, to cry out in all keys, Bravo, bravo, bravo, and to wish you very many years, very many years, very, very, very many years. I beg you to give the whole company my greetings, my warm and hearty greetings. Yours, Sergei Rachmaninoff. Dresden, on the fourteenth of October, in the year of nineteen hundred and eight, *anno domini: Post scriptum* – My wife seconds this.[19]

Three days later on the 17th, Igumnov premiered the Piano Sonata in an all-Rachmaninoff programme in Moscow. During the period of its composition he had made a number of alterations, shortening the recapitulation in the first movement and reopening some cuts in the finale. A lengthy review in *Russkiye Vedomosti* by Engel, although finding much to like in it, puts a finger on its weakness: 'The new sonata appeals with its mastery of form, its abundance of interesting details just as, for example, do the piano concertos, but it does not have their freshness of fantasy, nor comparable thematic inspiration.'[20] On 9 November, Rachmaninoff conducted his Second Symphony in Amsterdam. On the 27th, he repeated it in Antwerp, adding Moussorgsky's *Night on the Bald Mountain*, Glazounov's Violin Concerto with Mischa Elman, and he also played his Second Piano Concerto.

'The orchestra is large,' he wrote. 'The attitude of the players is fine but their playing bad.'[21] From there he journeyed to Berlin appearing on 2 December with members of the Czech quartet playing the piano in his trio, and also found time to hear Nikisch conduct Brahms's Second Symphony 'wonderfully'.[22] On the 10th, back in the low countries, he played his *Second Concerto* in Amsterdam, repeating it on the 12th in The Hague and the next day in Amsterdam again. 'It's the same orchestra, on tour – and a splendid orchestra, too, Mengelberg conducts it everywhere – it is he who will conduct at Frankfurt am Main when I play it next week. He accompanies perfectly. It's such a pleasure to play with him.'[23]

With the American tour again preoccupying him, he details the financial arrangements in a letter to Morozov dated 11 December: 'I sent them my new terms: twenty-five concerts, with a guaranteed minimum of 1,000 rubles a concert. I'm afraid they may agree! Though the earnings could be appreciable, which to some extent would console me, it will be very hard to have to endure such penal servitude; even these tiny European tours are a torture.'[24] The next news he had from New York was that Wolfsohn, of the Wolfsohn Bureau, which was arranging the tour, had died suddenly, 'so it looks as though I am not going.'[25] In December he received the Glinka Award of 1,000 rubles for his Second Symphony, the third time he was awarded it. Far from cheering him, the news seemed only to depress him: 'I'm terribly afraid I'll soon go to the devil,'[26] he wrote to Slonov. On 3 January, he appeared in concert in Moscow conducting a violin concerto by Julius Conus – one of the three brothers he had known since their student days. On 21 March, with the projected American tour preoccupying him again, he complained to Morozov: 'I've already talked of this to no purpose that it's become disgraceful to go on repeating myself, but what's to do, if negotiations will drag on and on. The trouble lay with one clause, now we're agreed on that, but it's so difficult because of the distance.'[27]

At the beginning of the next month, Rachmaninoff left Dresden for good, returning to Moscow with his wife and daughters. Natalia had not liked being so far from home and 'I promised her we would not spend more than three years abroad,' he told Taneyev. No sooner were they back than he was invited to conduct the Moscow Philharmonic in lieu of Nikisch, who had withdrawn; rumours had reached him of an outbreak of cholera. The first concert on 15 April included Scriabin's First Symphony, Strauss's *Til Eulenspiegel*, Wagner's *The Siegfried Idyll* and Liszt's *Tasso*. Grigory Chereshev, in *Moskovskiye vedomosti*, wrote: 'he was capable of making one forget even the most felicitous moments of Nikisch's appearances as conductor'.[28] At the second concert on the 17th, between his own Second Symphony and Moussorgsky's *Night on the Bald Mountain*, he introduced the first performance of his new symphonic poem, *The Isle of the Dead*, which he had completed in the first three months of that year.

Rachmaninoff first saw a reproduction of the Swiss artist Arnold Boecklin's painting *The Isle of the Dead* in Paris in 1907. He later came to see the different versions, both originals in galleries in Berlin and Leipzig. 'Had I seen the original first, I might not have composed it,' he later told Basanta Roy. 'I am not much moved by colour. I like the picture best in black and white.'[29] There seems something fitting in this, as it was clear from his meeting with Scriabin and Rimsky-Korsakov that associations between music and colour do not seem to have meant much to him. The painting shows the Isle of Ponza, off Gaeta to the west of Italy. The lugubrious atmosphere comes over effectively when the painting is reproduced in black and white, and it is that atmosphere that must have appealed to Rachmaninoff. The artist – reversing Canaletto who took the Mediterranean sky up north with him when he went to paint Dresden, Cambridge and London – brought lowering storm clouds down from the alpine heights. The music is dominated by a three-note rocking figure, representing the sound of the oars in the water as the dead are ferried to the island (a boat and oarsman appear in the painting). This may be an affecting device but although one of his most successful works without piano, the lack of rhythmic variety inhibits it and it does not rank for musical inventiveness with either his second or third symphonies.

The Isle of the Dead is the only piece of Rachmaninoff's music that Toscanini ever conducted, which is curious. He did so in concert at the Augusteum in Rome seven years later, at a time when Rachmaninoff had not yet appeared in Rome. Toscanini's indifference to Rachmaninoff's music was because, we are told, 'he had a low opinion of Russian music in general and Rachmaninoff's in particular'.[30] Nevertheless, Toscanini conducted quite a lot of Russian music; his programmes included works of Borodin, Moussorgsky, Tchaikovsky, Rimsky-Korsakov, Prokofiev and Stravinsky. His concerts also included compositions by Bossi, Busi, Cowen, Creston, de Venezia, Faccio, Fuchs, Gillet, Girard, Keenan, Kozeluch, Loeffler, Mignone, Mossolov, Pedrollo, Rieti, Rocchi, Siegmeister, Strong, Trucco, Veprik and Wetzler. Nowadays it is necessary to be very familiar with classical music and all its by-ways to have heard of any of them. Although Toscanini was always reverential in his attitude towards the dead – for Verdi and Wagner he appointed himself high priest – it was another matter with living ones. His relations with famous living composers were worst of all, as those with Puccini and Strauss testify.[31] Not only did Rachmaninoff literally tower over Toscanini but, as RCA Victor record producer Charles O'Connell related, 'Rachmaninoff was invincibly convinced of the rectitude of his musical ideas, and with the most implacable determination would enforce them upon his colleagues. When he could not do this with reasonable amiability on both sides, he simply wouldn't play. This, as he told me himself, was why he would not play with Toscanini.'[32] Toscanini was adroit, we may feel, in affecting a distaste for Rachmaninoff's music. Rachmaninoff

not only conducted himself, but played the piano and also composed, and a combination of such skills in the measure he had
would hardly have allowed enough room for an ego the size
of Toscanini's.

A new honour came for Rachmaninoff that spring from
St Petersburg when Princess Hélène of Saxe-Altenburg, who
had been appointed president of the Imperial Russian Music
Society (a sinecure held by a member of the Imperial family),
invited him to become vice-president. There were two such posts
– one was a musical appointee, and the other an administrator.
Founded in 1862 by Anton Rubinstein, the Musical Society soon
came to enjoy Imperial status. It set standards of musical education for all the conservatories throughout the empire. Although
these were high in St Petersburg and Moscow – Glazounov was
Director of the former and Ippolitov-Ivanov had succeeded
Safonov at the latter – it was another case in the provinces. It was
decided to appoint a musician of Rachmaninoff's competence
and stringent standards, one who was familiar with musical circumstances and had appeared in concert widely, to take on the
role of inspector. No sooner had he accepted than he set himself
the task of transforming the Music College of Kiev into a conservatory, and improving the standards of tuition by attracting
distinguished teachers under the direction of Reinhold Gliére,
his contemporary and a composer.

His last concert deputising for Nikisch took place at
the Conservatory on 27 April. The programme included
Glazounov's Prologue in Memory of Gogol (a centenary
tribute), a suite and air from Rimsky-Korsakov's *Christmas
Eve* (with soprano Aurelia Dobrovolsky), Levko's air from
Rimsky-Korsakov's *May Night* (with tenor Dmitri Smirnov),
Tchaikovsky's 'Perevechky' polonaise and Moussorgsky's
Introduction and Gopak from *Sorotchinsky Fair*. On 6 June, the
Rachmaninoffs retired to Ivanovka for the summer. Although
little more than half-way through his life, he was only thirty-six,
he was again lamenting to Morozov:

my health, or rather, strength, has clearly begun to decline, at most I have only about two or three hours a day when I feel strong. There is only a couple in the morning and, for some reason, one in the evening. Now I've taken up a new work and if health does not hinder me, I shall work on it steadily.[33]

It was then that he received notification from a New York bank that the Wolfsohn Bureau had deposited 2,500 dollars in his name. Notwithstanding the death of Wolfsohn, he was still wanted in America.

The new work he began composing was his Third Piano Concerto. He dedicated it to Josef Hoffmann, although Hoffmann never played it. A look at the score explains why Hoffmann's small hands would have had too much difficulty encompassing much of the piano writing, particularly the cadenza. Indeed, at Hoffmann's concerts the piano he used always had keys which had been specially shaved down. 'Rachmaninoff had enormous hands, capable of stretching a twelfth and enabling him to grasp even the most rapid and widespread chords of his own compositions with total security.'[34] Rachmaninoff's apparent inability to appreciate Hoffmann's physical limitations was similar to his refusal to understand why Chaliapin declined to sing in *The Miserly Knight*. Both works inhibited them technically; their failure to undertake them was not for temperamental reasons, nor from any personal animosity. Rachmaninoff remained on good terms with Chaliapin for the rest of his life, and with Hoffmann too, until he became a victim of alcoholism.

Rachmaninoff explains something of the concerto's inspiration in a letter he wrote to the American musicologist Joseph Yasser in 1935:

The first theme is borrowed neither from folk song forms nor church sources. It simply wrote itself. If I had any plan in composing this theme, I was thinking only of sound. I

wanted "to sing" the melody on the piano, as a singer "sings"
it, and to find a fitting orchestral accompaniment, one that
would not drown the "singing".[35]

It is his complete mastery of the piano that enables him to
express his musical ideas so completely. The Third Piano
Concerto is the ultimate romantic piano concerto; even when
compared with his Second Concerto, the piano is more strongly
assertive. The first movement culminates in a cadenza, of which
Rachmaninoff composed two versions. The first, which he
recorded and seems to have played more often, is shorter and
easier than the second. A recording of a broadcasted performance of the second version by the great French pianist Walter
Gieseking is a beautifully characteristic and highly coloured
interpretation; it sounds like an old Pleyel. Although by no
means faultlessly executed, the playing is perfectly matched
stylistically to the orchestral accompaniment provided by the
Concertgebouw Orchestra under Mengelberg, and it remains
one of the very few performances to rival that of Rachmaninoff
and Ormandy.

Notwithstanding Rachmaninoff's success with the work,
there is some truth in Vladimir Horowitz's claim that 'without false modesty, I brought his Third Concerto to light.
I brought it to life, and everywhere!'[36] It was the only one of
Rachmaninoff's works for piano and orchestra that Horowitz
played after his international career began. He recorded it three
times; in 1930, 1951 and 1978. When he played it for the first
time at New York's Carnegie Hall in 1928, the brilliance of his
playing amazed. By 1978, when he played it in his first appearance with an orchestra for twenty-five years at the Academy
of Music in Philadelphia, the clamour to see as well as hear
him was such that it had to be televised. Although his performance is quite different from Rachmaninoff's, stylistically they
have something in common: their virtuosity dates from before
rhetoric in pianists' playing had become compromised by the

microphone. This was a fact that Horowitz understood for in his later years, when he was the last great pianist from an era long passed, almost all of his recordings were made live in front of an audience. By doing so, he reconfirmed the full effect of the concerto. John Culshaw, one of Rachmaninoff's first biographers, wrote in 1943: 'from Liszt and Chopin Rachmaninoff inherited, on the credit side, the power to write music which explored the full possibilities of the piano, both as lyrical and percussive instrument; on the debit side, he furthered their sense of rhetoric.'[37] The first part of that evaluation now seems inarguable. In the second, Culshaw uses the word *rhetoric* in a modern sense, as one might expect of one of the twentieth century's greatest recording producers. However, had he looked in the *Oxford English Dictionary*, he would have read that rhetoric used to be reckoned with grammar and logic in a trivium of the liberal arts.

1909–1911

*First American tour: Introduces Third Piano Concerto: Appears
in concert many times playing Second and Third Piano Concertos:
conducts* The Isle of the Dead, *Second Symphony and works of
Moussorgsky and Tchaikovsky: Proceeds enable him to purchase Satin
family's estate: Writes Liturgy, 13 Preludes, Polka de W.R. and
9 Etudes-Tableaux.*

'During the first decade of the twentieth century, Rachmaninoff's
fame in Russia as a composer grew rapidly. He enjoyed an unex-
ampled popularity bordering on idolatry, it is no exaggeration to
say that he became almost as popular as Tchaikovsky had been in
his day.'[1] He spent most of the week-long voyage to New York
at a dumb keyboard assiduously practising his new piano concerto. Waiting to greet him at the pier was Modeste Altschuler,
whom he had known since their conservatory days. Altschuler
was founder and conductor of the Russian Symphony Orchestra,
which he had started in 1904 with a number of Jewish émigré
musicians driven out by pogroms. He was one of the first of
Rachmaninoff's transatlantic friends, and had introduced
The Crag in the orchestra's first season. The Wolfsohn Bureau
had arranged a number of recitals for Rachmaninoff as well as

appearances with the New York Symphony, Boston Symphony, New York Philharmonic and Philadelphia Orchestra. Other engagements would depend on the reception these earned.

His first engagement began, as was typical with tours, out of town with a recital on 4 November at Northampton, Massachusetts. He played his own compositions: the First Sonata and a selection of preludes (Op. 3 and 10) including the inevitable one in C sharp minor. This was the first occasion when he appeared in a recital entirely on his own, and then he was thirty-six. On the 8th, he played his Second Concerto at the Academy of Music in Philadelphia with the Boston Symphony under Max Fiedler. Repeat performances took place at Baltimore and New York on the 13th. Richard Aldrich, writing, in *The New York Times*, is somewhat restrained in his appraisal:

> Rachmaninoff, who is perhaps the tallest known pianist, is one of the youngest modern Russian composers … His Second Concerto has been given in New York in the last few years a number of times, somewhat out of proportion with its intrinsic merits. But with the assistance of the orchestra, which counts for a great deal in this composition, he made it sound more interesting than it ever has before here. He is a pianist of highly developed technique, as who must be who plays this concerto, and he has ample resources upon the instrument, though a beautiful and varied tone is not conspicuous among them.[2]

This is one of the very few occasions when we read any adverse criticism of his piano playing from a critic who knew what he was writing about. The reservation about lack of tonal variety suggests that his technique may not then have been fully developed. In the next few years, as he began to play the piano more frequently, so it becomes more complete. The worth of his music, on the other hand, was more debatable. Philip

Hale, another reputable critic, is dismissive. 'The concerto is of uneven worth. The first movement is laboured and has little marked character. It might have been written by any German, technically well-trained, who was acquainted with the music of Tchaikovsky.'[3]

After New York, he went on to Hartford, Boston and Toronto with the same orchestra and conductor, repeating the programme. Back in New York on the 20th, he appeared in another recital. Aldrich commented: 'A plaintive Russian note wandered through all the music. In fact, towards the end of the programme many of the listeners began to feel as if they were bound for Siberia.'[4] In Philadelphia on the 26th and 27th, with the Boston Symphony, he conducted Moussorgsky's *Night on the Bald Mountain*, his own Second Symphony, Tchaikovsky's 1812 Overture and as encores he played three of his own preludes. This was the great Russian pianist-composer-conductor's first appearance on an American podium and also the beginning of his long and warm association with what he would later call 'one of the greatest orchestras the world has ever heard'.[5]

The next day, the 28th, he introduced his Third Concerto under Walter Damrosch with the New York Symphony Orchestra. W.J. Henderson in *The Sun* wrote critically:

> It was too long and it lacked rhythmic and harmonic contrast between the first movement and the rest of the concerto. The opening theme in D minor is tinged with melancholy. Russian present-day composers have been charged before now with falling under the stress of recurring periods of political and social unrest. Rachmaninoff has been looked to among the younger men as likeliest after Glazounov to attain a broad nationalism of idea and expression. He has not done so in this concerto unless the outside world is labouring under a delusion as to what real Russia is. The new concerto then, may be taken as a purely personal utterance of the composer. It has at times the character of an impromptu, so unstudied

and informal is its speech and so prone, too, to repetition. The same mood of honesty and simplicity and the single pursuit of musical beauty, without desire to baffle or astonish, dominated Rachmaninoff's playing. The pianist's touch had the loving quality that holds something of the creative and his execution was sufficiently facile to meet his self-imposed test. Sound, reasonable music this, though not a great or memorable proclamation.[6]

Two nights later on the 30th, the concert was repeated. On 3 and 4 December he was in Chicago conducting the Theodore Thomas Orchestra in *The Isle of the Dead* and playing his Second Concerto under Frederick Stock. After a recital at Pittsburgh, he did the rounds touring Boston, Cincinnati (where Stokowski was conducting) and Buffalo, repeating his Second Concerto. On the 17th and 18th in Boston, with the Symphony Orchestra, he conducted *The Isle of the Dead* and played his Second Concerto under Fiedler. On 9 January 1910, he appeared in a Sunday concert at the Metropolitan Opera in an all-Rachmaninoff programme. He accompanied Russian contralto Anna Meitschik in two songs and then played Melody (Op. 10 No. 4), Barcarolle (Op. 10 No. 3) and Humoresque (Op. 10 No. 5). After the interval he added three preludes: F sharp minor (Op. 23 No. 1), G minor (Op. 23 No. 5) and C sharp minor (Op. 3). He finally brought the concert to a conclusion accompanying the Polish bass Adamo Didur in two more songs. While at the Sherry-Netherland Hotel in New York, he found time to respond to a letter from his young cousin Zoya Pribitkova: 'You know in this accursed country, where you're surrounded by nothing but Americans and "business" – they're forever doing "business" – clutching at you from all sides and driving you on – it's extremely pleasant receiving a letter from a Russian girl.'[7]

On the 16th, he played his new concerto with the New York Philharmonic under Mahler. Years later Rachmaninoff had not forgotten the rehearsal:

At that time Mahler was the only conductor I considered
worthy to be classed with Nikisch. According to him, every
detail of the score was important – an attitude unfortunately
rare among conductors. I still remember one incident characteristic of him. We had reached a difficult violin passage
involving some rather awkward bowing. 'Stop! Don't pay
any attention to the markings in the score play it like this,'
and he indicated a different kind of bowing. Some minutes
later, however, the player next to the leader put down his
violin. 'I can't play it with that kind of bowing.' 'What kind
would you like?' Mahler asked. 'As it is marked,' the violinist replied. When Mahler found [that] the leader agreed
he tapped the desk again: 'Then play it so,' he said. The
incident was a definite rebuff for him yet he remained unaffected. We did not begin to work on my concerto until there
was only half an hour left but he did not pay the slightest
attention to this. Forty-five minutes later he announced:
'Now we will repeat the first movement.' My heart stopped
beating – there would be a dreadful row, or at the least a
heated protest from orchestra players but I didn't notice a
single sign of displeasure. They played the first movement
with a keen or even keener concentration than they had
before. At last we had finished. I went up to the conductor's desk and together we were examining the score, when
some musicians in the back seats began quietly packing their
instruments. Mahler looked up – 'What is the meaning of
this?' The Leader replied, 'but, Maestro, it's gone half-past
one.' 'That makes no difference! As long as I am sitting [in
those days the convention had conductors sitting down] no
musician has the right to stand up![8]

On the 27th, he rounded his first American tour in New York
conducting *The Isle of the Dead* and playing his Second Concerto
under Altschuler with the Russian Symphony Orchestra.
Aldrich in *The New York Times* sums up:

Rachmaninoff's music in particular, is weighed down with a melancholy, which seems to be racial in its insistence. It is but natural that this composer should turn with a sort of gruesome delight to so congenial a subject [*The Isle of the Dead*] for his inspiration. It is possibly the composer's intention to show that death is as empty as life. Under the inspiration of the composer's baton the band developed qualities of sonority and precision which it has hitherto given little evidence of possessing. The programme ended with a performance of Rachmaninoff's Second Piano Concerto, which he played himself. This is a work which is not worth such frequent performances as it has received this season, and not in any way comparable to his Third Concerto.[9]

It is worth noting the general attitude of the American critics to Rachmaninoff, as composer, pianist and conductor: as composer, none seems to have cared much for his music; although to judge from the number of concerts where he played either his Second or Third Concerto, the public must have done. As a pianist, in spite of Aldrich's initial caveat about his tone, the same reviewer is later more appreciative of his playing, as is Henderson too, of his first performance of the Third Concerto under Damrosch. As a conductor, although inevitably Aldrich devotes more space to the music, he suggests that the inspiration of Rachmaninoff's presence alone seems to have been enough to metamorphose the playing of even a routine ensemble like the Russian Symphony Orchestra.

With the retirement of Fiedler as conductor of the Boston Symphony Orchestra imminent, board members were looking for a successor and Rachmaninoff's appearance on the podium encouraged them to offer him the position. But he declined; he was only too pleased to leave. Upon arrival back in Moscow he told a reporter from *Muzykalni Truzhenik*:

I am weary of America and have had more than enough of it. Just imagine: almost every day for three months I have

been playing my own compositions exclusively. I was a
great success and was recalled to give encores as often as
seven times, which is a great deal, considering audiences
there. They were remarkably cold, spoiled by guest performances of first-class artists, they were always looking for
something extraordinary, something different. Newspapers
would notice how many times the artist was recalled to take
a bow. For the public this was, if you please, the measure of
your talent.'[10]

Back in Russia on 6 February, he appeared at one of Siloti's
St Petersburg concerts, at which he was due to have introduced
his Third Concerto but as the orchestral parts had not arrived
from New York, he substituted the Second. Afterwards, he
played his Second Suite for two pianos (Op. 17) with Siloti.
At the beginning of March, news reached him of the untimely
death of Vera Komissarzhevskaya, the actress who had played
Monna Vanna. It seems to have been she who fascinated him sufficiently to become preoccupied with writing an opera on the
subject. To her memory he dedicated the song 'It cannot be'
(Op. 34 No. 1), which he would include in the 14 Songs, completed in June 1912. This was the third death in a short time to
affect him, following those of Vera Skalon, his childhood sweet-
heart, and his grandmother Sophia Butakova.

That spring, his cousin Serge Siloti wrote from St Petersburg
requesting permission to allow the leader of the Imperial
Marine Guard Band to arrange the *Polka Italienne*. He readily
agreed, even adding some fanfares, which proved very successful. Eventually, on 4 April, he played the Russian premiere of
his Third Concerto in Moscow with the Philharmonic conducted by Evgeny Plotnikov. It was part of an all-Rachmaninoff
programme in which he conducted *The Isle of the Dead* and his
Second Symphony. The critic in *Russkiye Vedomosti*, Grigori
Prokofiev, suggests it was far more enthusiastically received than
it had been in America:

The new concerto mirrored the best sides of his creative power – sincerity, simplicity and clarity of musical thought, a freshness that does not aspire to discover new paths. It is sharp, laconic in form as well as simple, brilliant orchestration–qualities that will secure it both outer success and enduring love by musicians and public alike.[11]

In the summer of 1910, the Satins' estate became Rachmaninoff's. What made Rachmaninoff so much a Russian of the Old School is apparent in his close feeling for the land. He may have lived much of his life in urban surroundings but it was memories of his childhood that he never forgot. Though his father had been obliged to sell the family estates, the opportunity to return could never have been far from his thoughts. His American tour, for which he earned his first appreciable fees, gave him the opportunity of realising this ambition and taking over the management of Ivanovka from his brother-in-law, Alexander Satin. He set out to modernise and re-equip it by bringing the latest agricultural machinery over from America. In the fashion of Russian landowners of former days, he took a keen interest in the land and was just as absorbed by the simplest work. On 4 June, he wrote to Morozov:

I've spent the whole month planting willows. This is a totally absorbing occupation. For it I bought a bore, with which I drove holes down two feet then planted the cuttings so now they stand about five feet high. I've planted about a hundred and twenty of them! I watered and watered them with such precision, patience and persistence, I know it is worthy of a better cause – but still, how great was the satisfaction when I saw a fresh bud. I am keeping a strict account of the number of trees that take root – there are now forty-three. Congratulate me, please![12]

Whilst at Ivanovka that year he completed the *Liturgy of St John Chrysostom* (Op. 31). Though not conventionally religious,

Rachmaninoff was representative of his class, and the Orthodox ritual meant a great deal to him. The Liturgy in the Orthodox Church is equivalent to Communion in the Church of England or Episcopalian Church, and Mass in the Roman Catholic Church. The work consists of twenty numbers for mixed choir. On 31 July, he wrote to Morozov: 'I've finished the *Liturgy*, which may surprise you. I first thought about it long ago but only set about it unexpectedly. I was at once carried away by it and finished it very quickly. I haven't composed anything in a good while, not since *Monna Vanna*, with such pleasure.'[13] It had in fact taken him less than three weeks to complete, between 3 and 21 June, although it took another two months to produce a final version. It was first performed that November in Moscow by the Synodal Choir, but in a concert performance. This may seem surprising but like Tchaikovsky's setting, composed in 1878, it greatly displeased ecclesiastical authorities. Anna Trubnikova remembers a religious instruction teacher telling her that 'it was absolutely wonderful, but too beautiful, with such music it would be very difficult to pray'.[14] This opinion matched critical opinion in *Russkaya Muzykalnaya Gazeta*, reporting the occasion when the composer conducted a dozen numbers from it in March the following year at one of Siloti's St Petersburg concerts: 'There were many remarks afterwards about it not being church music; that it contained operatic nuances and symphonic refinements. It is written highly musically, but it stands apart from a stylistically conventional work; the composer could never have intended it to fit that formula.'[15] Rachmaninoff seems to have lost interest in it. In 1934, Evgeni Somov (then the composer's secretary) told Nicolai Afonsky, the conductor of the Russian Chorus in Paris who wanted to know whether Rachmaninoff would permit him to perform something from it: 'I don't think it will please him very much. I know definitely he is not in sympathy with this composition.'

Composing his 13 Preludes (Op. 32) proved more demanding than the *Liturgy* and he spent much of that summer working on it. 'I don't like this, it's always difficult for me. There's no beauty or joy in it,'[16] he complained to Morozov. Martyn points out that two of the set had already been played that April as encores during the premiere of the Third Piano Concerto in Moscow. It is hardly surprising that some of them reveal the influence of church music, given that he was working on them at the same time as the *Liturgy*. Certainly the eleventh, in B major, shows 'the development in pianistic terms of an idea left over from the *Liturgy*'.[17] The tenth in B minor, considered one of the best,[18] recalls a tale of Moiseiwitsch's which he recounted in his obituary of the composer. He told Rachmaninoff that it seemed to him reminiscent of a painting by Boecklin, *The Return*, 'in which an old man is sitting by a still pool, his reflection in it, gazing at a cottage nearby.' Rachmaninoff expressed his astonishment, admitting that that had in fact been his inspiration. Like Boecklin's *The Isle of the Dead*, there is a similar potent stillness in the image.

In September, Rachmaninoff was off on another tour giving a dozen performances in western Europe. In London, he played the piano, and in Leeds, he conducted his Second Symphony on the 13th. He travelled on to Vienna, Berlin, Amsterdam and Frankfurt-am-Main, appearing in concert with Mengelberg. It was whilst in Vienna that a rather indiscreet interview with Rachmaninoff was published in Moscow's *Uttro Rossii*. In it, Rachmaninoff stated that he would never return to the Bolshoi, no matter how much money was offered him. He accused Chaliapin of being a brawler and declared that everyone was scared of him. Backstage at the theatre was like a saloon bar, he claimed, where people drank, shouted, swore and used gross language. Circumstances, he maintained, made creative work there impossible. They needed someone like Chaliapin – at least they had to hide from him to avoid trouble. The article caused a frightful rumpus. A delegation went to director Telyakovsky to insist that he deny there was any truth in it. At first Rachmaninoff chose to ignore it but when he heard that it had a depressing effect even on Chaliapin, he wrote a letter to *Russkiye Vedomosti* at length, explaining precisely what he had meant.

> I said that we often have regrettable confusion backstage. There was little or no quiet there, nor what so impresses one abroad – everyone assisting the common cause to the best of his ability. If one must speak during a performance then one whispers, and if one must walk then one tip toes. I also said that I had heard rumours that since Chaliapin had been appointed stage-director in operas in which he sings then things were much better backstage. And that is all I said![19]

On 28 November, he appeared in the Russian Music Society's Jubilee Concert in Moscow conducting, for the first time in the twentieth century, his symphonic poem *The Crag*. He also conducted his Second Symphony and played his Third Concerto under Emil Cooper. His next concert appearance, also in Moscow, took place on 15 January 1911. He again played his Third Concerto, this time under Pomerantsev, and conducted Brahms' *Tragic Overture*, Glazounov's *Finnish Fantasy* and his own *Spring* (with the bass Vassily Petrov and the Bolshoi choir). Afterwards, he went to Kiev where on the 21st he played in a concert under Khodorovsky, and on the 27th, he appeared in a recital. Between performances, in his capacity as vice-president of the Russian Musical Society, he paid a visit to his old friend from student days, Nicolai Avierino, who was then Director of the Rostov Music School. Years later Avierino describes how when they met at the station he invited him to stay at his house, but he declined. He was there, he said, in his official capacity. The next day he came to the school where he scrutinised the accounts; so business-like was his sharp questioning that he even made the bookkeeper uneasy. The next day he sat in during classes, sometimes up to half-an-hour, making notes on the teaching. His visit ended with Avierino conducting the student chorus and orchestra. At the end, much to Avierino's relief, he congratulated everyone – staff and students. It was when they were alone that he told Avierino: 'You know – I was afraid to inspect your school. It's hard to inspect an old friend, and I wasn't sure of you. I was seriously wondering whether it might have been better had I not come to Rostov at all!'[20]

It was on 11 March that Rachmaninoff completed the *Polka de W.R.*, dedicating it to the pianist Leopold Godowsky. Rather atypically for him, it is a delightfully gay piece and, as his recording confirms, shows off his characteristic rhythmic *élan*. On the 29th, he conducted an all-Tchaikovsky programme with the Moscow Philharmonic. The programme included: *The Tempest* Overture, the First Piano Concerto (with Siloti) and the Second Symphony. He spent that summer at Ivanovka again. Estate problems seem to have taken their toll to judge from a letter he wrote Zoya Pribitkova, a cousin: 'I don't think I have ever had so strenuous, exhausting and fatiguing a summer. From tiredness (or, perhaps, old age) I have become inexcusably forgetful. Every evening when I go to bed I remember how many things I had forgotten to do that day.'[21] This is dated 9 August, but by 8 September he had still managed to complete a new set of nine piano pieces called *Etudes-tableaux* (Op. 33). Although they are more complex and elaborate than the Preludes, the title does not seem to indicate any formal difference. This may account for why, when he included the first and seventh at a St Petersburg recital that December, they were entitled *Préludes-tableaux*. In 1929, when he agreed to Respighi orchestrating five of them, he did provide him with programmes but at the time of their composition these were not included. According to Riesemann,[22] the source of inspiration for No. 8 in G minor was another of Boecklin's canvases named *Morning*. Six of them appeared in April 1914 but he withheld Nos 3, 4 and 5. He included No. 4, in A minor, recast, in a second set (Op. 39) in 1917. He cut No. 5 in D minor, perhaps because, as Martyn states, 'it is the least interesting of the whole set'.[23] The fate of No. 3 is indicative: a page from it appears

slightly recast in the coda of the second movement of his Fourth
Concerto, written in 1926 eight years after he left Russia. Since
there is no record of him having brought it with him, the music
must have been in his head.

In the autumn of 1911, he went once again to London where he
played his Third Concerto under Mengelberg. *The Times* reported:

> He is one of the very few pianists, and probably chief among
> them, who have succeeded in adding types of effect to the
> resources of the piano which are not the natural outcome
> of Liszt and his school. The climaxes are built with wonder-
> ful power, but the musical ideas from which they spring are
> also distinctive.[24]

An interesting and apposite comment that we shall have occasion to recall in the light of another critic's observation, when he
reappeared there some years later. He spent the autumn touring
through southern Russia as pianist. On 10 December, he conducted a concert in Moscow that included Tchaikovsky's Fourth
Symphony, Strauss's *Don Juan* and Scriabin's Piano Concerto
in F sharp minor (with the composer at the piano). This was
the only time they appeared in concert together. Perhaps that
is not surprising for, as his wife reports, Rachmaninoff had
the greatest difficulty holding the piece together – Scriabin
had been drunk, and left out and muddled up passages. On the
13th, Rachmaninoff played some of his new *Etudes-tableaux* and
Preludes (Op. 32). Engel makes a telling comparison between
Rachmaninoff's preludes and those of Chopin:

> Instead of Chopin's two-page and sometimes even half-page
> preludes, Rachmaninoff's are four, six or even eight pages
> long. This is a development to be admired when it comes
> from a natural tendency for a musical idea to reveal itself as
> fully as possible. But when a thematic embryo, whose chief

interest is as a brief sketch, insists on being expanded so far,
then one is sorry for the piece and the composer.[25]

On the 15th, he appeared conducting a special concert
in aid of needy students organised by baritone Georges
Baklanoff. As well as Liadov's arrangement of the 'Gopak'
from Moussorgsky's *Sorotchinsky Fair* and Grieg's 'Peer Gynt'
Suite, the programme included the Baron's monologue from
The Miserly Knight sung by Baklanoff. This was the last time
Rachmaninoff would conduct any of his own operatic music.
Baklanoff had sung this scene the previous year with Henry
Russell's Boston Opera Company before performances of
either *Don Pasquale* or *Pagliacci*, or in a triple-bill with Debussy's
L'Enfant prodigue and *Cavalleria Rusticana*. On the 18th, revers-
ing their concert the previous March, Siloti conducted while
Rachmaninoff played Tchaikovsky's First Piano Concerto
for the first time, and afterwards accompanied the contralto
Zbruyeva in some of his own songs.

Whereas in Rostov he had come to hear the students of the
Music School play, at the St Petersburg Conservatory he played
for them. A large audience was present. It was not a formal
occasion; between pieces he talked with the large number who
had come to hear him, announcing the programme as he went
along. He played mostly his own works including some of his
recent *Etudes-tableaux*. When a bouquet of lilacs was brought
in, he seemed touched. The students went on applauding a long
time before finally allowing him to bring the proceedings to a
conclusion with his *Polka de W.R.* Afterwards the conservatory
director, Glazounov, thanked him warmly and, turning to those
present, announced that his visit was an occasion worth com-
memorating. The students were allowed to take the rest of the
day off. Rachmaninoff must almost have felt as if he were a
member of the Imperial family.

1912–1914

Friendship with Marietta Shaginyan: She assists him selecting texts for 14 Songs (Op. 34) and 6 Songs (Op. 38): Conducts works in Moscow by Mozart, Lalo, Grieg, Liszt, Tchaikovsky, Strauss, etc: Goes to Rome to write The Bells: *Completes Second Piano Sonata: Gives concerts in many Russian cities and in Western Europe: Purchases American tractor for Ivanovka.*

In February 1912, Marietta Shaginyan and Rachmaninoff began a correspondence that was to last five years. According to his biographers, Bertensson and Leyda, 'they entered into one of those strangely remote friendships that seem so characteristically Russian.'[1] But in those days many celebrated friendships were literary affairs; they were by no means then exclusively Russian. That between the playwright Bernard Shaw and the famous actress Ellen Terry is legendary, and they met even more rarely than Rachmaninoff and Shaginyan did, although they were often in the same town at the same time, sometimes even in the same theatre.

Shaginyan, born in 1888 of Armenian descent, remained in Russia all her long life until her death in 1980. Her father taught at the University of Moscow and as a young intellectual she studied Kant, Hegel and Goethe. Since her teens she had written short-stories and poems, and some articles on art, literature and music. She describes life in Russia in those days:

> They did not clean the heavy snow from the streets. The winter silenced street noises; inside the houses one did not feel the city shiver. Full, deep, cotton-like quiet enveloped the nights. Heavy snow lay on the pavements, the roofs and eaves of the houses. The gardens looked as though they were dressed in snow and along the wide boulevards sleighs glided softly through the snow.[2]

She tells how 'in February 1912 such a snow storm was raging that one felt lost even in the centre of the city, as if one were swept out on to the Russian steppes, into a snow storm of Pushkin. It was then that I wrote a letter to Rachmaninoff.' At the time he was conducting six performances of *Pique Dame* at the Maryinsky, the last time he would conduct an opera. From that first letter Shaginyan used a *nom de plume*, 'Re', which she continued to use long after she and Rachmaninoff had met. Although none of her letters have survived, she published those he had written to her after his death.

The letters throw some light on his moods, to judge from one dated 15 March[3] – the response to her offering to assist him in some way:

> I need texts for songs. Can you suggest something? I imagine that "Re" must have a great deal of knowledge in this field. Whether the author is living or dead makes no difference. So long as the piece is original and not a translation, not longer than say eight or twelve lines, or at most sixteen. And something else too; the mood should be sad rather than gay. Light, bright tones don't come easily to me.

Two weeks later he was chiding her for her 'merciless criticism of Galina's [Countess Einerling] doggerel',[4] whose texts he used in three songs: 'How fair this spot' (Op. 21 No. 7), 'Sorrow in Springtime' (Op. 21 No. 12) and 'Before my window' (Op. 26 No. 10). She rebuked him for attempting a cheap music-hall success, but he replied that it is a song's lyricism and not its lyrics that causes it to endure (as these songs prove, for they number among his most felicitous inspirations). On 28 April, he wrote her 'just a few words of thanks for your dear funny letter and for the book of poems which you have copied out with so much patience and perseverance'.[5]

By 19 June, he had completed twelve out of the 14 Songs (Op. 34), and 'almost half are written on poems from your [Shaginyan's] notebooks'. They include: 'The Muse' (No. 1), 'Storm' (No. 3) and 'Arion' (No. 5), all of which are written by Pushkin; 'The Soul's Concealment' (No. 2) by Korinfsky; 'A passing breeze' (No. 4) by Balmont; 'The raising of Lazarus' (No. 6) by Khomyakov; 'So dread a fate' (No. 7) by Maykov; 'Music' (No. 8) and 'Dissonance' (No. 13) by Polonsky; 'The Poet' (No. 9) and 'The Morn of Life' (No. 10) by Tyutchev; 'With holy banner firmly held' (No. 11) and 'What wealth of rapture' (No. 12) by Fet. With the exception of 'The Muse' (which he dedicated to Shaginyan), 'So dread a fate' and 'Music', the others are dedicated to singers. These include Chaliapin, the tenor Leonid Sobinov, Nezhdanova (for whom he wrote 'Vocalise' (No. 14) and the soprano Félia Litvinne – a distant relative of his grandmother Butakova. Rachmaninoff finishes his letter to Shaginyan: 'I succeeded in writing them without suffering much – Please God I shall always be able to work like this.' Flushed with her success, Shaginyan straight away sent him an anthology including works by a variety of other poets. However, he did not care for all of these; 'I was horrified by some,' he wrote. Nevertheless she did not give in and eventually three poems (by Blok, Bely, Bryusov) would be set to music in 1916 in his 6 Songs (Op. 38).

Rachmaninoff had known Nicolai Medtner for some while, but it was Shaginyan who was responsible for bringing them closer together. The Medtners were a cultured family of

German extraction who came from Riga in Latvia, a typically cosmopolitan port then in Imperial Russia. They spoke Russian, German and French fluently. The composer had three brothers: Karl (a business man), Emil (a philosopher) and Alexander (a viola player). It was with them that Shaginyan came to spend, as she describes it, her Athenian period. On 8 May, Rachmaninoff wrote her a lengthy letter, which seems at first to contain even a hint of jealousy:

> It occurred to me that what you wish to see in me you could find closer at hand in Medtner. You would like to attach to me a part of what is in fact part of him. It is significant that a half of your last letter is about him. But you must not think I am prejudiced against him – on the contrary. I love him very much and consider him to be one of the most talented among modern composers. He is one of those rare people, musician and human being who only grow in stature the better you know him. Medtner is young, healthy, strong and energetic, with a lyre in his hand, whereas I am old and ageing. Teach me to have faith in myself, dear Re, even half as much as you have in me. If there was ever a time I had it that was long – long, long ago – in my youth![6]

He goes on in the same melancholy vein for several sentences finishing, 'I wonder if I should not make up my mind perhaps to abandon composition altogether and become a professional pianist?' Written in 1912, this was prophetic.

He goes on with a dollop of heavy-handed Russian humour:

> The windows are now closed, a lamp on the table lit. Because of the cold, the cockroaches you love so, and which I detest, have not yet been born. Against the windows are great wooden shutters closed and bolted together. I feel more secure that way in the dark. Of course I know this is just timidity and cowardice. I am afraid of everything – mice, rats, cockroaches, bulls, burglars, etc.; I am afraid when the wind blows and howls

down the chimney; I am afraid when the rain lashes against
the windows. I'm afraid of the dark; I don't like attics and am
ready to believe ghosts are everywhere. It's difficult to know
what I'm not afraid of, even in the daytime when I'm left in
the house alone, I'm afraid.' There must be some question how
literally he should be taken, for the lifestyle of the patrician
class could not have been so lacking in comfort.

The autumn concert season at the Moscow Philharmonic
began that year on 6 October with a further burgeoning of
Rachmaninoff's repertory. Until 1 December he conducted
eight concerts, five for the Philharmonic Society, in which
none of his own music was included. It is doubtful that he had
heard, much less knew, all of the music programmed, so intensive preparation would have been necessary. The first concert
included Berlioz's *Symphonie fantastique*, Lalo's Cello Concerto
(played by André Hekking) and Glazounov's 'Ballet' Suite
(Op. 52). On the 20th, he conducted Mozart's Fortieth
Symphony, Arensky's Variations on a Theme of Tchaikovsky,
the overture to Weber's *Oberon*, Tchaikovsky's Piano Concerto
and Liszt's First Concerto (the latter two were played by
Hoffmann). Grigory Prokofiev, writing in *Russkiye Vedomosti*
thought Hoffmann did not play the Tchaikovsky concerto as
well as Rachmaninoff had the previous year, nor did he care
much for Rachmaninoff's conducting of Mozart's symphony:
'he took some tempi too slowly treating the music too for-
mally.'[7] Neither did Sabaneyev: 'The Mozart symphony was
not for Rachmaninoff. It came out inflated, losing its lightness
and simplicity.'[8] Medtner, however, did not agree: 'I shall never
forget this Mozart of Rachmaninoff's, so unexpectedly coming
upon us, pulsating with life, and authentic all the same. I shall
not forget the alarm of some individuals at the deceased resusci-
tated, the joyful amazement of others, and the sombre, gloomy
dissatisfaction of Rachmaninoff himself.'[9]

On the 22nd, the fifth anniversary of Grieg's death, he conducted an all-Grieg concert including the 'Peer Gynt' Suites

Nos 1 and 2, the 'Lyric' Suite and the Piano Concerto played by Mark Meychik. Engel was ecstatic:

> Rachmaninoff is a truly "God-given" conductor who stirs both audience and orchestra. He may be the only Russian conductor to be compared with such figures in the west as Nikisch, Colonne and Mahler. For Anitra's Dance alone, as conducted by Rachmaninoff, I would trade the whole of the Moscow Arts Theatre's production of Ibsen's play.[10]

On the 27th, he conducted Mendelssohn's 'Scotch' Symphony, Wagner's *Wesendonck Lieder* (Mottl's orchestral transcription), Grieg's 'Lyric' Suite and 'The Last Spring' and Liszt's 'Mazeppa' and 'Lorelei' (sung by mezzo soprano Ilona Durigo). On 3 November, his programme included Tchaikovsky's Fifth Symphony, 'Wotan's Farewell' and 'Magic Fire music' from Wagner's *Walküre* (with Baklanoff), after which he accompanied Baklanoff in his own 'Spring Waters' (Op. 14 No. 11) and 'Fate' (Op. 21 No. 1). He finished by conducting Strauss' *Til Eulenspiegel*.

In a letter to Shaginyan on the 12th, we can get an idea of how much the effort of having to learn so much new repertory cost him:

> Yesterday at another concert [the programme included a Schubert march arranged by Sakhnovsky, two excerpts from Berlioz's *La Damnation du Faust*, Liszt's First Hungarian Rhapsody and some of his own songs], for the first time in my life, at one point, I forgot what to do next, my mind just went blank. I tried for what seemed ages before remembering what came next. I pray God I shall get away from here soon.[11]

Unsurprisingly, on the 17th he cancelled his next engagement. On the 23rd, however, he was well enough to conduct a special programme to help raise money for the family of Ilya Satz, the thirty-seven-year-old composer of incidental music at the

Moscow Arts Theatre who had died suddenly. On 1 December, he conducted his final concert that season. The programme featured: Borodin's Second Symphony, Glazounov's *Spring*, Rimsky-Korsakov's 'Battle of Kerzhenets' from *The Invisible City of Kitezh* and Dvorak's Cello Concerto (played by Pão Casals). While this hectic schedule was going, two leading musicians visited Russia: the composer and pianist, Ferrucio Busoni, and the pianist Harold Bauer. Both recorded meetings with Rachmaninoff. Busoni's account was brief: 'In my last days in Moscow I was visited by Hoffmann and Rachmaninoff – both of them musical darlings in Russia.'[12] Bauer's account was fuller:

> I met a number of distinguished musicians at Koussevitzky's home in Moscow. The man who interested me most was Rachmaninoff. During dinner we spoke of music in France, and Rachmaninoff, who had recently played his Second Concerto there with immense success, expressed surprise at the catholic French musical taste. 'They like everything' he said 'even their moderns.' I asked him if he played Debussy's piano pieces, and he said no, he did not care for that music. Koussevitzky, after dinner, asked me to play some Debussy, which I did. Rachmaninoff sat silent for a few moments, and then suddenly started up and began haranguing Koussevitzky. 'Speak French or German' said the latter. Rachmaninoff turned to me and attempted to explain exactly why Debussy's music displeased him, but he was too excited and lapsed into his native tongue again, so I never found out.[13]

On 5 December, the Rachmaninoffs departed Moscow for Berlin. From there they travelled to Switzerland for a month, so he could recuperate from his exhausting schedule of concerts, before proceeding to Rome, where they spent three months:

> I was able to take the same flat on Piazza di Spagna that Modest Tchaikovsky had rented for his brother in 1880. It is only

possible to compose when one is alone and there are no external disturbances to hinder the calm flow of ideas; these conditions were ideally realized in the apartment in Piazza di Spagna. All day long I spent at the piano or the writing desk, not until the sinking sun gilded the pines on the Pincio did I put down my pen. I finished my Second Piano Sonata (Op. 36) and the choral symphony *The Bells* (Op. 35). I had already sketched a plan for a symphony during the previous summer. Then one day I received a letter from a certain Mlle Danova, a pupil of my old friend the cellist Bukinik, suggesting that I read Balmont's translation of Edgar Allen Poe's poem. The verses were, she said, ideally suited for a musical setting and would particularly appeal to me. I read them through and at once decided to use them for a choral symphony. The structure of the poem demanded four movements. I worked on it feverishly and it remains today [1934] of all my works the one I like best.[14]

Interestingly, he refers to *The Bells* as a choral symphony, although it is not so styled in the score. In spite of the composer's affection for it and notwithstanding the enthusiastic reception it received at its Moscow premiere the following November, it took another seven years before the music was eventually published. Poe's poem had already, six years before, been used as a setting by the English composer Joseph Holbrooke, although it is doubtful whether Rachmaninoff knew of it:

Each of the four stanzas apostrophizes a different kind of bell, associated in turn with different stages in human life. Thus, silver sleigh bells symbolize birth and youth, golden bells marriage; bronze is the metal of fire alarm bells, the harbingers of terror, and the tolling of the iron funeral bell marks a man's last rites on earth.[15]

By making use of three soloists, a chorus and full orchestra (in his usual fashion with orchestra leading, chorus and soloists following) Rachmaninoff set out to produce a work of ambitious proportions. He dedicated it to Mengelberg and the Concertgebouw – indicatively Mengelberg, unlike his peers, did not conduct opera.[16]

Before the end of March 1913 the Rachmaninoffs' Rome sojourn came to an abrupt end. Their daughters, Tatyana and Irina, came down with typhoid fever, and not trusting Italian doctors, they left for Berlin. On 29 June he was again writing to Shaginyan: 'My children are now, thank God, quite well. As for myself I have been able to work the whole day for the last two months.'[17] Although his daughters recovered, it was too late to go back to Rome where they would have had to endure the summer heat, so they returned to Russia. He completed his Second Piano Sonata (Op. 36) at Ivanovka during August and September. So elaborate was the piano-writing that it would hardly be surprising to learn that it was a transcription of a piano concerto. Yet despite a certain formal resemblance to his Third Piano Concerto, the sonata's musical material had its own immediate unambiguous appeal. As Boris Tyuneyev writes:

> Although it is the composition of a mature and great talent, you will find Rachmaninoff the lyricist in it only to a very small degree – rather the contrary; there is about it a certain inner reserve, severity and introspection. The composer speaks more of the intellect out of the intellect than of the heart out of the heart.[18]

He dedicated it to Marvin Pressman, one of the conservatory students he had lived with twenty years before at Zverev's and kept in touch with. In 1912, Pressman (being a Jew) had been dismissed from the post of director of the school of the Imperial Russian Music Society at Rostov. Rachmaninoff lost no time in submitting his resignation; as he told the Music Society, if anti-Semitism was more important than musicianship, he could see no point his continuing in the post of vice-president.

At Ivanovka that summer, Rachmaninoff bought an automobile. Back in 1909 he had told Morozov: 'I can't tell you how much I would like one'. In those days they were still a novelty in Russia, especially in the country. Between bouts of work he would motor out into the steppe country, sometimes travelling more than 100 miles a day. On such occasions he would be seated in his new open coupé, goggles on, the wind against his face, with his chauffeur in the passenger seat: 'I breathe the air, bless freedom and the blue sky; and after such an air bath I feel bolder and stronger. When I conduct, I experience much the same feeling as when I drive my car – an inner calm that gives me complete mastery of myself and the forces, musical or mechanical, at my disposal.'[19] On 30 August he wrote to Shaginyan:

Today I heard from a committee which is arranging a celebration of Shakespeare's 350th birthday, they asked me to write a scene from King Lear – the scene on the heath. Tell me; is there a new translation of Lear? If not, which of the older ones is the best? Could I ask you to send me a copy immediately? Though I have neither envelopes, nor Shakespeare, at least I have a conscience. I swear I'll refund you the cost of the book and the stamps with my warm gratitude.[20]

His concert schedule began that autumn, on 17 October, with a performance of his Second Piano Concerto in Warsaw, Poland. The *Russkaya Muzykalnaya Gazeta* observed rather tartly: 'It's a pity he doesn't refresh his repertory, this is the fourth time he has played it here!'[21] He went on to give recitals in Kiev, Tiflis, Voronezh, Saratov and St Petersburg. Of the last, critic Karatygin in *Rech* adopts a similarly condescending tone:

The public worships Rachmaninoff because he has hit the very centre of average philistine musical taste. Elegance of externals and insignificance of content are found together in most of Rachmaninoff's piano works. They are overly 'sincere'. In them one hears an 'experience' of some highly emotional feelings. The most successful numbers on the programme were a clever arrangement of his songs 'Lilacs' [though quite hackneyed, the original song must be considered the best that he has yet written, and more poetic than its piano transcription] and his new sonata. The latter has no interesting or profound ideas. Piano virtuosity dominates its musical potential, but it has some fresh and, for Rachmaninoff, rather unusual harmonies and counterpoint. In certain passages, in the central movement, the composer shows an excellent inventive capacity for variations. It was interesting to note that this sonata with musical ambitions far higher than all his elegies, barcaroles, and preludes, was received by the public with considerable reservation.[22]

On 30 November, *The Bells* had its premiere in a Siloti concert in St Petersburg, conducted by the composer; the programme also included *The Isle of the Dead* and the Second Concerto. Critic Tyuneyev was appreciative:

Sincerity and spontaneity have always been close to Rachmaninoff's muse. Against this tragic, sorrowing background, the concentrated shades of hopeless anguish and despair that first appeared in *The Isle of the Dead* reveal themselves with unusual clarity in *The Bells*. In his new poem are heard with special force the pessimistic passion and sublime tragedy characteristic of a great artist and noble heart.[23]

Back in Moscow on 14 December he conducted Tchaikovsky's Fourth Symphony and 'Theme and Variations' from Suite No. 3 in G as well as Saint-Saëns's Cello Concerto with Casals. In January 1914, he journeyed to England to make eight concert appearances. At the last moment, he nearly didn't go; just before he was to depart Moscow, on the 5th, the French pianist Raoul Pugno was found dead in his hotel room during a concert tour.

Rachmaninoff was morbidly preoccupied that the same thing might happen to him, and was only with difficulty persuaded to go. During his visit, Henry Wood invited him to come again that autumn to hear the first English performance of *The Bells* in Sheffield. The outbreak of the First World War prevented it, however, and another generation was to pass before it was given there. On 8 February, he introduced *The Bells* in Moscow where it was received with warm acclamation. It was the last item in a programme which might then have been described as modern, and to judge from his conversation with Harold Bauer, not much to his taste. It included Ravel's *Valses nobles et sentimentales*, Debussy's *Martyrdom of St Sebastian*, Roger-Ducasse's *Au jardin de Marguerite* and even Franck's *Le Chasseur maudit*, all of which had been written since he was born.

After the concert ended, an enormous floral tribute was brought onto the platform – bells of all sizes made from white lilacs (this was February). It was from the 'lady with the lilacs', as she became known. Since Rachmaninoff had returned from his American tour she had sent white lilacs whenever he appeared in concert, no matter what time of year. She would arrange for them to be delivered to his home on his birthday, and if he was going away, they would be sent to the train, or when he arrived at the hotel where he was staying, he would find a bouquet waiting for him. With it she would enclose a brief congratulatory note signing it simply 'Lilacs', the title of his song. It took until after the war began for him to come to know who she was. When he left Russia he offered her his assistance to leave too, but she preferred to remain.

On 24 February, he was in St Petersburg to conduct his *Liturgy* (Op. 31) with the chorus from the Maryinsky. On 1 March, back in Moscow at another Philharmonic Society concert, he began developing his classical repertory, conducting Bach's prelude from a cantata (Op. 35) and Vivaldi's *Concerto Grosso* (edited by Siloti). The programme also included Brahms's Variations on a Theme of Haydn, Weingartner's arrangement of Weber's

Invitation to the Dance, Beethoven's First Concerto in C and Liszt's
First Concerto in E flat (the latter two both played by Lhevinne).
On the 22nd, Rachmaninoff conducted Glazounov's Sixth
Symphony, his own orchestration of Borodin's song *Romance*,
'To me, O Lord, within Thy power', from Tchaikovsky's
Moscow cantata (sung by the contralto Zbruyeva) and Rimsky-
Korsakov's *Russian Easter Festival Overture*.

At the end of March 1914, Rachmaninoff retired to Ivanovka,
much earlier than he was used to doing. An announcement
appeared in *Muzika* on 12 April claiming that he was at work on
a new piano concerto. However, when he returned to Moscow
after another seven months, unlike in previous years, he did
not bring with him any new finished compositions. In a letter
to Goldenweiser on 11 June, he claimed that he was starting
work on the concerto, but less than a week later, he denied it to
Siloti. Some undated fragments of the first and last movements
of the concerto survive in a sketchbook from that November,
which also contains a draft of his setting of *From St John's Gospel*.
Letters, however, provide no further evidence.

During that summer he seems to have been more preoccupied
with agricultural than musical matters. As he delighted in his
new coupé in 1909, so in 1914 he realised a dream for Ivanovka,
purchasing an American tractor. It had to be arranged through
the Ministry of Agriculture, but not without some difficulty:

> I had to go to St Petersburg to call on one of the directors at
> the Ministry, whom I happened to know, and explain to him
> what I wanted. He spent a considerable time and effort trying
> to dissuade me – with all the horses I had what did I need a
> tractor for? 'And if you do get it, what are you going to do
> with it?' I told him, 'I'll drive it myself.' Thinking, no doubt,
> I'd taken leave of my senses, at last he consented to put the
> order through. The tractor was to be delivered that autumn.
> But I never saw it, in August war was declared.'[24]

10

1914–1917

Composes All-Night Vigil *(Op. 37): Koussevitsky buys Gutheil's catalogue: Scriabin's death encourages him to play his works but a recording confirms he does so unstylishly: Relationship with mezzo-soprano Koshetz: Composes 9 Etudes-Tableaux (Op. 39): Welcomes February revolution: Revises First Piano Concerto: After October revolution determines to leave Russia.*

The First World War represented a watershed in Rachmaninoff's life: until it broke out he was best known as a composer, only secondarily as a pianist and conductor. After it began in Russia he conducted only twice again. On 25 October 1914, he conducted a charity concert with the Moscow Philharmonic that included six symphonic miniatures by Liadov (a Professor at Petrograd Conservatory)[1] who had died that summer, and his own Second Symphony. Two and a quarter years later, on 7 January 1917, he rounded out his career at the Bolshoi conducting *The Crag, The Isle of the Dead* and *The Bells*. The outbreak of the First World War in Imperial Russia in August 1914 did not then seem like the inevitable prelude to revolution. Notwithstanding the Russian empire's catastrophic defeat by the Japanese navy in 1905, historical inertia ensured its survival for another dozen years.

The tsarist regime may have proved just able to cope with the economic metamorphosis going on within its frontiers, but it was another matter when faced by Germany's mighty military machine; so febrile had it become, that it would not take long to be swept away.

In November 1914, Rachmaninoff played the piano in recitals devoted to Russian music in Kharkov and Kiev, in aid of war charities. Then back in Moscow, in an all-Rachmaninoff programme, he played his Second Piano Concerto under Koussevitzky who also conducted his Second Symphony and *The Isle of the Dead*. At the end of January 1915 he completed *All-Night Vigil* (Op. 37), an unaccompanied work for four-part choir consisting of fifteen chants. In later years he said that it was a chance hearing of his 1910 *Liturgy* (Op. 31), which greatly disappointed him, that prompted him to write this new choral work. *All-Night Vigil* includes music sung in the Russian Orthodox Church before a holy day beginning with Vespers at six in the evening and continuing until nine the following morning. The chants are interrupted by prayers, litanies, readings, etc. Nine parts of the work are composed on traditional chants as used in church rituals, and only six are wholly original; although, as Rachmaninoff explains, he devised these as 'a conscious counterfeit of the ritual'.[2] He dedicated it to the memory of Stepan Smolensky, director of the Moscow Synodal School, an authority on early Russian church music who had first introduced him to manuscript music.

Upon completing *Vigil* he took it first to his old teacher, Taneyev, for him to correct any errors he might find in the polyphony. He was delighted when Taneyev handed it back unaltered, complimenting him. He then took it to Smolensky's successors, Alexander Katalsky and Nicolai Danilin:

> It pleased both of them when I played it through on the piano. They immediately asked my permission to perform it as soon as possible, which I gave with the greatest pleasure.

My favourite passage in it, which I love as much as *The Bells*, is the fifth canticle, 'Nunc dimittis'. I should like this sung at my funeral. Towards the end there is a passage sung by basses – a scale descending to the bottom B flat very slowly and pianissimo. After I had played this passage through Danilin shook his head, exclaiming 'Where on earth are we to find such basses? They are as rare as asparagus at Christmas!' Nevertheless, he did find them. I know the voices of my countrymen, and I well knew what demands I could make of Russian basses![3]

At the premiere in Moscow for war relief on 10 March the choir sang so well under the composer's direction and the work's reception was so warm and enthusiastic, that four more performances were quickly arranged. In spite of the work's particular nature and its essential *Russianness*, the revolution and the Soviet regime would adversely affect its establishment in the repertory. Martyn rates it 'by any standards a formidable creative achievement'.[4] We can hear the piece in a recording of 1965 with Klara Korka, Constantin Ognvoi and the Russian Academic Choir conducted by Alexander Sveshnikov.

In spring 1915, Rachmaninoff became preoccupied with the possibility of composing a ballet. For all his lyricism he had not proved a successful composer of opera, but like Tchaikovsky his style might have better suited ballet music. On 1 November, he wrote asking Siloti for a suitable subject:

Do you happen to know Fokine or anyone among Petrograd's dancers who you could ask? At this end I will try some Moscow dancers. A new director of ballet at the Maryinsky Theatre, Samuel Andrianov, approached to ask me to accept a commission for a ballet to be written this season; he suggested three subjects. I mentioned a large fee and he promised to think it over. I shall need a dancer who will be able to help me determine the number of bars, indicate tempi and so on.

Naturally not every subject might suit me, and one I like might not suit a ballet.[5]

However it was not Andrianov in Petrograd but a young Moscow choreographer, Kasyan Golyzovsky, who approached Rachmaninoff with an idea of Alexander Gorsky's, Director of the Bolshoi ballet, that he compose music for a ballet based on Balmont's poem *The Scythians*. But whether Rachmaninoff ever started the commission is a moot point. The only evidence that survives is a fragment of the text and a letter of 22 April from Golyzovsky to Rachmaninoff requesting permission 'to listen to sketches for the first scene and for the final symphonic dance'.[6] Years later, Golyzovsky claimed that music Rachmaninoff included in his 1940 *Symphonic Dances* is a reworking of the same material, but since this title dates from more than a generation later it seems highly unlikely. In March 1916, another proposition came that he should compose a ballet, this time from stage director Vsevolod Meyerhold and dancer Mikhail Mordkin. He wrote to Shaginyan begging her to suggest a suitable scenario but, with his customary caution, imploring her to keep his plans to herself. Shaginyan proposed a number of Hans Christian Andersen stories, including *The Little Mermaid*, *The Snow Queen* and *The Garden of Paradise*. Although he was interested enough in the latter to telephone her about it, according to Shaginyan,[7] nothing came of it. The nearest he came to writing a ballet suite was in 1939 when Fokine adapted his Rhapsody on a Theme of Paganini.

A plausible reason for his dropping the idea becomes apparent when we learn of the difficulties Rachmaninoff faced with publishers around this time. In 1915, Rachmaninoff, along with Scriabin and Medtner (both advisors to Koussevitzky's publisher, Éditions Russes de Musique), turned down Prokofiev's *Scythian Suite*. Koussevitzky was not so easily put off, however. Armed with his wife's money (he married Natalia Ushkova, the daughter of a millionaire tea merchant), he bought Gutheil's

catalogue, Gutheil having died earlier that year. He was therefore able to publish whatever he chose without having to
secure the permission of Editions Russes and he trumped
Rachmaninoff by becoming his publisher. Thus, there is no
need to wonder why, after settling in the west, Rachmaninoff
and Koussevitzky never appeared in concert together, or why
Rachmaninoff never wrote anything for Koussevitzky's new
publishing house in Paris. The nearest they came to any coop-
eration was in 1930 when Koussevitzky, anxious to find a
commission as popular as Ravel's orchestration of *Pictures at an
Exhibition*, offered Rachmaninoff sufficient financial induce-
ment to permit Respighi to orchestrate his *Etudes-tableaux*.

On 14 April, news came of the sudden death of Scriabin at
the age of forty-three from blood poisoning. Even back in their
conservatory days there had always been some rivalry between
them. In 1891, Arensky encouraged Rachmaninoff to sit his
finals in composition a year early, but when Scriabin wanted
to do the same, Arensky refused and Scriabin left the conservatory without graduating. When they met again in Paris in 1907
Rachmaninoff had become irritated by Scriabin's preoccupation
with the relationship between music and colours. 'What colour
is this music?', Rachmaninoff demanded to know ironically as
he played the opening chord of Scriabin's *Prometheus*. Scriabin
declared, 'It isn't music, only atmosphere enveloping the audience – a violet atmosphere.'[8] When they appeared together at
a Moscow Philharmonic concert in 1911, at which Scriabin
played his own concerto and Rachmaninoff conducted, the
report was that Scriabin was drunk.[9] Scriabin's music may not
then have been as popular as Rachmaninoff's but death elevated
it to classical status – nothing succeeds like death in concentrat-
ing public attention, as Rachmaninoff no doubt recalled some
years before when the composer Vassily Kalinnikov had died
indigent. To help raise money for Kalinnikov's widow and
family, Rachmaninoff took a quantity of his manuscripts to the
publisher Jürgenson, who immediately paid ten times what he

expected, and without demur. 'Don't imagine that I pay this tre-
mendous sum without good reason,' Jürgenson told him. 'I pay
it because death has multiplied the value of his works by ten.'[10]

Riesemann records Rachmaninoff's memory of Scriabin's
funeral:

> All the literary, musical and artistic figures assembled filled
> not only the church but the whole vast square in front of it.
> The Archbishop of Moscow gave the address, for the choir
> were chosen the most beautiful voices and best singers, so
> indescribably affecting was the singing it might have reduced
> the most obstinate heathen to tears and softened the heart of a
> hardened heretic.[11]

The following season Rachmaninoff planned a number of
Scriabin recitals to help raise money for his widow, and to do
so he set himself the task of learning a quantity of his music.
Goldenweiser tells how when he came to visit him:

> He thought his proposed programme too short and asked me
> to suggest some other works he might play. I asked him if he
> knew Scriabin's *Fantasy* (Op. 28). He replied that he did not, so
> I got out the music. He immediately played it through – it is
> one of Scriabin's most exceptionally difficult pieces – he liked
> it and decided to include it in recital three or four days later.[12]

Rachmaninoff's programmes were made up of mostly Scriabin's
early works. He included 11 Preludes (Op. 11), the Second Sonata
(Op. 19), the Piano Concerto in F sharp minor (Op. 20) and a
Poème in F sharp (Op. 32). Of his later works he played the 'Satanic
Poem' (Op. 36), three Etudes (Op. 42), and the Fifth Sonata
(Op. 53), which had been composed in 1908. More recently-writ-
ten works than that, he said, he was not prepared to play.

On 26 September, he travelled to Petrograd to play Scriabin's
Concerto under Siloti, which he had conducted in Moscow

four years before with Scriabin as soloist. He repeated it under Koussevitzky and afterwards undertook a tour through southern Russia with two programmes, one of his own works and the other of Scriabin's. On 18 November, back in Moscow for another recital, Shaginyan remembers:

> He was in an awful state, biting his lip, pale and angry. Before I could congratulate him, he began to complain how old he was growing, how he needed being put out on the scrap heap. We should write his obituary, how he had once been a musician, but now all that was over, he could never forgive himself. 'Didn't you notice that I missed the point?' he demanded. 'I let it slip.'[13]

He went on, explaining that in every piece there was a high point in its structure, and that a musician must approach this with the greatest spontaneity, yet also with the greatest art. It was like a tape breaking when a runner won a race. It might be anywhere in a piece, it might be loud or soft, but the pianist must know how to approach it, for if he let it pass without acknowledging it, then the piece would collapse and fail to make an effect.

Notwithstanding all Rachmaninoff's hard work, his Scriabin performances were not received altogether positively. The critic Grigori Prokofiev in *Russkaya Muzykalnaya Gazeta* wrote of the Moscow recital:

> Rachmaninoff played with his usual technical perfection and the musical quality natural to him, but in his approach to Scriabin's works, he did not—or could not—grasp the basic nature of this music—the emotional saturation of Scriabin's creative energy. It was as if in seeking to find some logic in Scriabin's structure, he showed us the harmony with extraordinary clarity, but in the process the spirit of the music was lost.[14]

The composer Sergei Prokofiev, who was also present at one of his Scriabin recitals, noted: 'When Scriabin used to play his Fifth Sonata somehow it all took wings, but with Rachmaninoff all its notes stood firmly on the ground.' The American musicologist Josef Yasser explains Rachmaninoff's interpretation: 'What he did was translate Scriabin, an already modern composer with all the characteristics of the Moscow School, into one trained in the tradition of Tchaikovsky.'[15] To understand what so upset the Scriabinists, listen to Rachmaninoff's only Scriabin recording, the Prelude in F sharp minor (Op. 11 No. 8) recorded in 1929 (indicatively, it was not published until 1973). 'He totally disregards the composer's marking "allegro agitato", playing the piece at about half speed, removes the Prelude's essential urgent restlessness, imposing on it an alien wistfulness.'[16] He plays it unstylishly, without having any sympathy for what to him then would have seemed alien modern music.

At the end of April 1916, Rachmaninoff's conservatory friend Avierino, director of the Rostov Music School, came up to Moscow to be married. On the night before he invited Rachmaninoff, with some trepidation, to a stag party:

> I knew his dislike of crowds, so I went personally to invite him, swearing I would take him home before midnight. He promised to come, and so he did. There was an excellent supper and throughout it many toasts – Chaliapin made some particularly witty ones. The noise and gaiety drove out of my mind my promise to Sergei Vasilyevich, it was two in the morning before I remembered and went to look for him. There was a loud burst of laughter – the actor Moskvin and Chaliapin were dancing a polka with Koenemann at the piano [and] hidden behind the piano was Rachmaninoff, doubled up with laughter. 'Well, Seryozha' I said when I could get to him. 'Time to go home, I promised to deliver you by midnight – and look at the time now!' 'Oh – I'm not going yet' he replied.[17]

That summer he took his vacation not at Ivanovka but at Khalila in Finland, near Siloti's home. While there, on 6 June, Taneyev died. To the editor of *Russkiye Vedomosti*, Rachmaninoff wrote a lengthy tribute finishing:

> Sergei Ivanovich Taneyev is gone – composer, teacher, the most scholarly musician of his time, a man of rare original-ity, and of rare spirituality. He was Moscow's musical leader, maintaining his high position with unwavering authority until the end of his days. For those of us who knew him, he was the best of all judges: wise, righteous, affable and direct. He was a model in everything, for everything he did was done well. Through personal example he taught us how to live, how to work, even how to speak, for he spoke in a peculiarly 'Taneyev way'; concisely, appositely and wittily. Only neces-sary words came from his mouth. All of us valued his wise counsel, because we trusted it, and it was always good.[18]

These deaths brought out the morbid and fanciful in Rachmaninoff. He wrote to Shaginyan: 'What is your attitude to death? Are you afraid of it?' He had been reading a fashiona-ble novel about death and was immediately stricken with terror. He had been afraid of robbers, epidemics and such like, but at least he felt he could cope with them. It was the uncertainty of death which affected him. It would be terrible indeed were there something afterwards. 'Better rot – disappear altogether – cease to exist.'

By this time Rachmaninoff was forty-three, but he seemed much older. To judge from Shaginyan's account, when they met that summer at Essentuki, the spa in the Caucasus, he sounds as if he were having a nervous breakdown:

> He looked haggard and spent. For the first time I saw tears in his eyes. In the course of our conversation he several times wiped them away but they welled up again. I had never seen

him in such total despair before. His voice kept breaking. He
said he was not working at all, whereas before he always used
to work at Ivanovka in the spring, that year he had no desire
to work. What galled him was being aware of his incapability
and the impossibility of ever being more than a well-known
pianist and mediocre composer. 'If I had always been only
that, and recognized it,' he said, 'it would be easier for me
now, but I did have talent when I was young. If you knew
how easily, casually, almost as a joke, I was able to sit down at
the piano and turn out any piece, to begin composing in the
morning and by evening have it finished. I still have a need for
creative work, but the desire to bring it out, the need to bring
it out – all this has gone for ever. Until I was forty I had hopes
but after forty only memories, and that sums up the whole of
my life.'[19]

After Rachmaninoff had been going on in this fashion for some
while, Shaginyan tried cheering him. She brought out a note-
book in which she had jotted down some forty-odd poems
suggesting that some might suit him for song settings.

While Rachmaninoff was away at Essentuki his father who,
after many years, had come to visit him at Ivanovka, died
suddenly. Although a great deal of Rachmaninoff's correspondence survives, there is little to suggest from it that he had seen
his father often or that he was ever on close terms with him.
Certainly his death at seventy-five does not seem to have affected
him anything like as much as that of Taneyev or even Scriabin.
In September he was writing to Shaginyan once again, this time
in a very different mood:

> I reread some of your letters to me, dear Re! I felt as much
> tenderness, gratitude and something more that is bright and
> good, that I was seized with the desire to see you at once, to
> have a good long talk with you. We could talk about you,
> me or anyone or anything you wish. Maybe we could just be

silent, but mainly to see you and sit next to you. Where are you, my dear Re? And how soon shall we meet?[20]

His spirits seem to have recovered after setting six of those texts which Shaginyan gave him.

This cycle (Op. 38) he dedicated to Nina Koshetz. He had first met Koshetz when she was a soloist at a Moscow concert in memory of Taneyev. Koshetz made some records about this time of Tchaikovsky's 'Lullaby' (Rachmaninoff later transcribed it for piano) and one of Tamara's arias from Rubinstein's *Demon*.[21] They show off a fresh and attractive sounding voice: the tone pure, focused and limpid on the breath and the high notes effortlessly produced. There is no question that she is a soprano here. Some of her later recordings, however – those for Brunswick after 1922 and HMV in 1931 – are equivocal. By 1939, when she ventured an album (including some songs by Rachmaninoff) for Schirmer she had smoked her head voice away. We catch a glimpse of her playing a bit part in a movie around that time, by which point she had come to look like the fat woman at the fair. At the beginning of her career she seems to have made an impression on Rachmaninoff, casting him in the role of father (he was a generation her senior, or so she maintained). At first, to judge from his letters, we can believe he was in love with her. He writes from Ivanovka on 1 September:

Highly-esteemed Nina Pavlovna, or dear Ninochka, or Ninunshka, or perfidious Naina! So you've abandoned Essentuki, and it can now enjoy peace undisturbed by your mischief and devilry. As to your appearing at the Siloti concert, I wrote him the day I received your telegram, asking him to change the order of the concerts. But my request came too late; the schedule had been set by then, as he wired you. So there's nothing to be done about it. For programme changes there is plenty of time. Let him print what he likes, we can always change it. You must sing the new songs. I'll give you them when I come to Moscow.'[22]

They appeared together at a recital on 24 October 1916 in Moscow, at which she sang the first performance of his new songs, and they repeated the programme in Petrograd and Kharkov. Engel wrote, 'on most occasions the singer is the centre of attraction and no one bothers much about the accompanist, but for once it was the other way about.'[23] Before they were to appear in Kiev, and other southern cities, Rachmaninoff heard that Koshetz had signed up for further performances without telling him. He wrote rebuking her:

Is this really true? Why didn't you tell me? Is it possible that you signed up without showing the contract to an adult? Did you limit the length of the tour? Has the itinerary been shown you? In such matters you are worse than a child. Merely because you've chatted with some acquaintances you are ready to sign anything. This, unfortunately, is very like you.[24]

By the following summer relations between them seem to have deteriorated further. Shaginyan describes them together at a recital at Kislovodsk on 28 July: 'Rachmaninoff appeared nervous and irritated: he did not want to accompany her, but she pouted and refused to sing without him, so finally he consented.'[25] This was the last time they appeared together, and it was also the last time that Shaginyan and Rachmaninoff met – she stayed in Russia, eventually even writing a biography of Stalin. After Rachmaninoff left Russia in December 1917, in spite of pleas by Prokofiev, he declined to assist Koshetz escape. It was not until the beginning of the Second World War, when he had moved to California and she was living in Hollywood, that he came to hear of her indigence and in a burst of sentimentality offered to accompany her once again in recital. But it was too late, by then she was quite voiceless.

In the autumn of 1916, he composed a further set of *Etudes-tableaux* (Op. 39), his last new compositions to be performed before he left Russia. He introduced the first eight of these at a Petrograd recital on 29 November. Perhaps it was the number of deaths in his circle that accounts for an excessive preoccupation with the minor mode; *Dies irae* recurs through them like a leitmotif. As a pianist he was growing in stature, notwithstanding the hiccough his progress had suffered with his Scriabin concerts. In Moscow, when he played there again, Engel asked: 'Who among Russian pianists is strongest, and most radiant? For me the choice is plain – it is Rachmaninoff. It is not surprising that with such pianism the music should seem no more than an accessory.'[26] Sabaneyev, an old acquaintance, wrote similarly in *Muzykalni Sovremennik*: 'for me Rachmaninoff's personality as conductor and especially as pianist must be placed before his career as composer.'[27]

In the days of his youth it had been his music that had always been the centre of attraction; he rarely played compositions other than his own. By this time, however, his music seemed increasingly old-fashioned and hardly representative of contemporary taste, even beside the works of Scriabin. Inevitably, he came to play the compositions of others. By so doing, as reviews testify, it was at least possible to make a more objective appraisal of his piano-playing. The Russian Revolution may have encouraged him to defer composing, yet the quantity of his new works had been declining since before the war and his decision to concentrate on piano virtuosity can be traced back to Scriabin concerts. As he himself later stated:

At the first Philharmonic concert in Petrograd on 26 September 1915 following Scriabin's death I played his Piano Concerto. This was the first time since my days at the Conservatory that I played the work of another composer with orchestra in public. It is a significant fact in that it marks the beginning of a new period in my artistic career which has lasted up to this day [1934].[28]

On 26 February 1917, the Russian Revolution took place in
Petrograd. Demonstrations had developed into a general strike
and the fact that the army was at the front fighting a war only
exacerbated the situation. The old regime was swept away, the
government resigned and the Tsar was obliged to abdicate. On
that day Rachmaninoff gave a recital in Moscow, half of the
proceeds of which went to aid the army's sick and wounded.
The next day Russia was a republic. Like so many others, he
welcomed the change and immediately waived the rest of his
fee, donating it to army charities and assisting newly released
political prisoners. During March he appeared as a soloist in
three concerts in Moscow: on the 13th he played Tchaikovsky's
B flat minor Concerto under Koussevitzky (with the proceeds
being donated to the Union of Artists); on the 20th, Liszt's E
flat Concerto and on the 25th, under Emil Cooper (in aid of the
sick and wounded) he added his own Second Concerto to those
of Tchaikovsky and Liszt. Today this may not be regarded as the
novelty that it undoubtedly was ninety years ago, but, as the
Decca/London record producer, John Culshaw stated,[29] still it
is quite a feat. With these concerts, he wrote finis to his concert
career in Moscow.

That spring, while his wife stayed in Moscow with his daughters (who were still at school), he departed for Ivanovka to assist
in the planting of crops. As he observed dryly, 'the impressions
I received from my contact with the peasants, who felt themselves masters of the situation, were unpleasant. I should have
preferred having friendlier memories.'[30] At the end of the school
year he returned to Moscow after which the family left for a
month in Essentuki. On 1 June, Rachmaninoff wrote to Siloti:

> I've spent about a 120,000 rubles at Ivanovka. But am prepared
> to write it off – I can see another crash coming. Living condi-
> tions in Essentuki are so much better than in Ivanovka that
> I've decided not to return. I've about 30,000 rubles left but
> I fear another crash, everything affects me and I can't work.

I am advised to go abroad temporarily – but where to? How will it be possible? Can you ask Tereschenko [the Foreign Minister] for his advice? Can I count on getting a passport for my family, if so might we go to Scandinavia? But it makes no difference where – anywhere will do! Could I obtain a passport by July? Can I take any money with me? Please do talk to him! Perhaps he could suggest something! Have a talk with him please do, only send me an answer quickly!'[31]

Unfortunately, the turmoil at the time either prevented Siloti receiving the letter, or prevented Rachmaninoff receiving the reply.

In August, the family left for the more tranquil circumstances at Cimiez in the Crimea. On 5 September, at Yalta, Rachmaninoff made his last appearance in Russia, playing Liszt's Concerto in E flat. By this time, it was apparent that the revolution had hardly alleviated the basic problem – the war. In Galicia the Russian army suffered defeat from the Austro-Hungarians, another soon-to-be disintegrating empire. Kerensky's government was a coalition of many diverse interests. Its failure to be able to take any firm decisions, and the decline of the country into anarchy, led to an attempt by General Kornilov to seize power, but this too failed. Although circumstances were too upsetting for Rachmaninoff to write any new compositions, he did manage to fulfil an oft-postponed rewriting of his First Piano Concerto. He was busy with this on the night of the second Russian Revolution, the 25 October. He was so preoccupied that he scarcely noticed the shots and machine gun rattles. In Moscow, in the new age of Bolshevism, he found himself required to attend meetings with other tenants and to take his turn conscientiously guarding the house at night. He did not much care for this kind of communism. By the time he completed the revised version of his piano concerto on 10 November, circumstances were scarcely conducive to beginning any major new compositions. There was nothing left for him to do but practise the piano. He did, however, complete three short piano works on 14 and 15 November, the last works he would compose in Russia. Of these, the 'Oriental Sketch' is the most interesting. It was not in fact published for another seven years, and did not receive its first performance until he played it in recital at Juilliard School, New York in 1931.

In the nick of time as it seemed, three weeks after the October Revolution, Rachmaninoff received an invitation for a tour of ten concerts in Scandinavia. The money was no more than a pittance, and a year before he would have turned it down at once, but by then it seemed like the perfect escape to neutral countries. He decided to accept and quickly secured passports and visas. The family was allowed to take only 2,000 rubles in cash, but the exchange rate had collapsed, leaving them virtually penniless. When he expressed concern at this, a friend pointed to his hands saying: 'You should be the last to worry – these are your best exchange!'[32] Before leaving Russia he gave a copy of the revised First Piano Concerto to Koussevitzky, so that it could be published. The only music he is known to have taken with him included the first act of his opera *Monna Vanna*, the three piano pieces referred to above and a score of Rimsky-Korsakov's *Le Coq d'or*. When he stopped in Petrograd on the 23rd December, the city was at it bleakest: it was one of the shortest days in the year and power cuts had plunged the city into darkness. They planned to travel with an old friend, Nicolai Struve, who had been obliged to leave Dresden for Russia at the beginning of the war and was now obliged to leave Russia. Since the train service had been disrupted by the revolution, they had no choice but to travel north through Finland in a peasant sledge until they reached the Swedish frontier. At the time, Rachmaninoff could not wait to get away; he could not have known it then but he would never return.

Some years later when the stage-director Feodor Komisarjevsky invited him to return on behalf of the Soviet government, Rachmaninoff replied: 'If you wish to stay in a brothel go ahead; I will not'.[33] But he was always ambivalent; he could never stop being Russian. At the time of his departure, his position was not so dissimilar to that of Glinka sixty years before, who had then felt obliged to leave Imperial Russia and move to Berlin. Upon reaching the frontier Glinka stopped his carriage, leant out, and spat on the ground saying: 'May I never see this accursed country again!'[34] It would take three-quarters of a century, half a century after Rachmaninoff's death, for the effects of the Russian Revolution to dissipate.

11

1917–1920

Exiled from Russia, economic circumstances oblige him to take up career as piano virtuoso and for it he has to acquire a repertory: Tours Scandinavia: Departs for New York: For the next five years he is based in America: Critics confirm his reputation as pianist: Makes Ampico rolls and records first for Edison and later RCA Victor.

With Struve, the Rachmaninoffs arrived in Stockholm on 24 December 1917.[1] Getting out of Russia safely had been their major preoccupation, but now, Christmas going on all around them, the mixture of the familiar and unfamiliar in an alien environment, they felt alone and cut off. In the New Year they lost no time departing for Copenhagen, where Struve assisted them in finding a house to rent so that he could practise the piano exhaustively prior to his Scandinavian tour. As he recalls, living standards were prosaic: 'the house's principal distinction was its defective stoves which it was my daily duty to light. My wife did the cooking and housework, and our daughters, with the aid of a bicycle, kept up communications with the town nearby.'[2]

His first concert took place on 18 February 1918, when he played his Second Concerto. A week later came a recital. During the next few months, engagements quickly followed.

On 12 March, he was in Stockholm again repeating the Second Concerto and adding Liszt's E flat Concerto. On the 14th, he played the Tchaikovsky concerto and on the 18th gave a recital. On the way back to Denmark, he stopped off at Malmo for another recital on the 22nd. In Copenhagen, on 16 April, he played the Tchaikovsky concerto and his Second Concerto. From there he departed for Oslo where, on the 20th, he repeated the first Stockholm programme, appearing at recitals on the 24th and 26th. On 2 May, he returned to Stockholm, this time to accompany the soprano Adelaide von Skilondz, another Russian ex-patriot. The tour ended at Copenhagen on 10 July, when he played his Second Concerto.

The 1918/19 season began with recitals in Lund on 18 September and Malmo on the 19th. During the next four weeks he played fourteen recitals – one every other day! To cope with such a schedule, his first task was to add an appreciable proportion of new pieces to his repertory, so keeping his programmes fresh and vital. This would remain a major preoccupation for the rest of his life. That summer in Copenhagen, he had begun rehearsing a selection of his own shorter works (taken from Op. 3, 10, 23, 32, 33 and 39) to which he added Scriabin's Second Sonata (Op. 19), some preludes (Op. 11) and etudes (Op. 42) from his Scriabin commemorative recitals three years before. To augment his repertory, he went back to his early years reworking some pieces he had last played more than a quarter of a century previously: Beethoven's Sonata in D (Op. 10 No. 3) and 32 Variations in C minor; Schubert's *Moments musicaux* (D. 870); Chopin's Waltz in A-flat (Op. 42), Polonaise in C minor (Op. 40 No. 2), Nocturne in C-sharp minor (Op. 27 No. 1) two studies (Op. 10 No. 3 and Op. 25 No. 12) and the Sonata in B minor (Op. 58); Liszt's Second and Twelfth Hungarian Rhapsody; Rubinstein's Barcarolle in A minor (Op. 93 No. 7); Medtner's three *Fairy Tales* and *Tragedy Fragments* and Tchaikovsky's *Troika en traineaux* (which he had learned as a surprise present for Zverev's birthday in 1886). He made a gesture too in the direction of the classics with the Bach/Busoni Chaconne in D minor, Haydn's Variations in F minor, Godowsky's arrangements of Dandrieu and Loeillet, the 'Turkish March' from Mozart's Sonata in A (K. 331) and a couple of Scarlatti sonatas.

In the summer of 1918, the Soviet Union hastily signed the Treaty of Brest Litovsk with Germany, which obliged it to free Finland, Poland and the Baltic states. The communists assured their continued rule by withdrawing from a war with which Russia had been manifestly unable to cope. The Germans were left free to intensify hostilities in the west. Scandinavia, although at peace, was isolated and since the opportunity to leave looked effectively blocked indefinitely, Rachmaninoff had time to take stock of the situation. With the war going on in Europe it was America that beckoned. It had, in fact, been on his mind even before his departure from Russia. In the autumn of 1917 he enquired of the US consul in Moscow whether there was any possibility of his giving concerts there, but was told: 'they were more concerned then about the war than about concerts'.[3]

Three opportunities were open to him: compose, conduct or play the piano – on the face of it, an embarrassment of choices. That winter he received a cable from concert manager Charles Ellis, with a renewal of an offer made six years previously by the Board of Directors of the Boston Symphony Orchestra to become its conductor. Karl Muck had then succeeded but he was a German and the entrance of the US into the war obliged him to resign. The directors had approached Ossip Gabrilowitsch, conductor of the Detroit Symphony Orchestra, but he declined suggesting they should try Rachmaninoff. However, for Rachmaninoff to have accepted would have meant retuning Rachmaninoff the musician; he would not only have had to learn a collection of non-Russian classics, but it would have been intolerable for him to conduct a repertory that included the works of contemporaries with whose style he was so obviously out of sympathy. He turned the offer down, as he did the Wolfsohn Bureau when it offered him the post of conductor of the Cincinnati Symphony in succession to Stokowski, who had gone to Philadelphia.

As composer, however, he could not expect to earn enough to keep him in the style he had become accustomed to in Imperial Russia, even if the times had been more conducive. The more he thought about it the more he realised that he had no choice; he had to be a pianist. Kirena Siloti, daughter of his cousin Alexander, assured Seroff that by this time Rachmaninoff's piano-playing had altogether changed, 'the soft lyrical approach given way to a new conception built on an iron rhythm and power'.[4] But he still had a problem – although he had played the piano with increasing regularity during the last ten years and his technique was irreproachable, he knew comparatively little music, aside from his own. At the age of forty-five he was reversing Liszt's precedent; Liszt had given up a career as an internationally famous pianist when he was only thirty-five, exclaiming – 'Always concerts! Always to be a valet of the public! What a trade!'[5] It is a testament to Rachmaninoff's strength of character that he managed to survive such a career for a quarter of a century. During that time, as recordings and reviews attest, both his technique and his art became ever more refined and responsive. Notwithstanding an inevitable lacuna in his creative activities so as to be able to learn sufficient repertory to become a travelling virtuoso, he did begin to compose again in his later years.

By 1918, the presence of the United States in the war in Europe was beginning to be felt. In the autumn, the German army collapsed and by the end of October peace was only weeks away. On 1 November, the Rachmaninoffs were able to secure places on the Bergensfjord from Oslo bound for New York. Not being able to save much from his Scandinavian tour, he was only able to go thanks to the assistance of the émigré Russian banker Alexander Kamenka. Upon arrival in New York, on 11 November, the Rachmaninoffs moved into the Sherry-Netherland Hotel, which stood on Fifth Avenue,

opposite the Plaza between 58th and 59th Street. The family
had hardly got to bed that night when the din coming up
from the square outside rudely awoke them. As English was
not yet a familiar tongue, it took them some time to persuade
themselves that New York was not being occupied and the
public was only expressing relief at the news of the Armistice.
News of Rachmaninoff's arrival spread quickly. In only days
Hoffmann, Kreisler, Zimbalist, Elman and Ysaye and even
Prokofiev (having fled Russia the other way, via Japan) called
on him. Notwithstanding there being little love lost between
Rachmaninoff and Prokofiev, in the alien environment where
they now found themselves, it was better to be friends. So,
on the 20th, Rachmaninoff was present at Prokofiev's debut
recital at Aeolian Hall. Prokofiev played three Rachmaninoff
preludes, including that in G Minor (Op. 23 No. 5). Huneker,
in *The New York Times*, swept aside Prokofiev's playing and
Rachmaninoff's music in half-a-dozen words: 'his treatment of
trifles is brutal.'[6]

The first thing Rachmaninoff did in New York was to procure the services of the secretary, Dagmar Rybner Barclay. She
describes coming to the Sherry-Netherland and being greeted
by Natalia Rachmaninoff: 'There was no sign of him, but after
a while the curtains of the adjoining room moved slightly, and
out of the corner of my eye – I saw him peering at me. Soon,
very timidly, he came in, with his equally shy younger daughter
Tatiana. I understood his aversion to meeting strangers, however after a few moments of halting conversation, I sensed his
decision that I seemed to be a safe person and could be trusted.
He pointed to the piano covered with letters, telegrams, and
messages and asked me to help him with "all that".'[7]

The next thing he needed was an agent and to acquire one
he solicited the advice of each visitor; although as Hoffmann
later enjoyed reminding him, he made the decision who to
work with himself. He signed an agreement with the concert
manager Charles Ellis. Ellis managed Melba and Kreisler and

also Paderewski, but since Paderewski was about to become the first Premier of newly independent Poland, Ellis was left with a vacancy. Rachmaninoff's arrival, which he heard of through Harriet Kreisler (the wife of the violinist) must have seemed singularly propitious and he lost no time in offering Rachmaninoff his services.

The next few weeks were filled undertaking musical fixtures: Rachmaninoff rented a piano from Steinway for practice; signed contracts to make Ampico piano rolls and Edison recordings; and even at that late date, the season having already begun, Ellis secured him thirty-six recitals. At first he led an active social life in New York, accepting invitations to dinners, cocktail parties and receptions; but after the initial impetus spent itself he was content to see mostly Russians. To some extent this was a matter of personal disposition, but it was also reinforced by his having little facility as a linguist. Although he was to spend a quarter of a century giving concerts regularly in America, it took him some years before he came to speak English easily. Although he read English classics, they were always in translation and there was only one novel, Upton Sinclair's *Main Street*, that he toiled through in the original.

He had only been in New York a matter of weeks when he was stricken with Spanish influenza (the epidemic at the time). On 8 December, though barely well again, he played in public for the first time in Providence, Rhode Island. He began with his own arrangement of *The Star-Spangled Banner*, which he seems to have written at the last moment for, to judge from a piano roll, it was not nearly as full of effects as those transcriptions by Godowsky and Horowitz; nor is it anything like as original as his own later transcriptions of Kreisler's *Liebeslied* and *Liebesfreud*. At a recital at the Symphony Hall in Boston on the 15th, to judge from the review of Philip Hale, he had recovered from the flu, even if the 'bronchial audience'[8] hadn't. In the *Boston Evening Transcript*, H.T. Parker (known engagingly by the acronym Hell-To-Pay) may have been a stringent devotee to high standards, yet he was completely in Rachmaninoff's thrall from his first appearance:

No more impressive figure had crossed the stage of Symphony Hall these many years than Rachmaninoff when he came first to the piano yesterday afternoon. His height nearly topped the doorway through which he entered; the breadth of his spare body nearly fitted it; the black that clothed him heightened this austerity of presence. The head, the face were unmistakably Russian from the close-cropped dark hair to the long jaw, the firm chin. The forehead sloped upward broad and high; the eyes kept the gravity of contemplation. Obviously Rachmaninoff lives much within himself, wears no surface-moods and emotions, cultivates no manner for audiences, shuts himself from the world except as far as his music and his playing may reveal him. Therein speaks the man who, having found his means of self-expression, first makes himself unobtrusive master of them; who by this mastery discloses more amply, more exactly the treasures of a penetrating, reflective, many-sided mind, of a grave yet ardent imagination, of a quick, yet measuring spirit – a man in whom all things run deep and strong, devotions and ideals, passions and affections, sensations and achievement.

He has given himself to music – to the writing of it, to the playing of it as conductor and pianist; yet, as with Paderewski, it is possible to feel that upon any other career he would have stamped his individual mark. Once embarked upon performance he neither regards nor disregards his hearers; he merely bids them hear. With hands, with body he has not a trick of physical or technical display. There he sits, wholly absorbed in his task, entirely concentrated upon it, summoning, marshalling into it all that his faculties may give... The piece ends; with grave courtesy Rachmaninoff acknowledges the applause with which the audience yesterday heaped him; seeks neither to emphasize nor to prolong

it; returns as quietly, as briefly, to the next item in the programme of the day. Similarly with the inevitable extra pieces,
the pianist waits not to play them until time and again clap-
ping has recalled him. He sees to them at once, plays them
generously; quite understands that sooner or later, before an
English or American audience, he must play his Prelude in
C sharp minor. With grave good will he fulfils every obliga-
tion to his hearers – and vanishes.[9]

In those days American critics had, as the evidence of recordings
goes some way to confirm, the highest, most stringent standards.
Their concern for excellence inevitably reflected the accomplishment of the greatest virtuosi, most of whom were appearing
there then. At the same time too, classical music was still a popular and vital art-form, albeit not as vigorous as it had been in
the nineteenth century. Rachmaninoff reminds us of a division
of opinion between critics: the so-called classicist, Parker, who
shows how well he understood and valued Rachmaninoff's
musical restraint, and the romantics, like Huneker, who may
have approved of his concert program but took his restraint for
coldness. Huneker, in *The new York Times*, begins his review of
Rachmaninoff's New York recital on 22 December:

No! He did not play it at Carnegie Hall yesterday afternoon.
That is the doubly distinguished composer and pianist, did
not play his celebrated Prelude in C sharp minor, though the
Rachmaninoff 'fans' – and there were hundreds of them in
the audience – clamoured for the favourite piece of Flatbush
'flappers'. They surged toward Sergei in serried masses. They
clustered about the stage. They raised aloft their arms as they
supplicated the Russian to give them his recollection of the
Henselt concerto. But to no avail. He played the G minor
Prelude (Op. 23 No. 5), first made known here by Josef
Hoffmann, who does not play it so rapidly, thereby getting
a more sonorous tone. It is dangerous however to criticize

the interpretation of a composer. So please do not accept our opinion as official. He also played his 'Humoresque', which we didn't know until a friend prompted us. It is truly humorous with more than a moiety of the devilry that lurks in the dark forest called the Russian soul. The other three encores were salon music, clever, not very original, though effective. But the chief thing is the fact that Rachmaninoff did not play IT. All flapperdom sorrowed last night, for there are amiable fanatics who follow this pianist from place to place hoping to hear him in this particular prelude; like the Englishman who attended every performance of the lady lion tamer hoping to see her swallowed by one of her pets.

Otherwise the programme was far from exciting – old-fashioned, it could have been called. Mozart's familiar Variations in D, and the D major Sonata of Beethoven (Op. 10 No. 3), began the afternoon. The oldsters were reminded of von Bulow. The same cold white light of analysis, the same incisive touch, the strongly marked rhythms, the intellectual grasp of the musical ideas and the sense of the relative importance in phrase-groupings proclaimed that Rachmaninoff is a cerebral, not an emotional, artist ... Nevertheless there were some disquieting details in the reading to conservative Beethoven students. The principal one hinged on the question of tempo. The first movement is a presto. It was taken at a prestissimo, plus a prestissimo. Not a blurred outline was there, yet the speed detracted from the essential weightiness of Beethoven's proclamation. The largo was better, the minuet most ingratiating, the rondo full of the quizzical human interest in its challenging theme. Both the Mozart and the Beethoven were as clear as dry-point etching. ...

We have said that Rachmaninoff is not emotional, but that must be taken in a limited sense. Josef Hoffmann is not emotional, as was his master, Anton Rubinstein, yet there is a colour, a glow, not in Rachmaninoff, whose touch is like a boulder of granite in chord playing, whose piano voice in cantilena is not velvety. The C sharp minor Nocturne (Op. 27 No. 1) by Chopin was thoroughly satisfactory because of its superlatively fine adjustment of tonal dynamics with the tragic mood-picture. It reached the head, not the heart. The A flat Valse (Op. 42) was brilliant, while the best of the group was the Polonaise in C minor (Op. 40), seldom heard – Paderewski loved it – and when heard seldom played in the profoundly significant manner that the virtuoso delivered its moving measures yesterday. It is a pendant to the popular 'Polonaise Militaire', and might be the obverse of the heroic medal; after the bugle blasts, the proud panoply of war, follows fast the awful penalty. 'Home they brought the warrior dead!' is the motto of this processional elegiac polonaise, its melancholy muted, its resignation worn like crepe in every bar. Rachmaninoff played the work nobly.

His own compositions were enjoyable, and with the C sharp minor Rhapsody of Liszt dazzling. He gave a polka [*Polka de W.R.*] that made one long to be dancing. Rubinstein in *Le bal* has a fetching polka, and the form is of the ragtime persuasion. After the Chopin polonaise we were most impressed by the encore, which appropriately trod on the heels of the Beethoven sonata. It, too, was from a Beethoven Sonata, in A flat (Op. 31 No. 3) – the scherzo-like allegretto, which von Bulow played so overwhelmingly. Rachmaninoff took it quicker than the nimble little Hans and with the same clarity and electric precision. The Russian is a master etcher on the keyboard.[10]

After another Boston recital, on 10 January 1919, in which Rachmaninoff's programme included Haydn's Variations in F minor and Beethoven's 32 Variations, he made his first US appearance with orchestra since 1910: on the 12th, playing his Second Concerto with the New York Symphony conducted by Damrosch. Two weeks afterwards, with Altschuler and the Russian Symphony Orchestra, he introduced the new version of his First Concerto. For his third recital in Boston, on 22 February, he played an all-Russian programme including a group of Scriabin's works, three of Medtner's *Fairy Tales*, his own Variations on a Theme of Chopin (Op. 22) and *Etudes-tableaux* (Op. 33). In response to a reporter who demanded to know their programmes, he replied: 'Ah! That is for me, not for the public. I do not believe in the artist disclosing too many of his images. Let them paint for themselves what it most suggests.'[11] By this time, as Huneker puts it, 'it would seem to have become a Rachmaninoff season'.[12]

With so much of the man and his music about, antipathy to his music can be traced back to that first post-war season in America. Rosenfeld, in *The New Republic*, cannot say precisely what it was he did not like about it, but equivocated:

> The music of Rachmaninoff is never quite completely new-minted. Has it a melodic line quite properly its own? One doubts it, nor can one discover in this music a distinctly original sense of either rhythm or harmony or tone-colour. In all the music of Rachmaninoff there is something strangely twice-told. From it there flows the sadness distilled by all things that are a little useless.[13]

His first US season came to a close with three charity concerts. On 8 April, he appeared at the Metropolitan Opera in concert with the soprano Geraldine Farrar under Stokowski and played his Second Concerto; on the 14th, he joined Casals in his Sonata for piano and cello; and on the 27th, he included in the programme his *Star-Spangled Banner* and Liszt's Second Hungarian Rhapsody, and for an encore – *the* Prelude.

Between concerts, on the 18th, 19th, 23rd and 24th, he went to Edison's recording studio in New York to make his first ten records. Edison, inventor of the phonograph, had taken out patents for cylinder recording apparatus as long ago as December 1877. Unfortunately the discovery was not in response to any musical prompting and he soon forgot about it, becoming pre-occupied instead with the challenge of providing light for New York City. It took until 1895 for the flat disc to be copyrighted by Emil Berliner – from a positive master via negative stamper, any number of discs could be produced easily and cheaply. It was only when Edison came to realise what he had accidentally stumbled across that he set up his own company to produce records. Unfortunately these were not laterally cut, but vertically (what became known as the hill-and-dale process). The records had to be sufficiently thick to absorb the tracking device and three masters were cut for each – better safe than sorry. Edison liked to demonstrate the fidelity of his records at what he called 'Tone Tests': in a concert hall, a singer or instrumentalist would stand next to the gramophone and start singing or playing, the lights would then gradually dim until at some point the record would take over – the audience was challenged to state precisely when. In view of the generally poor quality of reproduction in Edison records, it is hard to believe that anyone could have been taken in except, of course, for Edison who was deaf; the deaf, *pace* Beethoven, are not noted for musical sensitivity.

In June, the Rachmaninoffs left for California for the first time, renting a house on the south-west of the San Francisco Bay, near Palo Alto. This period of rest from the concert circuit was not a vacation for Rachmaninoff, and every day he would practise pieces for inclusion in the next season's concerts. These included studies by Alkan, Chopin, Rubinstein, Schloesser and Schumann; Beethoven's Sonata in D Minor (Op. 31); Chopin's Fourth Ballade (Op. 52), First Impromptu (Op. 29), Polonaise in E flat minor (Op. 26), Scherzo and two waltzes; Liszt's 'Gnomenreigen', 'La Campanella' and Waltz from Gounod's *Faust*; Mendelssohn's *Song Without Words* No. 34, *Rondo capriccioso* and *Variations sérieuses*; and Schumann's *Carnaval*.

One day a local boy from Menlo Park, the avant-garde composer Henry Cowell, then twenty-one, called on Rachmaninoff. Cowell remembered the meeting thirty-six years later:

He received me kindly and, picking out *Fleeting*, from a great pile of works I brought, looked at it intently with no comment for two hours, while he marked tiny red circles around forty-odd notes, saying 'You have some wrong notes.' Seeing my confusion, he quickly added: 'I too have sinned with wrong notes in my youth, and therefore you may be forgiven.'[14]

In 1923, Cowell made his European debut playing the piano in London. He created something of a sensation, not so much on account of any prodigious virtuosity, as by his use of the forearm as well as fingers on the keys. *The Morning Post* observed waspishly: 'something quite new in piano technique, but a dangerous precedent. The next step obviously, is a part for the player's nose!' Perhaps it was Cowell's forearm that accounted for some of those forty wrong notes Rachmaninoff found in *Fleeting*.

His 1919/20 season began on 31 October, again in Boston, this time with Monteux conducting the Symphony Orchestra. The programme spanned the extremes of contemporary music with Stravinsky's *Firebird* and Rachmaninoff playing his Third Concerto for the first time in America since the Russian Revolution. Olin Downes, later of *The New York Times*, but then a young critic of *The Boston Post*, posed a question to Rachmaninoff in an interview:

He phrased in a manner both crafty and subtle. 'Do you believe,' he asked, 'if a composer can have real genius, sincerity, profundity of feeling, and at the same time be popular?' Rachmaninoff replied: 'Yes, I believe it is possible to be very serious, to have something to say, and at the same time be popular, I believe that. Others do not, they think – what *YOU* think,' with a long indicating finger and a look of such evident comprehension that Rachmaninoff's questioner was left high and dry, not a word to say![15]

On 6 February 1920, Stokowski conducted the Philadelphia Orchestra with Rachmaninoff for the first time, in a programme devoted to his works. In due course Stokowski would conduct the world premieres of Rachmaninoff's Fourth Piano Concerto, Three Russian Songs, Rhapsody on a Theme of Paganini and Third Symphony. On this occasion, the composer played the Third Concerto. Afterwards came the American premiere of *The Bells* (then known as Third Symphony), the soloists were Florence Hinkle, Arthur Hackett (brother of tenor Charles) and Frederick Patton. When the concert was repeated in New York, Pitts Sanborn in *The Evening Telegram* called it 'a great deal of noise about very little indeed'.[16] It was sung by Fanny Copeland in an English translation – not of the Russian text but of a German translation by Berthold Feiwal. This must have made for a strange linguistic concoction for it was originally the work of Edgar Allen Poe, translated into Russian by Constantin Balmont. *The Bells* was also programmed by Damrosch for a performance in his New York Music Festival at the 71st Regiment Armory, but was cancelled. Instead Rachmaninoff played his Second Piano Concerto. In a slip in the programme the composer pleaded 'an attack of neurosis'[17](neuritis, surely) which prevented his playing the piano and conducting in the same concert, so instead Damrosch conducted his cantata *Spring. The Bells* seems to have been jinxed: performances were announced in Sheffield for 1914 under Wood, and in Vienna for 1938 under his own direction, but neither took place due to wars.

Between 1919 and 1929 Rachmaninoff made some thirty-seven Ampico piano rolls, but all but six of them were subsequently re-recorded. These six were: his arrangement of *The Star-Spangled Banner*, Chopin's Nocturne (Op. 15 No. 1) and Second Scherzo in B flat minor, Rubinstein's Second Barcarolle in A minor (Op. 45), his own Elegie in E flat minor (Op. 3 No. 1) and *Etude-tableaux* in B minor (Op. 39 No. 4). In the days of acoustic recordings, they must have sounded more life-like; nowadays they sound, as Philip puts it:

Like someone ... having a go at imitating Rachmaninoff
and making quite a job of it ... Performance[s do] not quite
hang together ... because the melodic fragments do not sing
out as [they do in his recordings] and fail to achieve the right
balance with the accompan[iment] ... One of the results is
that [Rachmaninoff's] subtle rhythmic dislocations sound
messy, like failures to co-ordinate rather than purposeful
expressive devices.[18]

A year had passed since Rachmaninoff had made his first
records for Edison. Edison's airy casualness, capriciously publishing whatever took his fancy without even bothering to tell
Rachmaninoff (and no one was more particular), soon brought
relations to a conclusion. On 21 April, Rachmaninoff signed
a new and exclusive five-year contract with Victor; he would
make twenty-five records annually and receive an advance of
15,000 dollars against royalties. On the 26th, he went down to
Camden for the first time. On 30 June, he took part in a special benefit given by Victor artists for the National Association
of Talking Machine Jobbers at the Ambassador Hotel, Atlantic
City. He shared the occasion, the only time he ever did, with
the great tenor Enrico Caruso who, like Rachmaninoff and
Chaliapin, was born in 1873 – an *annus mirabilis* indeed.[19]

12

1920–1924

Method of piano practice: Writes first new composition since the war: Health problem: Friendship with Medtner: Composes transcriptions: Gives the largest number of concerts throughout the length and breadth of North America, appears in Canada and Cuba: Reappears in London for the first time since the war: Composes Fourth Piano Concerto.

For Rachmaninoff's annual respite in the summer of 1920 he rented an abode some seventy miles upstate of New York at Goshen. Some days he would drive his automobile out into the Shawangunk mountains with his chauffeur-cum-mechanic, far enough from the city to recall *autre fois, autre meurs* – lazy days at Ivanovka. On most days he would spend some time at the piano. Arthur Hirst describes him mastering additions to his repertory:

> When he began work on a new piece, first of all he learned the layout of each bar and decided on the fingering, in his opinion half the work was then done. He played his exercises very slowly, diligent pupils would have been heartened to hear at how slow a tempo this greatest of pianists used to practise and with what painstaking attention he monitored the sound

of each note and the work of each hand. Once I heard him
playing like this from another room, and although each note
of the piece he was practising was familiar to me, I could not
recognize Liszt's 'Waldesrauschen.'[1]

That season he added to his repertory four pieces from Debussy's
Children's Corner Suite. Notwithstanding the hostility he had
shown Debussy's music in Bauer's presence only a few years
before, he was beginning to catch up with public taste, albeit
slowly. Other selections he added included: a Bach prelude;
Mozart's Sonata in A (K. 331); Beethoven's Sonata in E minor
(Op. 90); Chopin's Ballade in G minor (Op. 23), Barcarolle
(Op. 60), Mazurka in A flat (Op. 59), Nocturne in F sharp
minor and three waltzes; Liszt's *Rhapsodie Espagnol*; eight more
of Mendelssohn's *Songs without Words*, Schumann's *Papillons*,
Daquin's *Le Coucou*, Grieg's *Mountain Tune*, a Scriabin study,
Weber's *Momento Capriccioso*, a Tchaikovsky waltz and *Trepak*,
and a couple of Medtner's *Novellen*.

During that summer he also made a gesture in the direction
of composing again. When a couple of years later, in 1922,
Rachmaninoff met the Satins again they asked him: 'Is it possible that in all these years you have not written a single note?'
"Oh yes," he replied smiling, "I have written a cadenza to
Liszt's Second Rhapsody."[2] He may have written nothing of
consequence since before the war but his muse had not been
completely silent. He finished three arrangements of traditional
Russian folk songs. The first, *The little birch torch*, was a favourite
of Chaliapin's, who recorded it twice before the revolution. The
second, *The Apple Tree*, he harmonised for inclusion in Alfred
Swan's *Songs from Many Lands*, published the following year.
As Martyn states, 'his contribution, though consisting of little
more than a few chords, lends it a characteristic wistful melancholy'.[3] The third, *Along the Street*, was arranged for the folk
singer Nadezhda Plevitskaya. The following March, for Victor,
he would record a piano transcription of the 'Gopak' from

Moussorgsky's *Sorochintsky Fair*, but did not include it in concert until November 1923. He had conducted an orchestral arrangement by Liadov in Moscow, but although more elaborate than Moussorgsky's original piano version, it is hardly typical of his later more complex transcriptions.

Rachmaninoff's 1920/21 season began on Armistice Day, 11 November, the second anniversary of his own arrival in New York, with a recital at Ann Arbor in Michigan. It was then that he learned of the shocking death of his friend, Nicolai Struve, in a lift accident in Paris. That autumn he replied to a letter from Avierino, who had fled Russia. Obliged to eke out an existence playing the violin in an Athens hotel orchestra, Avierino wanted to know whether there was any point in coming to America. 'God keep you from trying to come here,' Rachmaninoff replied:

> There are ten candidates for every one musical position. In any case, you'd never get a visa with the government's recent ruling caused by the unprecedented flood of immigrants. Go to Paris, or London, or wherever you wish to in Europe, but forget about the 'Dollar Princess'. Today I am sending you 1,500 drachmas. I know it's little but forgive me, I can't manage more. No matter how poorly you are living it can't be compared with conditions in present-day Russia. I have my mother and a sister [this is the only mention in any of his letters of his surviving sister Varvara] but there's nothing I can do for them.[4]

It took some years before he managed, with the aid of the American Relief Administration, to send his mother a regular income. But Avierino did eventually get to America and there found employment.

Rachmaninoff's health, even in Russia before the revolution, had not been perfect. He often complained of severe pains in his right temple when writing music. He maintained that if they didn't get better he might be obliged to give up composing altogether. After the war, he found it difficult to find time to compose, and the pains grew steadily worse. He consulted doctors who ascribed them to all sorts of things – neuralgia of a facial nerve, an infection of some sort, perhaps of the jaw or teeth. He was persuaded to submit to surgery, but an operation proved to no avail. Today the problem looks more like a recurrence of the psychosomatic ailment that had afflicted him years before. By this time, in his late forties, it does not seem unduly imaginative to believe that his inability to compose, and the resultant bottling-up of his feelings, might have led to just this kind of affliction.

In May 1921, the Rachmaninoffs rented a town house in New York on Riverside Drive, but they were not able to move in until the autumn. In the meantime, they took a vacation retreat on the shore of the bay at Locust Point, New Jersey, some fifty miles from New York City. It was their habit to reproduce, as far as they could, a Russian lifestyle, with Russian food and Russian visitors. That year Rachmaninoff secured a young Russian, Evgeny Somov, to work for him; a great deal of correspondence would pass between them during the rest of his life. That summer he took his driving test but failed in the oral examination – a reflection on his inability to master English rather than any lack of skill as a motorist.

Great was his relief that autumn when news came from Dresden that the Satin family had finally managed to escape from the Soviet Union. This was followed in early October by news of Medtner's escape; he had written from Riga in newly independent Latvia that he was on his way to Germany. His letter was full of news: he was writing a new work which he had entitled *The Art of the Fugue*.[5] Rachmaninoff replied discussing the possibility of being able to secure him contracts with Steinway and Duo-Art. Although he promised to work hard on his behalf, he warned how difficult getting established in America could be. Since Medtner intended to stop a while in Germany, he advised him to try giving concerts there. He recommended writing to Koussevitzky, who was then in Berlin, about the possibility of publishing some of his works. He insisted that composers were better off in Europe than in America. This letter from Rachmaninoff is in German but his response to another from Medtner, after arriving in Germany, is in Russian. 'I am so happy that you are in western Europe, now we can meet again, and you'll be able to live and work peacefully. As for the estrangement you feel, I confess I sense it too, I see few real, sincere musicians here. You are the only one left.'[6]

The 1921/22 season commenced on 10 November, when he gave a recital in St Paul, Missouri. As in the previous season, he made a substantial number of additions to his repertory including: Beethoven's 'Pathétique' (Op. 13); Chopin's Third Ballade (Op. 47), Nocturne in D flat (Op. 27), Polonaises in C sharp minor and A flat and Third Scherzo; Dohnanyi's *Etude-caprice* (Op. 28); Handel's Variations in B flat; Liszt's Ballade in B minor, *Grand galop chromatique*, Petrarch Sonnet No. 104 and 'Tarantella'; Medtner's *Fairy Tale* in A minor; his own transcription of his own song *Daisies*; Grieg's Ballade in G minor (Op. 24); Schumann's Novellette in F sharp minor (Op. 21 No. 8) and the Weber/Tausig *Invitation to the Dance*.

On the 20th, he introduced another new transcription in Chicago: Kreisler's *Liebesleid*. Like Kreisler's *Liebesfreud* (which he would transcribe in 1925) and unlike his Moussorgsky and Bizet transcriptions, his new arrangement was a brilliant piece of work, using Kreisler's simple melodies as a point of departure. 'The surprising transitions, the outré harmonies, the startling cadenzas, the sudden modulations whisking the hearer aside from the expected course, the final glissando, the Kreisler themes, and extensions of the Kreisler moods'[7] arrested attention when it was first played. It is interesting that in returning the compliment, Kreisler transcribed Rachmaninoff's *Daisies* and the theme from the second movement of his Second Piano Concerto, but neither is successful. This may seem a criticism of Kreisler, but it is because Rachmaninoff's melodies depend on the elaborate harmonies they are decked out with and do not stand up to bald revelation, even when played in Kreisler's disarmingly insouciant fashion.

On 7 December, Rachmaninoff was in Boston for another recital. Hale, in *The Herald*, captured the measure of his peculiar genius in a few sentences: 'His playing is distinguished by its clarity. His dissection of a composition is not, however, pedagogic. He is far from being a dry analyst, but he delights in exposing the structure of a work in an eloquent manner. In this he has no rival.'[8] On the 15th he played his Second Concerto in New York with the Philharmonic conducted by Josef Stransky. The programme also included Strauss's *Til Eulenspiegel*. Strauss was in the audience, he had in fact conducted *Til Eulenspiegel* in New York only the previous month with the Philadelphia Orchestra. It was strange that nobody thought to get both composers performing at the same concert. Each would only have had to perform half as much but ticket prices could have been more than twice as much, so from a box-office point of view the whole would certainly have been much greater than the sum of the parts.

For Rachmaninoff's American tour that season, he stepped up the number of engagements he undertook, travelling to less familiar locations. He gave fifty-nine recitals and made five appearances in concert with orchestras. By this time he was becoming increasingly popular. In January 1922 he played, for the first time, a new transcription of the minuet from Bizet's *L'Arlésienne*, in Tulsa, Oklahoma. It must have been different from the four-hand arrangement of the same piece he made in 1900 and played with Goldenweiser, although a manuscript of the solo version was also, as Martyn observes, 'if the date on it is to be believed, completed on 13 September 1900'. Certainly there is no record of him bringing the original transcription with him to America. On the 24th, he stopped off for a recital in Lincoln. After the performance, when the Chancellor of the University of Nebraska conferred on him the degree of Doctor of Music, he replied: 'I am very sorry that my poor English prevents me telling how proud and glad I am. I thank you very much for this honour.'[9] There was something appropriate in his acceptance speech running to just two short sentences, for Nebraska is one of the least populated states in the union.

His intense schedule increased his health problems. Inevitably there were some engagements when his bad health was apparent to a critical ear, like that at Parker's in Boston:

> Not that he was careless after the fashion of sundry pianists when they are out of vein. Rather he was dry exactitude to the last curl of the last letter. Not until the end of the concert, and he played Liszt's Second Rhapsody, did he let his hearers forget the piano as an instrument. Only the native wildness of Liszt's Rhapsody, laced and interlaced with his own ornament as well as the composer's, warmed Rachmaninoff out of his dry and dull mechanics.[10]

He brought this tour to a conclusion with two benefit concerts in New York. On 2 April, his forty-ninth birthday, he played his Second and Third Concertos under Damrosch; the proceeds for the American Relief Administration amounted to 7,500 dollars. On the 21st, he gave a recital for the relief of Russian students in the United States. On the 25th, he left for Europe on the *Mauretania*.

In London that May, his first visit for nine years, his reputation had only grown. *The Observer* noted: 'He filled the Queen's Hall yesterday, and sent people away disappointed. Hoffmann half-fills the Queen's Hall and Busoni plays in the Wigmore Hall, but then they never wrote *the* Prelude.'[11] In a letter to his secretary, Dagmar Rybner, he tells of his reaction at being in London again:

> The concert was a success. I played well and the hall was sold-out. Some scolded me in the press but that's only to be expected. They'll praise me as others are praised, only when

I'm dead, and then everyone does. I'm very bored here, I
think of America often, I extol America to the English, they
get so angry![12]

A notable change from his attitude in 1910 when he left the
United States after his first visit.

Although he did not venture as far as Italy that year, he must
have been satisfied when news came that he had been made honorary member of Rome's Accademia di Santa Cecilia, along with
composers Paul Dukas and Henri Rabaud. In Dresden, again
with his wife and daughters, the family was reunited with the
Satins. The pleasure his wife got from seeing her elderly father
and mother affected him deeply. He used the excuse of another
letter to his secretary, who was soon to be married, cautioning
her to show love and attention to her parents; the lack of close
relations with his own seems to have been much on his mind.
In 1916, his father came especially to Ivanovka to await him
but died before his son returned from Essentuki. There was not
much likelihood of his ever seeing his mother again for she was
still in Russia. We are not surprised he was troubled by perennial headaches. He wrote to Medtner, who was then in Stettin,
regretting the necessity of treatment for them for it made it seem
unlikely that they would be able to meet again that year. 'My last
tiny hope is to be able to sneak over to see you from Hamburg,
where we'll arrive on the evening of 19 August.'[13] But it was not
to be.

On the 22nd, the Rachmaninoffs left for America. Back at
Locust Point he resumed practising, adding to his repertory
Beethoven's *Appassionata*; Chopin's 'Funeral March' Sonata,
three nocturnes, *Fantaisie-impromptu* and the Liszt arrangement
of *Maiden's Wish*; Liadov's Etude in A flat; one of Medtner's
Improvisations; Moszkowski's *La Jongleuse*; and the Schultz-
Evler transcription of Strauss's 'Blue Danube'. On 9 September
he replied to a letter from Vladimir Wilshaw, a friend from his
conservatory days; it was the first contact they had had since he

left Russia, Wilshaw wanted to know what he had been composing since they last met. Rachmaninoff wrote:

> For the whole time – not one note. I only play the piano and give a great many concerts. For four years now I have been practising hard. I make some progress, but actually the more I play the more clearly do I see my inadequacies. If ever I learn this business thoroughly, it will be on the eve of my death. Materially I am quite well off – bourgeois! But my health fails; it would be strange to expect anything else when one remembers that my dissatisfaction with myself throughout my life has scarcely ever allowed me to feel calm. In the past, when I composed, I suffered because I was composing poorly, now it is because I play poorly. I feel I can better both – that keeps me alive![14]

At the time he was preoccupied by news of troubles in the Soviet Union; in the Ukraine the harvest had failed and famine was rife. The country was destitute and people were starving. He did his best to alleviate the crisis by sending money, food and clothes. Letters of thanks reached him from musicians, writers, teachers, the staff of the Kiev Conservatory and the chorus at the Maryinsky in Petrograd. Constantin Stanislavsky, from the Moscow Arts Theatre, wrote to him: 'You cannot know how your attention and memories touch our hearts. It is a very fine thing you are doing, the artists are really starving.'[15]

In 1922/23 he played a total of seventy-one concerts; sixty-eight in the United States, one in Canada and two in Cuba. Sixty-three of these were recitals and eight concerto performances, which worked out collectively to seven concerts every two weeks, from 10 November to 31 March! Such a pace was certainly exhausting. This was his busiest season to date, and the largest number of performances he would ever undertake. It is not surprising that by the time he reached Dallas, he was lamenting to Somov:

I moan and groan and take no pleasure in deducting the passing days from the sum total of my life. Material and moral
satisfaction afforded by my concerts are middling. But no
one's material effects are very good now, so I seem no exception. As for the moral side – better not speak of it. Five years
ago I thought I would get satisfaction playing the piano but
now I realize it is unattainable.[16]

For his tour that year he took his own train which was equipped
with observation-car, bedroom, bathroom as well as room for
a piano. In such fashion he travelled from place to place, as had
Rubinstein, Adelina Patti and Paderewski when they crossed
the States. At first he enjoyed the luxury, and the opportunity
of being able to practice at will whenever and wherever he
chose, but it was not long before he became disenchanted and
gave it up.

In January 1923 cheering news reached him: the arrival in
New York of the Moscow Arts Theatre for a special Broadway
season. He had always admired the Arts Theatre. Chekhov
was its most popular dramatist, and there was no one whose
plays he enjoyed more. Stanislavsky, its director and one
of its founders, he greatly respected. The prospect of again
encountering so many Russians whom he had not seen in
years made him very happy. After years of enforced separation
suddenly, once again, surrounded by his fellow countrymen,
New York felt like home. It was as if the mountain had come
to Mohammed. He spent as much time as his concert schedule permitted backstage at performances with Stanislavsky,
the actors Moskvin and Kachalov, and the actress Knipper-
Chekhova (widow of the dramatist). Other Russians such as
his cousin, the pianist Siloti (who had recently come to New
York via London and joined the staff at the Juilliard School)
and the choreographer Fokine, were also assiduous visitors
and would often come to his home on Riverside Drive. There
he would listen to the:

sharp and lively stories by Moskvin about backstage life, told
in the idiomatic fashion of Moscow speech, catching every
word and watching every movement of his expressive features. Rachmaninoff's face would become almost childlike,
his deeply graven wrinkles vanish, as he surrendered himself
to the happiest and most carefree laughter, throwing back
his head, and brushing away tears of joy with the back of
his hand.[17]

On 2 April he celebrated his fiftieth birthday, though it took
another eight months for a cantata composed in his honour
by his Russian colleague Gliere, with text by Wilshaw, to
reach him.

> From your far-off native country
> We send you joy and our greeting,
> And from our hearts and souls we say
> Long live Rachmaninoff Sergei![18]

It could not have been the quality of the verse, but the sentiment
that found Rachmaninoff short of words to thank them with.

   That year, after receiving news that his old friend Morozov
was unwell, they resumed their correspondence.[19] He wrote, 'I
should like to talk with you again and, of course, argue, as we
used to do.' In his next letter he is apologising: 'I am dictating
this as every unnecessary hand movement tires me. Because of
fatigue I am not now going to Australia as was planned on the
20th.' He then touches again on a subject Morozov had taxed
him with – his writing new works:

   I am not now drawn to it, or only rarely drawn. This only
   takes place when I think about two major compositions
   I started not long before leaving Russia. When I think of
   these, I long to finish them. This perhaps is the only way
   of shifting me from this dead-lock, but to begin something

new now seems unattainable. If I get a bit stronger perhaps
I'll try again this summer. Your advice and new subjects will
have to go into reserve and wait there until my reawakening
or renaissance.

Morozov suggested some new subjects: a four-movement suite,
a symphony with a programme based on the seasons; a biblical
work drawn from Genesis; a Shakespeare opera possibly based
on *Anthony and Cleopatra* and some new studies for piano. As for
the 'two major compositions' that Rachmaninoff mentions he
had started 'before leaving Russia', one is definitely the Fourth
Piano Concerto. As we saw, Moscow Conservatory teacher
Constantin Igumnov claimed he was working on this in April
1914. The other may have been *Monna Vanna*, which he had gone
to the trouble of bringing out of Russia with him, even though
copyright restrictions necessitated his resetting it to another
libretto. If that seems improbable, then composers are like
mothers: they will spend what may seem an inordinate amount
of time, energy and perseverance on a weak work, even though
the outcome does not justify their effort.

One night in July 1923, when the Rachmaninoffs were again
at Locust Point, they gave a dinner party. The guests included
Chaliapin, who had been singing that season at the Metropolitan
in New York and the Chicago Opera, as well as undertaking a
concert tour throughout the United States. Also present were
the actors Moskvin and Ramsh from the Moscow Arts Theatre;
Ivan Ostromislensky, Professor of Chemistry; and Somov. After
dinner, Chaliapin entertained with everyone sitting on the floor
in Turkish style. He regaled them with a variety of roles: a drunk
with his wheezing accordion being dragged off to jail, a lady
arranging her veil in front of a mirror, an old peasant crossing
herself at prayer in church. At two in the morning, when someone made a move to leave Chaliapin stopped him, demanding
to know where he was going, and insisted on him sitting down
again. With Rachmaninoff at the piano, Chaliapin sang through

a quantity of his song repertory – peasant songs, love songs and gypsy songs. It was not until after five, after a final rendition of *Ochi Chornye* (Black eyes), that the party finally broke up. That same morning Ostromislensky was surprised to find Rachmaninoff pacing the garden only hours later, the bags under his eyes the more conspicuous from the night's revels. He stopped him, demanding to know which song he liked best. Not giving him time to reply, he insisted 'I'm sure it was "Ochi Chornye" – I have no doubt of it. Oh! How he sighed, the villain! How he sobbed "you have ruined me"! I couldn't sleep for thinking of it. How God has endowed Chaliapin beyond other men!'[20]

In 1923 Charles Ellis died, and Charles Foley took over Rachmaninoff's engagement schedule. In the 1923/24 season additions to his concert repertory included Bach's English Suite No. 2, the Delibes/Dohnanyi 'Naïla' Waltz, a Chopin nocturne, Liszt's *Liebestraum* and *Funerailles*, his own transcription of Schubert's *Ave Maria*, Tchaikovsky's *Theme and Variations* and the Wagner/Brassin 'Magic Fire Music' from *Walküre*. He told Morozov: 'this year my season has been shortened to the minimum. From today, 18 November, until 15 December I have fifteen concerts, I shall then rest until 15 January, studying my next programme. After which, until 20 February, I then have only another fifteen concerts.'[21] A month later he wrote to Morozov again to complain:

> What is bad is that after you had read several books you promised you would write me about them, but you haven't. How many times I've told you I love your letters and they bring me joy. I finish my concerts on 1 February and then at the end of March plan to leave for Europe.[22]

On 5 April, the Rachmaninoffs arrived at Naples on the *Duilio* and were cheered by the sight of spring in Italy, everything in flower. They stopped in Rome before going on to Florence. From there Rachmaninoff wrote to Somov:

We've been here three and a half weeks. I feel better and seem
to have gained some weight. Altogether life is pleasant. I've
been entertained by the Medtners, who were here when we
arrived and are coming with us when we leave for Zurich.
I've listened many times to his playing; I can't tell you what
sincere pleasure and satisfaction I get from his compositions
and his playing of them.[23]

It was during this, their first meeting since before the revolution that, inevitably, Medtner asked him why he had given
up composing. He shrugged: 'How can I compose without
melody.'[24] Perhaps as Martyn conjectures, 'Medtner stung him
into action',[25] for only two months later, on 20 June, he wrote
to Medtner from Dresden reporting that he was writing music
once again. No matter what he may have said, the idea of writing music again can never have been far from his thoughts. Some
brief sketches for the last movement of the Fourth Concerto
appear on the back of the draft for the cadenza to Liszt's Second
Hungarian Rhapsody, performed for the first time in January
1919. Others appear in a sketchbook he had apparently given
Siloti, after his arrival in New York in 1921.

Several reasons account for the cut in the number of concerts
he undertook that season. Firstly, the health problems he was
suffering from. Secondly, the attitude of even appreciative critics, like H.T. Parker, persuaded him that he needed to take more
time off. Thirdly, he was now sufficiently secure financially.
But fourthly, and most significant, was his need to start writing
music once again.

1924–1927

Love of jazz: Writes more transcriptions: Rents country estate in France: Music Studio of Moscow Arts Theatre comes to New York with Aleko but he declines to conduct: Correspondence with Medtner: Appears in USA introducing his Fourth concerto, but without success: Another new work, Three Russian Songs for orchestra and chorus based on folk music, is much admired.

On 24 September 1924, Sergei and Natalia's elder daughter, Irina, married Prince Peter Wolkonsky in Dresden. Rachmaninoff wrote to Wilshaw: 'We shall stay here until the wedding; the next day I leave for England.'[1] There he undertook a three-week tour playing six recitals and two performances of his Second Piano Concerto. On 22 October, with the young couple still in Europe, the remaining Rachmaninoffs left for New York. Back in America, Rachmaninoff went to hear the Symphony Orchestra play *The Isle of the Dead* in Boston, before giving a recital, on the afternoon of 23 November. 'When the audience discovered him they gave him as much of an ovation as is decorous in Symphony Hall,' one journalist stiffly observed.

After playing another afternoon recital on 7 December at Providence, Rhode Island, he stayed on to hear Paul Whiteman.

This was the age of Jazz and Rachmaninoff, an admirer of Whiteman's, had been present in New York the previous February at the Aeolian Hall when Whiteman introduced Gershwin's *Rhapsody in Blue*. In January 1925, appropriately in New Orleans, Rachmaninoff discusses Whiteman.

> He has the finest orchestra of its size I have ever heard. I have long been an admirer of his work, each month I send my daughter in Europe records made by this remarkable organization. The charm and interest of this orchestra for the musician is that it is undoubtedly new. That is to say, it expands its material in a characteristic and novel fashion which to me is absolutely fascinating. This may be certainly called authentic American music, for it can be heard nowhere else that I know of. My friend Medtner calls Whiteman the best storyteller he knows in music; storytelling is exactly what Whiteman's short pieces are: excellent pointed anecdotes, crisply told, with all the human breeziness and snap that are so characteristic of the American people.[2]

In 1925, the microphone was invented and the recording process electrified. The number of popular arrangements of the classics was increasing rapidly. Rachmaninoff had written to Morozov to deny a rumour that he had composed a series of Foxtrots; that this was but one of countless arrangements of his C sharp minor Prelude. Only a month after the prelude was first published in New York in 1898, it was played in a version by someone called William Lorraine. A quarter of a century later there were innumerable different editions, including that for saxophone sextet, entitled *The Russian Rag* by the Six Brown Brothers, and even one by Duke Ellington.

Rachmaninoff's recital programmes in the 1924/25 season included: Bach's Prelude in D Minor from *The Well-Tempered Clavier* and Liszt's arrangement of his Prelude and Fugue in A minor; Chopin's Ballade in F, Mazurka in E and the Scherzo in

E; Sgambati's arrangement of the 'Mélodie' from Gluck's *Orfeo ed Euridice*; Saint-Saëns' Caprice on a Theme from *Alceste*; Liszt's Sonata and Polonaise in E; Schumann's Twenty-second Sonata in G minor; and the Strauss-Godowsky *Kunsterleben*. On 16 January, he gave a recital in the presence of President Coolidge at the White House. The programme was made up of the Gounod-Liszt waltz from *Faust*, a Chopin group and some short encore pieces – anything too long might not have suited the President who was famed for brevity of expression. There is a tale told of a talkative journalist who took up a challenge that he would not be able to get more than five words out of him. After spending an hour with him and only managing to procure an occasional Presidential grunt, in desperation he told him of the wager. 'You lose,' Coolidge said.

From the east, Rachmaninoff set out west giving concerts across America to California. We get an idea how squalid conditions on tour could be from a description of one concert he gave at a school auditorium at Stockton, California:

> By reason of a temporary heating system, which blew out the curtain in an annoying way, it had been difficult to procure a proper setting. It suggested some cheap melodrama with rats running about. Had the 'Red Mill' set, used in last year's high school opera production been put up, it could not but have looked more appropriate.[3]

In April that year he recorded a piano transcription of the 'Gopak' from Moussorgsky's *Sorochintsky Fair* for RCA. He had been including it in recitals since November 1923, and before the war he conducted an orchestral arrangement of it by Liadov in Moscow. Moussorgsky never completed the orchestration but left a piano reduction, and although Rachmaninoff's version is more elaborate, it is in the more literal style he used for the minuet from *L'Arlésienne* rather than the one he used for Kreisler's *Liebesleid*.

During his travels he found time to tell Wilshaw about selling his Riverside Drive house. Despite claiming 'not to understand a thing about business – I hate it',[4] the post-war boom was still going on and property prices still going up. By the end of the season he decided: 'next year to drastically alter my style of living. My schedule here will last altogether only five weeks from 2 November to 5 December. In that time I'll give no more than between twenty and twenty-five concerts. Then two weeks recording.'[5] His daughter's marriage caused him to want to re-orient his career to Europe once again:

> I've liquidated my affairs in the States, and the house, which we all loved very much, I've sold. Where we'll live the rest of the time I haven't decided. Probably here, with my wife, part of the time; Tanya will stay in Paris with the Wolkonskys, and part of the time we will travel to Europe to be with the children.[6]

On 23 May, the Rachmaninoffs and Wolkonskys departed New York bound for Europe. After leaving Natalia in Paris, Rachmaninoff, daughter Tanya with the Wolkonskys had reached Dresden by 3 June. Once there, he took up residence German-style at a sanatorium 'from where I now write you', he told Wilshaw in a letter of 2 July:

> Tomorrow we'll have been here a whole month. I'm writing very badly; my hands are shaking – old age is no joke! Still, I am a little better, but only a little. These sanatoria have changed since the war, but so has the rest of the world. Tomorrow I move to a hotel, for a few days' freedom, afterwards we go to Paris where Natasha has found us a villa, and we'll remain there until 15 October.[7]

That summer the Rachmaninoffs rented Le Chateau Sorbeville at Orsai, Seine et Oise. There, he goes on:

I shall sit at the piano and do exercises for the fourth and
fifth fingers. About five years ago, Hoffmann told me that
our second fingers are lazy. I began to watch them, but then
I noticed the third finger has the same fault. And now, the
longer I live, the more I become convinced that neither the
fourth nor fifth work conscientiously. Only the thumb is left,
but that only temporarily. However I even begin to look at
that too, with suspicion![8]

In August tragedy struck the family: Irina's husband, Prince
Wolkonsky, a young man of barely twenty-eight, died suddenly leaving her a widow at twenty-two, with a daughter born
posthumously weeks later. Rachmaninoff would have preferred
to stay in Europe with his daughter and her baby, but contrac-
tual obligations convinced him to depart for America. During
that summer, on behalf of his daughters, he started the Paris
publishing house, Tair, an acronym of their names. It would
remain a publisher of his music for the rest of his life. For the
1925/26 season he cut the number of American performances
he would undertake to twenty-two. He continued to add to
his repertory: Bach's Partita No. 4 in D and a Saraband; Liszt's
Consolation in E and the 'Eroica' study; Medtner's *Fairy Tale*
in E minor; and Schubert's Impromptu in A-flat. He also introduced two of his own new transcriptions: Kreisler's *Liebesfreud*
and Schubert's *Wohin?*

He first played *Wohin?* in a recital at Stanford, Connecticut.
H.T. Parker of the *Boston Evening Transcript*, took a few sentences
to be won over:

In this new piece – for thoroughly new it is – the composer
raises a question. The style of the accompaniment is quite
frankly, though mildly, chromatic; while nothing could be
more naïvely diatonic than the melody. One can hardly deny
that the combination of such melody with such ornamental
figuration presents an anachronism. To many, this will be a

complete answer, and a damning one. Yet if one looks more
deeply, one finds that this gently modern background does
no violence to the melody, that the two fit as hand in glove,
that Rachmaninoff had written brook-music such as probably has never been penned, such as completely justifies itself.
And, through it all, ever present, like the song of a simple
peasant by the side of the turbulent brook runs the simple,
beautiful melody.[9]

To our ears today, his chromatic elaboration of Schubert's song
hardly sounds anachronistic. Now we enjoy the advantage the
distance time provides, not only from Schubert's song, but also
from Rachmaninoff's transcription which today is as old as the
song *Wohin?* was when he transcribed it.

In the autumn of 1925, Nemirovich-Danchenko, co-
founder of the Moscow Arts Theatre, enlisted the help of
Otto Kahn (Chairman of the Board of Directors of the
Metropolitan Opera) to persuade its manager, Giulio Gatti-
Casazza, to stage Tchaikovsky's *The Queen of Spades* with a
Russian troupe. They also had Rachmaninoff in mind as the
conductor. However Gatti refused bluntly. His hostility had
nothing to do with Rachmaninoff, but with the opera's outright failure at the beginning of his Metropolitan career in
1910, notwithstanding Mahler as conductor. That December,
when the Music Studio of the Moscow Arts Theatre came
to New York, Rachmaninoff's *Aleko* was among the operas
performed with Pushkin libretto. The choice of *Aleko*,
which had not been performed under the composer's baton
for many a year, may have been partly a thank-you present
to Rachmaninoff for his timely assistance providing food
and money for theatre personnel during the recent famine.
By this time, however, *Aleko* seems to have dropped from
Rachmaninoff's favour. As Julia Fatova, one of the singers,
describes: 'Timidly I went up to him at a reception and asked
him whether he would be present when we played *Aleko*.'

His reply was unequivocal: 'Not only will I not come; I am ashamed to have written such nonsense.'[10]

According to Fred Gaisberg, HMV's recording manager, Chaliapin would have liked to revive *Aleko* (appearing in it dressed as Pushkin) on the occasion of the centenary of Pushkin's death in 1937. His reason for doing so was because Pushkin's name was Alexander (Aleko is the diminutive). Since Aleko murders his wife Zemfira and her lover, the young gypsy, it would be necessary to make Aleko a sympathetic character. This could be done by revealing the opera to have been merely the poet's dream, but Rachmaninoff would have to be persuaded to compose a new prologue and epilogue. Chaliapin had last sung Aleko in Russia in 1921 when he may have appeared in Pushkin-disguise, but it is surprising he should still have been taken up with the idea after he had moved to the west. In New York, Pushkin's features were hardly familiar enough for there to have been any point in such make-up. Rachmaninoff poohpoohed the idea, 'too much water has run under the bridge since the days of *Aleko*,'[11] he told Gaisberg.

After the death of Morozov it was perhaps inevitable that Medtner, another Russian musician whom Rachmaninoff had known since before the revolution, became one of his regular correspondents and closest friends. He would dedicate his Fourth Concerto to Medtner. In a letter of 14 January 1926,[12] in response to one from Medtner complaining of a proposition by his publishers to let them own his music outright, Rachmaninoff observed:

There are three categories of composers: those who compose 1) popular music, that is, for the market: 2) fashionable music, that is, in the modern style, and finally 3) serious music – very serious music – to which category you and I belong. Publishers are very willing to print works in the first two categories – this is easily merchandisable – but most unwilling to touch the last – this moves very sluggishly.

The first two are for the pocket, the last for the soul. Once
in a while, however, a publisher does have a tiny spark of
hope in the future; that by the time the composer of serious
music is about to reach his hundredth birthday – or, more
likely, after his death, his compositions may end up selling
as well as popular music. The world has many publishers of
popular music, and modern music, but there's no one who
publishes serious music exclusively. Belayev was the exception but he proves the rule; it cost him his entire fortune. If
serious music ever sees the light of day, that is only because a
publisher compromises; seventy-five per cent of the first two
categories and twenty-five per cent serious music. The late
Gutheil was able to survive publishing a large quantity of my
music that he died of natural causes was because he also published thousands of popular songs otherwise he would have
hanged himself.

He concludes by encouraging Medtner to try composing chamber music for a contest to be held in Philadelphia, and advises
him not to be concerned with the advance, and not bother
about royalties.

The Fourth Concerto was going through a difficult period.
He had been working on it since he was in New York that
January and was still writing it that summer at Weisser Hirsch.
When at last he completed it and received back the two-piano
version from the copyist, he discovered while he was playing it
through that it had developed, as he told Medtner,[13] 'Ring-like'
dimensions: it was a 110 pages long. Recalling their correspondence about over-long works, he said he must reduce it. He was
not so worried about the first movement, although there were
eight bars that could go; it was in the last, he said, that he had
written far too much. He would have to go through it with a red
pencil excising what was repetitious. Another thing that both-
ered him was the orchestra, which was almost never silent. 'This
means it is not a piano concerto but concerto for orchestra and

piano – a big fault.' Medtner wrote back counselling him not to
worry about length:

> Naturally there are limitations to the lengths of musical com-
> positions, just as there are for the size of an artist's canvas,
> but it is not the length of a work that creates an impression
> of boredom, but rather the boredom that creates an impres-
> sion of length. A song without inspiration and only two
> pages seems longer than Bizet's *Carmen*, and Schubert's
> *Doppelgänger* seems much grander and more expressive than a
> Bruckner symphony.[14]

He then asked Medtner whether he had noticed a resemblance
between the theme in the second movement and that of the first
movement of Schumann's Piano Concerto. Whether Medtner
had or not, he does not mention it in their correspondence and
Rachmaninoff never did alter it; not until after its first performance did others too notice the resemblance.

Upon arrival in Weisser Hirsch, Rachmaninoff was suffering
from what may have seemed an injury to the little finger on his
right hand, but was in fact an arthritic joint. It would trouble him
increasingly with the passage of time. At first he kept it bandaged
but later he had a special hand-warmer made for him heated by
battery. With it he could withstand exposure waiting at stations
for trains between concerts during the often critically cold winters
of North America. From Dresden on 28 August he dispatched a
letter to Somov detailing family activities: Natasha was leaving by train for Nice via Paris, and Irina and he would be taking
a more direct route by car. The problem was getting everything
done before leaving for New York; being a Russian necessitated
visas for pretty well every country. He finished the letter with the
rueful observation that he had not played the piano in public for
eight months and was beginning to wonder whether he still could.

On 7 September, when he next wrote to Medtner,
Rachmaninoff had moved into a villa in Cannes with his wife

and younger daughter, where he was awaiting the arrival of a piano from Paris:

> The house belongs to a Rothschild – the rental price is to match! We have our own underground route to the sea. The garden is full of palms, both the heat and the mosquitoes quite overwhelming. All last night, until six in the morning, the three of us spent trying to catch them. I counted nineteen corpses lying on the bed. And still the piano does not come – how I'm to give concerts I dread to think.

Two months later he was back in New York. This season he would make twenty-eight recital appearances and play his Fourth Concerto six times. As usual he made additions to his repertory: Beethoven's Sonata in A flat; Chopin's Rondo in E flat, Nocturne in F (Op. 15 No. 1) and a posthumous Waltz in E minor; two studies by Mendelssohn, one in F, the other in A minor (Op. 104); Liszt's *Fifteenth Hungarian Rhapsody*; the Schubert/Tausig *Andantino and Variations*; Schumann's *Symphonic Studies* (Op. 13) and Brahms' Intermezzo in E flat minor. He played the latter in a New York recital on 19 February 1927, and the pianist Olga Samaroff singled it out for special attention in a review the next day in *New York Evening Post*:

> Rachmaninoff is a curiously complex personality. Reserved and inscrutable as a man, he is singularly frank and simple as a pianist, presenting music with a magnificent pianism and imposing general mastery, but with sometimes almost matter-of-fact directness, as in the Brahms Intermezzo. This destroys the mystery and half-lights which under the fingers of Gabrilowitsch seem to form the undeniably characteristic note of the piece. Brahms clearly indicated the establishment of the general mood in the opening section of this work by marking the first four measures 'piano', 'sotto voce' and the repetition of the phrase beginning at the fifth measure

pianissimo in the treble with a triple pianissimo in the bass. Rachmaninoff played all these measures forte or mezzo forte, thus throwing a clear, decisive light on the outlines of the music.[15]

On 18 March at the Academy of Music, Philadelphia two of his new works were introduced for the first time conducted by Stokowski. Richard Stokes in *The Evening World* describes the effect of the juxtaposition of the Fourth Concerto and the *Three Songs* on the same bill:

> The opening attack was made with a new concerto; Rachmaninoff came reeling back from the charge in disorder and defeat. But like Napoleon at Marengo, yesterday evening he turned the most disastrous rout of his career into decisive victory. After the intermission a chorus of twenty proceeded to redeem the catastrophe with his three latest settings for voice and orchestra of Russian folk songs. The chorus had the effect of a twenty-fold soloist. The composer uses the folk melodies as well as text, so that his creative office was restricted to the orchestra. But its comment on the narrative of the verses was that of a music drama.[16]

The idea for this seems to have gone back to his Russian days, for four pages of rough work on it survive from 1916. The songs are all folk settings, and as Martyn points out, 'they create the structure and coherence of a miniature three-movement symphonic work':[17] Moderato leading to Allegro assai, Largo and Allegro moderato. 'The verses are sung in unison by the choir, altos and basses, while the orchestra illustrates incidents in the text in a lively, humorous fashion.' The first, *Over the River*, comes from a traditional round dance and was first published in 1895 and then, with different words, arranged by Liadov. 'The words tell the pathetic tale of a drake escorting a grey duck over a bridge; the duck becomes frightened and flies away, leaving

the drake forlorn and weeping.' The second, *Eh Vanka*, the
song upon which it is based, was recorded unaccompanied on
more than one occasion by Chaliapin. 'It is the bitter lament of
a wife whose husband has been persuaded by his father to abandon her and spend the winter with him.' The third, *Powder and
Paint*, was a number performed by a popular singer from pre-
revolutionary Russia, Nadezhda Plevitskaya. 'It is the humorous
tale of an unfaithful wife who hurriedly removes the make-up
from her face as she hears her husband's unexpected return.' By
this time, Plevitskaya was living in America and had come to
know Rachmaninoff well. With him at the piano she had made
a private recording the previous February, which was eventually
published in 1973.

Thereafter the concerto was given again in Philadelphia
and then repeated in New York, Washington and Baltimore.
Notwithstanding subsequent tampering he was to make with
it, in the course of which he reduced it by nearly 200 bars, it is
doubtful that it sounded very different to his 1941 recording. At
any rate this is what Lawrence Gilman's review of its New York
premiere on the 22nd suggests:

> For all its somewhat naïve camouflage of whole-tone scales
> and occasionally dissonant harmony, Rachmaninoff's new
> concerto remains as essentially nineteenth century as if
> Tchaikovsky had signed it. Sombre it is, at times, but it never
> exhibits the fathomless melancholy of such authentic masters
> of tragical speech as Moussorgsky. There is a Mendelssohnian
> strain in Rachmaninoff which relates him more intimately to
> the salon than to the steppes; and this strain comes out in his
> new concerto, as it does in all his music, sooner or later. The
> new work is neither so expressive nor as effective as its famous
> companion in C minor. Nor is it so resourceful in develop-
> ment. There is thinness and monotony in the treatment of
> the thematic material of the slow movement, and the finale
> begins to weary before its end. The imposing, the seductive

Rachmaninoff is still the unashamed and dramatizing senti-
mentalist of the Second Concerto.[18]

Pitts Sanborn in *The Evening Telegram* was even less enthusiastic:
'it is long-winded, tiresome, unimportant, in places tawdry.
The orchestral scoring has the richness of nougat and the piano
part glitters with innumerable stock tricks and figurations.
As music it is now weepily sentimental, now of an elfin pret-
tiness, now swelling to bombast in a fluent rotundity.'[19] Like
Rachmaninoff himself, Chotzinoff notes how 'the melody of
the largo was reminiscent of Schumann's Piano Concerto, the
opening theme of which appeared in it like a pale emanation of
itself.'[20] The Second and Third Piano Concertos remained, of
all Rachmaninoff's works, the most often performed in his own
day; so it is not surprising that the failure of the Fourth should
have taken up a disproportionate amount of newspaper space.

Whatever critics may have said, and by this time they were
scarcely enthusiastic about any of his works, its failure with
audiences is what counted with Rachmaninoff. He set to work
to make revisions. The next summer he told Julius Conus, then
living in Paris, 'after a month and half's hard work I have finished corrections to the concerto. The first twelve pages have
been rewritten, as also has the coda.'[21] It was published like this
by Tair in 1928. In November 1929, he played performances in
London, the Hague, Amsterdam, Berlin and Paris, but it was not
a success. Although he talked of revising again, it was not until
after the Second World War broke out in Europe in the summer
of 1941 that he found time. After fiddling a bit with minor
details, and striking out a further seventy-eight bars, he played
this version in seven American cities during that autumn, but its
reception was just as indifferent. He undertook it the last time in
December that year for the RCA Victor recording.

Rachmaninoff was an enormously successful composer in
the late Romantic style. Coming from the old Russian landed
gentry, an extinct breed by this time, it is small wonder that

musically he should have seemed born out of his time. It was inevitable, with the cataclysmic changes that had taken place in the West since the outbreak of the First World War, that works like his Second and Third Piano Concertos should have seemed to critical opinion hopelessly outdated by the 1920s. However, the radio and electrification of the gramophone had begun to bring music to a vast new audience who had never been to a concert hall or opera house and was quite unaffected by the style of modern composers like Schoenberg and Stravinsky. Its taste was still in tune with Rachmaninoff's music, though it took him a while to realise it. At first, with his Fourth Concerto washed up on the American shore, attacked by the critics, he sought to change and develop his style, but this he proved unable to do. It took him another eight years, and the prospect of his new home in Switzerland, for him to be himself again; it was then that he composed the Rhapsody on a Theme of Paganini.

14

1927–1930

Horowitz's New York debut with Third Piano Concerto: Kreisler and Rachmaninoff record Beethoven: Explains why he does not approve of broadcasts: Records The Isle of the Dead: *News from Russia of the death of his mother: Agrees to Respighi making orchestration of some of his* Etudes-Tableaux.

The Rachmaninoffs spent the summer of 1927 in Europe. At the beginning of August the family left Dresden and Sergei sent the Somovs details of their progress. They spent two weeks on holiday in Switzerland for health reasons and to please his wife, or so he claimed. They went to Glion, a resort 2,000 feet above Montreux, within sight of Lake Leman. Here they would sleep with the windows wide open at night, and during the day take walks through the mountains sometimes encompassing, or so it seemed to him, hundreds of miles. After a week, he was complaining that they had eaten enough for three. They returned to New York at Christmas.

Only a week later, Vladimir Gorowitz (not until his name was better-known was it transliterated into a more familiar form) arrived to make his American debut playing Rachmaninoff's Third Piano Concerto. It was on 1 January 1922 that Rachmaninoff first received a letter from Felix Blumenfeld, an erstwhile Russian colleague, telling of an exciting new pupil he had at the Kiev Conservatory: 'Since August 1918 I have had a graduate student, an extremely talented youth of seventeen, who is a passionate admirer of your music and of Medtner's. He graduated with your Third Concerto and later at his own concert played your B flat minor Sonata, quite well.'[1] Rumours of the prowess of the *wunderkind* had reached Rachmaninoff through Kreisler, who was present at Horowitz's Paris debut, when he also played the Third Concerto. Horowitz always admired Rachmaninoff, 'the musical god of my youth,'[2] he declared. As soon as he arrived in New York, he asked Alexander Greiner of the Steinway company to introduce them. Nothing could have proved easier and Rachmaninoff was delighted: 'I hear Horowitz plays my Concerto very well and I should like to accompany him'.[3] The meeting was arranged on 2 January 1928, ten days before Horowitz's debut at Carnegie Hall, in the basement of Steinway's on 57th Street where the pianos were stored. Horowitz played the Concerto through, while Rachmaninoff accompanied with a piano reduction of the orchestral part. In his typically undemonstrative fashion he said little, beyond making some suggestions about dynamics and occasional cuts, yet he was obviously very impressed. The composer Abram Chasins recalled later how he told him: 'Horowitz pounced on it with the fury and voraciousness of a tiger swallowing it whole'.[4]

On his tour that season he added to his concert repertory: two Bach/Busoni Organ Preludes; Chopin's Study in C (Op. 10 No. 1) and Waltz in D flat (Op. 70); Liszt's *Dante Sonata* and Paganini Study in A minor; Medtner's *Fairy Tale* in C minor; Scriabin's Fourth Sonata (Op. 30); the Strauss/Tausig *Waldweben* and Taneyev's Prelude and Fugue in G sharp minor (Op. 29). Between engagements, Charles Foley invited Rachmaninoff and Kreisler, both artists whom he represented, to dinner to coax them into making some recordings together. Foley wrote:

The idea of collaborating for the sonatas was born in my house in New York City during a talk about music – what else? – between these two great men, and my house was the place selected for the rehearsal for reasons you might call social protocol. The only listener to their rehearsals was a manservant I had, a Korean, who admired both but was not very much interested in occidental music. He made coffee for them, which they gratefully and copiously consumed. There they felt free to argue about tempi, shadings etc., and as you might say, let their long hair down.[5]

Today, these recordings are of special interest for these artists never appeared together in recital; the reverse of countless performances that we can now only read about but at which we should so much like to have been present: Rachmaninoff conducting Chaliapin in an opera; playing his Second Concerto with Siloti conducting or vice versa; accompanying McCormack with Kreisler providing the obbligato; playing with Horowitz in his *Polka Italienne* not to mention those other concerts he appeared at with, for example, Caruso (though they did not actually perform together).

The success of the first recording, Beethoven's Sonata in G (Op. 30 No. 3) made at the end of February, led to two others that year. In September, they recorded Grieg's Sonata in C minor (Op. 45) in Berlin at Electrola (German HMV) studios – the only recording Rachmaninoff made outside the United States. In December, they recorded Schubert's Sonata in A (D. 957). All six sides of the Grieg (originally on 78 rpm records), were recorded five times each before Rachmaninoff approved. 'So much labour did not altogether please Kreisler,' he told an interviewer. 'He is a great artist, but does not care to have to work too hard. Being an optimist, he will declare with enthusiasm that the first set of proofs is wonderful, marvellous. But my own pessimism invariably causes me to feel, and argue, that they could be better.'[6] 'Kreisler thought only of the beauties of their ensemble effort and artfully dodged the issue of doing the whole thing over again. He is like a flea; one just can't put a finger on him.'[7] When Rachmaninoff heard test pressings of the Schubert recording he told Kreisler:

From the musical point of view the records are good but the
general impression seems somewhat dull. Nevertheless, I con-
sent to their release. It irritates me a little that in some places
we do not play absolutely together; we were too far away
from each other. The defect is very small but you and I will
notice it, which is why I am not satisfied.[8]

The Rachmaninoff/Kreisler partnership was certainly untypical
and extraordinary; both men had profoundly different tem-
peraments. Kreisler gave concerts regularly throughout the year,
whereas Rachmaninoff *force majeure* would spend the summers
assiduously practising next year's repertory – it was he who
observed that if you played as regularly as Kreisler did then you
did not need to practise. Kreisler was disarmingly candid about
it, practising would, he felt, have staled his performances. As
recordings show, whatever Kreisler's technical failings, his art is
always inimitable, fresh and spontaneous. Since boyhood days
he almost never took up the violin except to make music. When
a reporter once asked him how many hours a day he practised
he chuckled: 'Twenty-four – twenty-five years ago!'[9] It was
during the recording sessions of one of these sonatas, so the
story goes, that Kreisler had a sudden lapse of memory. Turning
to Rachmaninoff under his breath he hissed, 'Where are we?' 'In
the recording studio,' came the reply. *Se non e vero e ben trovato.*

On 23 May, Rachmaninoff was in London again playing a
recital. He told Somov next day that the Queen's Hall was about
three-quarters full, and although he had a considerable artistic
success, he felt he played only so-so. A very fashionable critic,
Ernest Newman for *The Sunday Times*, however, found it worth
noting that he filled the hall. Newman went on,

his Bach and his Chopin playing was a pure delight, we lis-
tened with special interest to his performance of Liszt's
'Fantasia quasi sonata' and 'Après une lecture de Dante'.
For it is out of the Lisztian rhetoric that a good deal of

Rachmaninoff's own music has come. He makes a more
worthy thing of the Fantasia, I fancy, than Liszt himself was
in the habit of doing.[10]

However, we feel inclined to accept Rachmaninoff's appraisal,
not only of the size of the audience (he had a vested interest in
it), but also of his own playing. Certainly his music owes little to
Liszt – nothing like as much as it does to Tchaikovsky.

The Rachmaninoffs crossed to the continent at the beginning
of June to take their vacation near Villes-sur-Mer, Normandy.
It was a country house, Les Pelouses, 'surrounded by flowers,
and orchards and meadows.'[11] There, on the 17th, he told the
Somovs about the rigorous regime he was following. 'I lead an
exemplary life: doing gymnastics, walking a lot, going to bed
punctually, drinking milk and smoking only a little – that is,
considerably less than I am used to doing. Results are good, I
sleep better, headaches are less frequent, and I eat more.'[12] But
he could not have cut his smoking very much, to judge from
the 1,000 cigarettes he puts at the top of a list of requests he
asked the Somovs to send over. He also asked them to send
over the music for Liszt's 'Etude d'exécution transcendante,
No. 7, Eroica', as it was unobtainable in Europe, and Chopin's
Preludes and Rondos, which they would find in the library, as
well as ensuring that two volumes of his songs had been sent to
Washington for copyright registration.

By the beginning of August, he was writing to the Somovs
again with news of the full house they had almost every day
from morning to night. The Medtners had also come and were
staying nearby. Every evening family and guests would gather *à
la Russe* to take tea together over which Natalia would preside.
Their two daughters were also present. One night was especially
memorable, 29 August, when music was made. In company
with Julius Conus, Rachmaninoff played through the new
two-piano version of his Fourth Concerto while Medtner, its
dedicatee, was present. Olga Conus, Julius's wife, remembers:

'he also played a few of Czerny's Studies (Op. 740). His playing was so beautiful that all of us begged him to include them
in his concert programme. The trills were a big thrill and the
arpeggios impeccably done, with different expression, bravura,
light and shade.'[13] As we saw from Hirst's account of his method
of practice, this technical finish was typical of his playing. That
year still in France he began work on the next season's concert programme earlier than he was used to doing. As well as
adding Beethoven's Sonata in E (Op. 109), Medtner's *Fairy Tale*
in D minor, Mozart's Sonata in D (K. 576), two Scarlatti sonatas
and Scriabin's Study in D flat, he included what must then have
seemed to him advanced works: Debussy's *La Fille aux cheveux
de lin* and *Les Jardins sous la pluie*, and Ravel's Toccata from *Le
Tombeau de Couperin*.

Save for his Scandinavian sojourn in 1917/18, that October
he made his first appearances in continental Europe since before
the war. On the 2nd, after undertaking the first of two dozen
recitals at Copenhagen, he wrote to the Somovs: 'I love to go to
Denmark, but it's not very profitable. I do so out of sentiment.
The Danes are about one hundred years behind in music, which is
why they still have heart. Very soon this organ will be atrophied
because of its uselessness and soon be a curiosity.' One might
wonder, bearing in mind his concert programme, whether it was
not he who was a hundred years out of step. After giving recitals
at Oslo, Bergen, Stockholm, Upsala, The Hague, Amsterdam and
Rotterdam, his reception in Berlin was particularly warm, even
enthusiastic. In the heyday of the Weimar Republic, Berlin was
noted for its progressive culture: George Groz, Vassily Kandinsky,
Berthold Brecht, Max Reinhardt and Schoenberg were all living
there then. A review of Rachmaninoff's recital on 9 November in
8 Uhr Abendblatt was uncompromising in its praise:

> One had almost forgotten how Chopin's works should be played,
> there is no piano classic more sinned against. Rachmaninoff
> approaches him with incomparable art and unpretentious

virtuosity. Only a great musician can take a Nocturne as slowly and still produce a breathless tension without its collapsing. And how Rachmaninoff plays a rondo, a scherzo – rhythm, tempo, colour and form are forged into one.[14]

Two nights later he confirmed his success when he played his Third Concerto with the Berlin Philharmonic under Furtwängler. His long absence from Berlin (this was his first appearance since 1908) prompted one critic to remark: 'So it is possible to grow famous away from Berlin, too!'[15]

After engagements in Dresden, Prague, Vienna and Budapest, the tour ended in Paris on 2 December. There he gave an interview:

Radio is not perfect enough to do good music justice, but my chief objection to it is on other grounds. It makes listening too comfortable. People often ask why they should have to pay for an uncomfortable seat at a concert when they could stay at home, smoke a pipe, put up their feet and listen comfortably. But I believe that one should not be too comfortable. To appreciate good music, one must be mentally alert and emotionally responsive. Music, like poetry, is a passion and problem. You cannot enjoy it and appreciate, as it should be, just sitting at home with your feet up.

Hardly surprisingly such an opinion stirred up a hornets' nest. In *The New York Times* on 23 December, the sometime conductor/ composer Walter Damrosch sought to justify his position as a proselytiser in the name of classical music. We may believe that he was acting on behalf of the principal source of his income, David Sarnoff and the National Broadcasting Company:

Rachmaninoff is so fine an artist that I think I could convince him of the error of his ways if he would sit in with us for one of our radio symphony hours and then during the following week read the letters that pour in from that great

audience which he believes to be too lazy and comfortable to
enjoy music. If Rachmaninoff is correctly reported he must
be woefully ignorant of the enormous factor the radio has
become in the development of good music.[16]

No doubt Rachmaninoff's opinion must have seemed obso-
lete and antiquated, to attempt to preserve the past in a rapidly
changing world was hardly likely to meet with approval. And
Damrosch was right, the radio did reach, in a large country like
the USA, a vast new audience, but it was a moot point whether
it contributed to 'the development of good music'. In the nineteenth century, away from metropolitan centres, people had to
make music for themselves around the piano, playing an instrument or singing. Amateurish they may have been, but they
were amateurs in the real sense. Today, the radio, records, tape-
recordings, CDs, television, viseos and DVDs, etc. have certainly
brought classical music to millions, but only passively. By holding
a mirror up the media have inevitably exhausted it, as if it were
standing in the way and blocking off any further development.

Rachmaninoff returned to America at the beginning of 1929
to play thirty-one recitals. At this time he finished another transcription, Rimsky-Korsakov's *Flight of the Bumble Bee*, the only
composition he had been busy with since his *Three Russian Songs*
in 1926. After an appearance at Detroit on 5 February, *The
Evening News* reported: 'something seems to have come over
Rachmaninoff these past few seasons. Not only did he take to smiling a couple of times, but now he has definitely joined the ranks of
the pianistic pyrotechnicians, and in Orchestra Hall Tuesday evening gave a performance that was positively dazzling.'[17] Although
he was continuing to make music as usual, without regard to critical temper, that did not stop him endeavouring to discover what
was written about him. He could not always understand English
so he sent this notice to Somov quizzing him: 'at last I too, for the
first time in my career, have joined the pyrotechnicians – I could
not understand all of it: do they praise, or scold me?'[18]

In March, Greiner of the Steinway company wrote to know whether he would be prepared to conduct three concerts of his own music with the New York Philharmonic the following season. No, he told Greiner, he had no wish to conduct.[19] He could not expect an orchestra to pay him enough to justify his interrupting the recital schedule. If ever he felt the desire to conduct then he would hire an orchestra himself and play whatever he liked – that he stated would make surer sense. In any case, the public believed he had written nothing save the Prelude in C sharp minor, and since no one wanted to hear any more of his music, what point was there in trying to interest another conductor in it either? He went on, he would prefer to stop playing altogether and retire but that he could not yet afford to. However, the idea of conducting then could not have been so far from his thoughts. In April he took up the baton once again, for the first time since his Russian days, when he went down to Philadelphia to record his symphonic poem *The Isle of the Dead*. There too, with the orchestra under Stokowski, he played his Second Concerto again and this time, recording now being electrified, with the full complement of players.

On 30 May, back in Paris, he was again writing to Somov: 'Yesterday, with Natasha, and the former cook and a new chauffeur – a new broom, if it's Russian, sweeps cleanest – we moved into the new villa. Although we are not quite satisfied with it, it was the best to be had – according to Natasha.'[20] Nevertheless they returned there regularly in the course of the next few years. Riesemann also went there when writing his biography of Rachmaninoff.

An hour's drive from Paris lies the tiny village of Clairefontaine. As one enters it there rises a wall with a high gate, which opens to the pull of a bell. Through the wrought-iron work of the gate one can see the corner of an unpretentious manor-house. It is 'Le Pavillon' the country place in which Rachmaninoff has spent his recent summers.

Before the house stretches the broad pelouse, surrounded
by magnificent old chestnuts and lime-trees, through which
one catches a glimpse of the tennis court, where immediately
behind the lawn an arrow-straight avenue, flanked by grey
beech trunks and silver birches of the park, seems to dwin-
dle into infinite distance. These are ponds close by bordered
by lush meadows and soaring woods – loud with the croak-
ing of frogs. 'I would not exchange this concert for the most
beautiful chorus of nightingales,' says Rachmaninoff. For the
rest there is silence. It seems as if the high surrounding walls
arrested every sound from the outside world; for the stillness
beneath the trees remains unbroken.[21]

Undoubtedly much of the attraction of Le Pavillon for
Rachmaninoff had to do with its evoking something of the
atmosphere of Ivanovka and pre-revolutionary Russia.

In another letter to the Somovs, written on 14 July, he was
lamenting the shortness of the holidays, how he loved sitting in the garden in a hammock lazing away the hours. The
holiday made him feel better; he had even managed to put on
a few pounds. During the month he suffered less from headaches – he had even gone as far as to forget he ever had them.
His wife noted how much fitter he was looking. Nevertheless,
he still had the piano much on his mind. He would soon have to
begin working on the next season's additions to his repertory:
Beethoven's Sonata in F sharp; Chopin's *Fantaisie-Impromptu*
(Op. 66), Mazurka in B minor (Op. 33 No. 4) and Nocturne in B
(Op. 32 No. 1); Liszt's *Valse-Impromptu* (G. 213); Medtner's *Three
Hymns in Praise of Toil* (Op. 49); the Schubert/Tausig *Marche-
Militaire* and Liszt's transcription of 'The Spinning Song' from
Wagner's *Fliegende Holländer*.

A jolt from the past reached him at the end of the summer with
news of the death of his mother in Novgorod on 19 September.
Although they had never been close since he left Russia, he had
been diligent in sending her an allowance and they had kept in

regular correspondence. On the 29th, he was again writing to
the Somovs about business matters. There was a letter he had
received from Stokowski, who wished to broadcast a concert.
He requested them to give it to Foley and told Stokowski that
the decision rested with him. He wanted to know whether the
new recording of his Second Concerto had been published yet,
and if so, whether the recordings could be made available in time
for his performance of the same piece at the Concertgebouw in
The Hague under Mengelberg on 1 October. There were two
other matters on which he needed advice: should he permit a
broadcast of his Berlin recital on 5 December (it was already sold
out) and if so, how much should he ask? The previous year he
earned 9,000 marks (these were the days of crippling inflation
in the Weimar republic) and if a similar proposition was made to
him in London, should he accept?

In London on 3 November he gave a recital in the vast sepul-
chral circumstances of the Albert Hall. 'Beyond my expectations
the barn's acoustics turned out to be quite good. The instant I
touched the piano I was reassured. I calmed down and played
quite successfully. Thank God! The audience was large, but
I have no idea how many seats were sold. The hall holds nine
thousand!'[22] He played fifteen concerts that season in the UK.
On the 18th, with the London Symphony Orchestra under the
Russian-born Albert Coates and he introduced his Fourth Piano
Concerto after only two rehearsals. The critical reception was
no warmer there than it had been at its American performances.
On the 21st, *The Bells* was conducted by Hamilton Harty with
the Hallé Orchestra in Manchester, but since he was playing elsewhere the following night his wife went instead. It was not until
the 23rd that he came to Manchester to give a recital. Neville
Cardus, in *The Guardian*, writes so intelligibly and eloquently
we might almost have been there:

> Consider the programme, the main works in it: Beethoven's
> Sonata in F sharp [Op. 78]; the Schumann Novelette in F sharp

minor [Op. 21 No. 8] ; the Nocturne in D-flat and the Valse
in E flat of Chopin; the Chopin Scherzo in C sharp minor;
Tchaikovsky's Variations [Op. 19 No. 6] – who would cross
the street to hear music so hackneyed? This music, one would
have sworn until Rachmaninoff played it us, could contain no new delights, no pleasures that long and mechanical
acquaintance had not staled years ago. It was Rachmaninoff's
achievement to make these standard works seem fresh from
the forge, every note vital and full of meaning. Incidentally
he caused us to think we have never before heard them played,
save in a mild, commonplace fashion. He expresses his power
by keeping, like an artist, within the range of his instrument.
His sonority is unforced, a matter of intensity, not of noise.
His songfulness, of which he is sparing, is never too yielding
in line; he seems always proud of the piano's essential keen-
ness of tone. He uses the pedal dexterously in his production
of light and shade. But he does not abuse this device, indeed
he is often austere in the niceness with which, by a perfection
of timing, he releases the sustaining pedal to avoid dissonance.
His attack is so intense that he commands our ears – and our
minds – at once. He has the composer's instinct for what is
important in a structure; he seems to see the end in the beginning and to lay out his proportions accordingly. Yet we never
get the effect of a merely studied interpretation, the sense of
form is quick and instinctive with Rachmaninoff.[23]

It is interesting that, as we know from his letter to Shaginyan in
1917, Rachmaninoff conceived his playing in exactly the fashion
Cardus relates.

The very next day, the 24th, he was back in London to give
another recital at the Albert Hall again. During the performance
he was afflicted with his perennial neuralgic pains, yet in spite of
acute indisposition, reviews do not suggest anyone could have
realised. He was obliged to cancel the two remaining concerts
in England, however. He went immediately to Paris to consult

a Russian specialist. By 1 December, he was well enough to resume his schedule, appearing there once again in recital. For the remainder of that autumn he undertook eleven more engagements in Europe. In Berlin, he appeared on two occasions playing his Second Piano Concerto conducted by Bruno Walter.

It was after he had arrived in New York in December 1929 that Koussevitzky, now conductor of the Boston Symphony Orchestra, approached Rachmaninoff through his music publishing house. He wanted to find out whether he might be interested in permitting some of his *Etudes-tableaux* to be orchestrated by Respighi. While in Paris, Koussevitzky had commissioned Ravel to orchestrate Moussorgsky's *Pictures at an Exhibition*; the premiere had taken place on 3 May 1923 and was a sensational success. It triggered off other arrangements by Granville Bantock, Lucien Cailliet, Henry Wood and Stokowski. We can understand that the works of another Russian composer should have seemed an appropriate follow-up, and who better to do the orchestration, Koussevitzky calculated, than Ravel's contemporary Respighi. Respighi too, whatever may be thought of his music, was certainly a consummate orchestrator. Indeed, he had been, albeit briefly, a pupil of Rimsky-Korsakov. The financial negotiations satisfactorily completed, Rachmaninoff wrote to Respighi on 2 January 1930:

> I am sure that in your masterly hands these 'Etudes' will be made to sound marvellous. Here are the programmes [he selected five]: The first [Op. 39 No. 2] represents the sea and gulls; the second [Op. 39 No. 6] Little Red Riding Hood and the Wolf; the third [Op. 33 No. 4] a scene at a fair; the fourth [Op. 39 No. 9] an oriental march; the fifth [Op. 39 No. 7] a funeral march.[24]

Respighi's reply was suitably respectful, although he arranged the pieces in a different order. The suite was not a success, for which it is of course easy to blame Respighi, but the *Etudes-tableaux*

could not have been reconceived for the orchestra. Whether the
arrangements sound flatulent, too lavish or overly percussive is a
matter of taste, but they are unfitting because they are inextricably pianistic. Respighi made the mistake of trying to translate a
work that could not succeed in any other language than its own.

Before commencing his American tour, Rachmaninoff went
to Carnegie Hall to hear Josef Hoffmann. This led to a short
exchange of letters. Rachmaninoff wrote to Hoffmann: 'What
a delight you gave me with your Suite and how marvellously
you played it – although the first part did seem a little monotonous! Can I make another remark? Why was the second half of
the Chopin Valse not played in the same character as the first?
The first was so beautiful!'[25] Hoffmann replied:

> I was very happy you liked my Suite and how I played it – the
> reason I try to play it well is just because the composition is
> so dull! As to the Valse: I do not plan how to play a com-
> position, it is just occasionally that it happens to sound well;
> which may explain why, on returning to the first part, it did
> not sound so well.[26]

That year Rachmaninoff played his first US concert date in
Hanover, New Hampshire, on the 21st. After his familiar tour,
with stops throughout New England and Canada, he returned to
New York where he found that he had a gap in his schedule and
told Foley. Foley thereupon arranged an additional couple of
concerts at Englewood, New Jersey, and Mount Vernon, New
York, notwithstanding the Depression. Rachmaninoff wrote,
agreeably surprised: 'All the tickets were sold and everything
went well, this can only happen in America. In the afternoon I
had tea at home, drove there and back in the car, played, earned
some money, and at night again had tea at home.'[27]

1930–1932

Records Chopin's B flat minor Sonata: Throughout his career his shortage of repertory obliges him to practice assiduously, which causes his playing through the years only to improve: Riesemann writes Rachmaninoff's Recollections: Riesemann introduces him to Switzerland: Dispute with Soviet Russia: Composes Corelli Variations: Builds new home.

On 15 February 1930 at Carnegie Hall, Rachmaninoff gave a recital. Henderson, another great critic, wrote a review worthy of him in *The Sun*:

For one listener this interpretation of Chopin's B-flat minor sonata – in which even the funeral march was played differently – closed itself with a magisterial *quod erat demonstrandum* which left no ground for argument. The logic of the thing was impervious; the plan was invulnerable; the proclamation was imperial. There was nothing left for us but to thank our stars that we had lived when Rachmaninoff did and heard him, out of the divine might of his genius re-create a masterpiece. It was a day of genius understanding genius. One does not often get the opportunity to be present when such forces are at work. But one thing must not be forgotten; there was no iconoclast engaged; Chopin was always Chopin.[1]

Three days later, he went down to Camden in New Jersey to record the same sonata for Victor, so happily, three-quarters of a century later, we have an opportunity of hearing it.

By six that evening, having completed the session, he continued his journey to Philadelphia where he stayed with his friends, the Swans. There he talked about making records:

> Today I recorded the Chopin, but I do not yet know how it has come out. I shall hear the test records tomorrow and then I'll know if everything was all right. When I make the final recording, and it will remain for good, then I'll get nervous and my hands tense. I am very pleased with the Schumann 'Carnaval' [this he made in April 1929]. It has come out very well.'[2]

No records Rachmaninoff made better exemplify a characteristic of his piano playing: 'The rhythmic "snap"', as Martyn calls it, 'an extra accentuation of the beat, sometimes accompanied by a slight crescendo to it or by the clipping of the final note, or notes of a group preceding it, is one of his most characteristic hallmarks as a pianist.'[3] Rhythmic control is a particular feature of the art of great performing musicians from the Romantic era, as can be heard in the recordings of, for example: Patti, Battistini, Paderewski, Chaliapin, Rachmaninoff, Caruso, Kreisler and Cortot. Rhythm is the heart beat of romantic music; it will not stay vital for long without it. Since the Second World War, and the increasing prevalence of artificial amplification, performances of romantic music have been steadily compromised by the growing influence of Afro-American popular music. This has led to a semantic confusion between rhythm and beat: beat is certainly rhythmic, the performer is locked into it; but rhythm, as we hear on Rachmaninoff's recordings, is much more subtle and does not just mean beating time.

The tour that year took him to Chicago, where he appeared on 23 March. He thought he had played well and was pleased, but backstage afterwards neither his wife nor other guests seemed particularly enthusiastic. The next day he wrote to Somov, regretting the fact that Elena, Somov's wife, had not been there: 'then there would have been none of those bitter moments – I would have been praised.'[4] On the 29th, he was back in Philadelphia again for a recital. Hoffmann, a professor at the Curtis Institute at the time, had been present and wrote to Rachmaninoff: 'There were many high spots but the Chopin Mazurka [in B minor, Op. 33 No. 4] was probably, musically, the best. Rubinstein once told me that when I knew how to play a Chopin Mazurka, then there was no need to worry about anything else. So, why should you worry?'[5] After the recital Rachmaninoff, his wife, the Swans and some friends who had come down from New York, went off in search of somewhere to dine. The problem in those days was prohibition. Eventually they found a sleazy restaurant where they took a private room so that wine could be served. Rachmaninoff was suffering from his usual post-concert neuralgia and throughout the meal the constant background-noise of a banjo player came from the next room; it was only with some difficulty that Swan was persuaded not to go and shoot him.

Upon arrival in Europe again, Rachmaninoff wrote to Somov: 'I haven't seen a doctor yet. But I am quite well. We're mostly loafing. Or we go visiting – or are visited. Natasha is off shopping every day in Rue de la Paix, from morning until evening. We hope to get our villa [Le Pavillon at Clairefontaine] back and will move in on 10 May.'[6] That summer there was again a stream of guests passing through the house, many of them friends of the Rachmaninoff daughters: Irina, now twenty-seven, and Tatiana, twenty-three. He was lamenting, perhaps not too seriously, how he was referred to as 'the one who suffers the financial losses. Our house is like a Babel; half Paris comes down at week-ends.'[7] He still found the opportunity to practise the next season's additions to his repertory: Tausig's transcription of Bach's Organ Chorale in A; Balakirev's *Islamey*; Chopin's Polonaise in F sharp minor and Scherzo in B flat minor; Liszt's ninth *Hungarian Rhapsody* (*Carnaval de Pesth*) and *Valse oubliée No. 1*, Medtner's *Funeral March* (Op. 31 No. 2) and Schumann's *Davidsbündlertänze*. Swan describes:

> one of the last days of June, when the mood at Le Pavillon was particularly light and jolly. A great many people had gathered. After dinner a game of poker was organized, in which Medtner was the principal loser. Rachmaninoff then went to the piano. 'Father, play Bublichki,' the girls called out. This was a vaudeville song just imported from Russia. To Rachmaninoff's accompaniment everybody sang it. 'And now,' he said, 'Natasha and I will play the Italian Polka. It's the only thing she knows!'[8]

Swan remembers Medtner telling him:

> I have known Rachmaninoff from my early years, all my life has passed parallel to his, but with no one have I talked so little about music as with him. Once I even told him how I wanted to discuss harmony. Immediately his face became very distant and he said, 'Yes, yes, we must, sometime'. But he never broached the subject again.

Swan goes on:

> The curious thing about these words was that Rachmaninoff expressed himself similarly of Medtner. Medtner's whole mode of life in Montmorency is so monotonous. An artist cannot give everything from within. There must be outward impressions. I once told him; "You should go out and spend the night in some den, get thoroughly drunk. An artist cannot always be a moralist."[9]

Notwithstanding their close friendship, although Medtner was usually careful what he said, he is quoted on more than one occasion expressing a scarcely disguised hostility after Rachmaninoff's death. After settling briefly in Paris and finally in London, Medtner was obliged to teach the piano. His works were never properly appreciated, but there was enough in common between their musical styles to explain his jealousy.

That summer, Rachmaninoff authorised his German-speaking friend, Oscar von Riesemann, to write his autobiography, and long conversations followed. A French literary agent had once before approached Rachmaninoff about his life story, to no avail. Published in 1934, Reisemann's account has always enjoyed a somewhat ambiguous reputation, not least because of another biography, *Sergei Rachmaninoff: A Lifetime in Music*, by Sergei Bertensson and Jay Leyda, which appeared in 1956. They describe Rachmaninoff's reaction[10] when Riesemann brought him the draft to read:

> His first shock was to see the title, *Rachmaninoff's Recollections*; his indignation at this unwarranted liberty mounted to anger when he found it contained long passages allegedly by him. Especially infuriating was a chapter in which he praised himself and his work. Though he found himself accurately quoted on many episodes of his youth and musical career, he could not tolerate the several embroideries and invented quotations in which he was made to judge and explain his compositions.[11]

Rachmaninoff told Riesemann that he could write whatever he chose, but the title would have to be altered, and some of the direct quotations changed or omitted. However, Riesemann declared that the publisher would not hear of changing the title. If any serious trouble was made then the whole project might collapse, and all the time and money he had spent would be wasted. Reisemann thereupon suffered a heart attack so

Rachmaninoff agreed, rather than inflict anything else on him, to pay for some cuts, including most of the offending chapter of self-praise.

Since neither Bertensson nor Leyda were present in London in April 1933 when Riesemann brought the draft for Rachmaninoff to read, whose evidence were they relying on? Almost certainly it was Rachmaninoff's sister-in-law since the following inscription appears on the title-page immediately below their own names: 'with the assistance of Sophia Satina'. But by then she was living in the United States; so how significant are the 'several embroideries and invented quotations' they mention? Seroff, another of Rachmaninoff's biographers who knew him, quotes a letter Rachmaninoff wrote to Wilshaw some years after the publication of Riesemann's biography:[12]

> The book is very boring. There is a lot in it that is not true, which proves that I did not dictate it, but Riesemann composed it out of his head. I was asked to give an authorization, but I only read three chapters. I didn't have the patience to go any further.

After consulting other available sources, Seroff found that 'Rachmaninoff's remark [was] unfair and could only have been based on a few unimportant errors and a certain slant which one feels is more Riesemann's than Rachmaninoff's, but [with] which, I am sure, at the time of their conversations Rachmaninoff was in accord.' Riesemann's book has been poached upon freely by every other biographer, including Bertensson and Leyda, who have by their own admission 'condensed as well as corrected quotations from it'.[13] According to Bertensson and Leyda, 'Rachmaninoff even furnished an ambiguously phrased letter that Riesemann could print as an "endorsement"'.[14] They do not, however, bother to reproduce it and it is interesting to read exactly what Rachmaninoff did write in his 'endorsement':

My dear Mr Riesemann.

I have read with interest the manuscript of your book and wish to thank you for the sympathetic understanding with which you have treated our intimate talks at Clairefontaine. If you have over-emphasized the importance of some of my achievements I am sure it is only because of our long and close friendship.

Believe me, sincerely, Sergei Rachmaninoff.[15]

Notwithstanding the heart attack that Bertensson and Leyda report Riesemann to have suffered, the Rachmaninoffs were invited to Riesemann's home on Lake Lucerne that summer. As a result of the visit they fell in love with the beauties of Switzerland and determined to build their own house there. For some years the possibility of going back to Russia had been getting ever more remote, and they wanted a property of their own. At first they tried to buy Le Pavillon near Paris which they often rented, but this not proving possible, they toyed with the idea of purchasing somewhere in Germany or even Czechoslovakia. Eventually they purchased an estate on Lake Lucerne at Hertenstein, and decided to call it 'SE[rgei] NA[talya] R[achmaninoff]'. There they would build their own home.

On 9 October, while Rachmaninoff was still in Europe, the Hindu poet-philosopher Rabindranath Tagore arrived in New York. In an interview by *The New York Times* he explained his dreams for the future of India, in the course of which he commended the great improvement during the last decade in the education of Russian peasants (he had recently returned from the Soviet Union) in comparison with those in India. Although taxed by journalists, he persistently refused to express any views on other questions – he was talking about education, not politics. Nevertheless, Tagore's views were widely misrepresented.

To make matters worse, in the last months of 1930 and the beginning of 1931, the Soviet government was conducting one of its periodic purges in which dissidents were imprisoned, sent to Siberia or shot. Inevitably a wave of resentment was building up in the west, especially among the large number of exiled white Russians.

Rachmaninoff began his European tour that season in Oslo on 25 October. During the tour he gave seventeen recitals, including five performances of the revised Fourth Concerto at Amsterdam, The Hague, Paris, Berlin and Zurich. He made his final appearance on 10 December and reached New York before the end of the year. Until that point, although frequently interrogated by inquisitive journalists, he always refused to express himself on any aspect of Russian politics. However, on 15 January 1931, in *The New York Times*, there appeared a letter under which his name appeared with those of Professor Ostromislensky and Count Ilya Tolstoy (a nephew of the author). It asks whether Tagore:

> is aware of the fact that all Russia is groaning under the terrible yoke of a numerically negligible but well-organized gang of Communists intent on reducing the peasants to a state of abject misery and that these unfortunate sufferers are being daily and systematically subjected to indescribable privations, humiliations and torture. At no time, in no country, has there ever existed a government responsible for so many cruelties, wholesale murders, and common-law crimes in general.[16]

Rachmaninoff's tour through America began without any reaction from Moscow. It was not until 9 March, preoccupied as Soviet Russia had been with the purge trials, that an opportunity was taken by *Vechernaya Moskva* to get its own back. After a performance given at the Moscow Conservatory of Rachmaninoff's *The Bells*, conducted by Albert Coates, the publication reported: 'The music is by an émigré, a violent enemy of Soviet Russia: Rachmaninoff. The words are also by another émigré, the mystic Balmont. On the podium was conductor Coates, formerly of the Maryinsky, who left Russia in 1917 and was back on a foreign passport.' The article even vented its wrath on members of the audience: 'decrepit old men in tails and old women in ancient silks smelling of moth-balls.'[17] *Pravda* went on in the same vein:

> Rachmaninoff, the former bard of the Russian wholesale merchants and the bourgeoisie – a composer played out long ago, whose music is that of an imitator and reactionary. A former estate owner who, as recently as 1918, burned with a hatred of Russia when the peasants took away his land – a sworn and active enemy of the Soviet government.[18]

Not coincidentally, it seems, after Rachmaninoff's last American recital that season, Edward Cushing in *Brooklyn Daily Eagle* writes:

> his art reflects the fluctuations of his mood to a degree not observable in the performances of pianists equally gifted. When he is not at his best, as was the case last evening, he can be very dull. He is sufficiently master of his instrument, sufficiently the musician always to play brilliantly, in a sense effectively; neither his technique nor his sense of values, or proportion, of style deserts him, but his pianism becomes spiritually, emotionally barren, and conveys to us little or nothing of the meaning of the music.[19]

We may believe his playing on this occasion was revelatory of his feelings, and not the air of simulated indifference he put on two days later when he was leaving New York and was asked by a *New York Times* reporter what he thought of the Soviet attitude towards himself and his music. He claimed to be indifferent and proud of being the object of its scorn.[20]

In the summer of 1931, although the Rachmaninoffs were again based at Le Pavillon in Clairefontaine, they spent the first two weeks of their annual European trip in Switzerland. This was spent partly inspecting the progress of the work on their new property, and partly at a Kurhaus near Lucerne. They returned to Le Pavillon on 27 May and Rachmaninoff immediately began work on a new composition, Variations on a Theme of Corelli (Op. 42). Corelli had used the theme in his Sonata in D minor (Op. 5). However, the theme 'La Folia' had been in use years before Corelli providing a source of variations for many different Spanish composers. When the musicologist Yasser drew this to Rachmaninoff's attention, he compromised by not printing Corelli's name on the cover, although it remained on the title page.[21] But, as Yasser states, 'the "Corelli problem" was, for Rachmaninoff, only of secondary importance'.[22] Although he may have written music which was then thought old-fashioned, how far back the theme could be traced for him did not signify – Corelli had used it, that was enough.

Martyn calls the Corelli Variations 'his most cerebral and least sentimental work'.[23] Although architecturally he adopts a similar three movement pattern to that of his Chopin Variations published in 1904, it is not a work whose style he managed to blend effectively with his own, as would be the case with Rhapsody on a Theme of Paganini. Prokofiev, who heard him play the Corelli Variations in a Paris recital the following March, observed: 'this is not the old Rachmaninoff of the Second and Third Concertos.'[24] As with the Fourth Concerto at this time, Rachmaninoff seems to have been taken up, so far as he was able, with trying to find a newer style that was more acceptable to modern taste. When he played it in Washington, Ruth Howell, in *Wahington Daily News* thought 'there were, perhaps, too many variations. The piece grew long, boring and the theme thickened so that even Corelli could not have found it. If the finale had been put in five minutes before, it would have been perfect. When it was finished, even Rachmaninoff looked a little disgusted.'[25] After including it in recital next season, as he told Medtner, 'I don't remember where – some small town – the coughing was so insistent that I only played half the Variations. My best record was in New York, where I played eighteen out of twenty!'[26] He seemed to have realised his failure quicker with the Corelli Variations than he did with the Fourth Concerto, dropping it from his concert repertory after only three seasons, and without spending any further time revising or re-editing it.

It was on 20 June that he took up his Second Piano Sonata again, cutting and revising it. He had written this at Ivanovka in the summer of 1913 directly after his return from Rome. 'I look at my early works and see how much there is in them that is superfluous,' he told Swan. 'Even in this sonata so many voices are moving simultaneously and it is too long. Chopin's Sonata lasts nineteen minutes and in that time all that it was necessary to say has been said.'[27] The matter of cuts in performances of music of the past has become disputatious. The proportions of a classic are an intrinsic part of it, or ought to be; cut it and it is robbed not only of content but form too. Although countless composers of the past often cut their works, nowadays when they are played there is a movement afoot to include every bar. Revealing a part which we have not heard before may be interesting but a composer's second thoughts are often more significant musically, no matter whether the tailoring be his own preference, as it was with Rachmaninoff, or simply a response to the economics of music-making.

The next season, he added the Sonata to his concert repertory, but it was not a success and he soon gave it up. It was not until the end of 1942 that Horowitz, as he tells with some trepidation, approached Rachmaninoff about the possibility of combining the best of both editions. To his surprise, Rachmaninoff agreed. 'You are a good musician. Put it together and bring it me and we'll see how it is,'[28] he told him. Although Horowitz played it shortly thereafter, it was not until he revived it in the 1960s that he enjoyed any real success with it. As his different recordings attest,[29] even by the 1960s he had not made up his mind about how much of which version to play!

It was a busy summer: not only were his compositions taking up time but there was also Senar to worry about. In August, the Rachmaninoffs left Clairfontaine for their new abode in Switzerland, although they had to camp out in an apartment over the garage. On the 8th he wrote to his sister-in-law, Sophia Satina:

> Of our four days here two have been very hot, and two have had uninterrupted rain. Nevertheless I feel wonderful. Stillness disturbed by no one! Yesterday evening we had guests, Riesemann came with violinist Nathan Milstein. As I had worked to my heart's content before their arrival I was pleased to spend the evening pleasantly, chatting.[30]

On the 28th, the Rachmaninoffs returned to Clairfontaine. Whatever may have been happening in Russia, for Rachmaninoff these were comfortable years:

> After tea, no matter how many guests there were, "[Le Pavillon]" would be plunged into silence; quietly and very inconspicuously, Rachmaninoff closed the doors of the drawing room and sat down at the piano. He did not practice in the strict sense of the word, he played something through, went with his fingers over the keys meditatively, and then suddenly the loud and victorious sounds of Beethoven's *Les Adieux* would be heard.[31]

This he added to his concert repertory next season along with the Corelli Variations; the new edition of his own Second Sonata and his *Oriental Sketch*; two of Brahms's ballades (Op. 10); the Gluck/Pauer Old French Gavotte from *Paride ed Elena*; Liszt's *Harmonies du soir* and Chopin's Nocturne in G (Op. 37) and Polonaise in A.

As usual, that autumn he was back in the States. At the Academy of Music in Philadelphia, Bell Telephone Laboratories (Western Electric) were conducting experiments in long-playing recording in stereophonic sound with Stokowski and the orchestra. On 2 December, in the midst of exploratory work, Rachmaninoff arrived to play a recital. In spite of his known hostility to broadcasting, Stokowski was sufficiently persuasive to encourage him to come to the session and make a couple of sample recordings: Weber's *Perpetuum mobile* and Liszt's B minor Ballade. In 1979, when a number of the orchestral records were finally published, an attempt was made by Ward Marston, the distinguished recording producer, to discover what had happened to the Rachmaninoff solos. Neither, alas, seems to have survived.

After Rachmaninoff's recital on the 5th, Swan remembers how enthusiastic the audience was and what a good mood it put him in. At the end he came backstage demanding to know what they thought of his *Oriental Sketch*. He rushed over to a piano, brushing his wife aside, and played it through again and again, each time faster, turning it into what he said Kreisler called the 'Oriental Express'. That season, Kreisler invited him to lunch to meet the Broadway composer Robert Russell Bennett, who was then working on *Of Thee I Sing* with Gershwin. After lunch, Russell begged to be excused so that he could write an overture for the orchestra to rehearse the next day. Rachmaninoff raised his eyebrows observing that that didn't leave much time; Bennett agreed but *that*, he shrugged, was show-business.

In 1930s America, diverse modern musicians seemed to have a fascination with Rachmaninoff. It was as if some familiar name from the distant past had suddenly come alive. We noted above the avant-garde Henry Cowell's reminiscences of him. Even Bartok would express a wish to have the score of Rhapsody on a Theme of Paganini to hand while composing his Third Piano Concerto. Musicologist Yasser tells of a meeting that he had with Rachmaninoff in 1932 to expound his treatise, *A Theory of Evolving Tonality*. He was pleasantly surprised not to find Rachmaninoff hostile. He said he would not deny the logic of Yasser's theory, but that it was only with difficulty that he could appreciate going beyond the limits of the twelve-tone scale. He asked Yasser if he knew of Taneyev's demonstration of musical evolution and thereupon went to the piano and played through several bars of an ordinary Viennese waltz, each time quite differently. Rachmaninoff's playing of those few bars revealed a musical subtlety which Yasser admitted fascinated him because it was impossible to be notated. In the end Yasser argued that all general trends in music were not the result of choice but of the irresistible march of history. He made an attempt to define this progress in the development of contemporary music, but Rachmaninoff interrupted to state that if a composer was consciously aware of the need for change then he might do so capriciously. In order to demonstrate that modern composers were not just capricious, Yasser asked Rachmaninoff whether he doubted the sincerity of Debussy or Scriabin. But Rachmaninoff was evasive: 'Well, Scriabin – but that was quite a special case,'[32] he replied.

Continuing his tour across the States that year, he played twenty-one recitals including two performances of his Second Concerto and four of his Third. One of these he played in Chicago on 15 January under Stock, who conducted an all-Rachmaninoff programme. It included *Vocalise*, *The Isle of the Dead* and Respighi's orchestration of *Etudes-tableaux*. Gunn wrote in *Chicago Herald and Examiner*:

With one impulse the audience rose and shouted its approval. Once on their feet the listeners remained to cheer long after the composer-pianist had brought Dr Stock to the footlights to share his honours. Never have I witnessed such a tribute, not in symphony, opera or recital. And never, it is my sincere conviction, has such response been so richly deserved.[33]

Back in Europe at the beginning of March, he stopped first in London to play his Third Concerto with Henry Wood. On this occasion he was presented with the Royal Philharmonic Society's Gold Medal by the Duchess of Athol. He then brought his concert peregrinations that season to a conclusion in Paris with a benefit recital on the 17th.

All the while he had been suffering from his usual neuralgia. Before leaving for Switzerland he was persuaded to undertake a course of treatment with Dr Kastritzky, which proved efficacious and resulted in the final disappearance of the malady he had suffered from for many a year. Save for a brief return visit to Paris at the beginning of May (for the marriage of their younger daughter Tatiana to Boris Conus, the son of his old friend, the violinist Julius Conus) they spent the next three and a half months in Switzerland supervising the building of their new abode. During the summer, the Swans and Milstein and Horowitz (who were staying at the Palace Hotel – a ten-minute drive from Rachmaninoff's new home) all came round to visit him.

Much of the summer was spent getting the new estate in order. There was a great deal to attend to: rocks had to be blown up and a road built out onto the promontory upon which the house would stand. He was called on frequently for consultations with the builders. A dispute with the head gardener culminated in his dismissal and he secured hired help with the assistance of a neighbour. How pleased he was that he had had the forethought to bring over some Havana cigars that he could thank him with. It was necessary to dig up much of the land using a two-bottom plough and a team of horses. Unfortunately it proved too stony for much cultivation and only trees could be grown. Six men with a big truck came over bringing four cypresses, two maples, ten plum trees and twenty rose bushes. These were added to the five birches, two pines, weeping willows and shrubs already along the lake-side. 'Oh! The grandeur of the place!'[34] he wrote to Somov. We do not know how much

money he got through that summer, but all the building seems
to have exhausted his accounts. As he told the Swans,[35] notwithstanding the Depression his deposits in American banks were
safe, yet his stock and bonds had plummeted in value so that they
were worth only two-thirds or half of what they had been. We
can well see the reason why he would step up the number of performances that he undertook the next season, almost doubling
them. He gave forty-seven recitals, and seven performances of
his concertos.

He found time to add to his repertory for the 1932/33 season:
Liszt's transcription of Chopin's song *The Return*; Haydn's
Fantasia in C; Schubert's Impromptu in F minor; the Schubert/
Liszt Serenade; three pieces from Schumann's *Fantasiestücke*
and his *Nachtstücke*; the Schubert/Liszt *Widmung* and Poulenc's
Toccata. The last represented the nearest he would ever come to
modern music. After playing it next season in recital in Brussels,
he described his affection for it in an interview in *La Nation*: 'A
single modern work has found favour alongside my undimin-
ishing passion for the classics. It is distinguished by spontaneous
inspiration, and is written for a musician of temperament'.[36]
There was little time left for him to compose anything, although
he completed two new piano transcriptions: the Scherzo from
Mendelssohn's incidental music to *A Midsummer Night's Dream*
and the Prelude from Bach's Partita in E for unaccompanied
violin. On 15 August, he wrote to the Somovs: 'At Senar domes-
tic problems don't decrease, they only increase. It costs a lot
of money and affords me little pleasure. I am bored with it all,
though I pretend to show interest.' By this time his eyes were
already turned to America: 'On 15 September Natasha and I go
to Paris, where we'll probably be at the Majestic, on 4 October
we sail for America from Southampton on the *Europa*.'[37]

On the way, he stopped in London. One night he was entering a restaurant when the band saluted him by playing Ferdy
Grofé's arrangement of his Prelude in C sharp minor. His reaction was one of uncharacteristic delight; a friend remembers

that he insisted how much he enjoyed every note.[38] Perhaps he recalled that occasion years before at a Moscow restaurant when he witnessed Tchaikovsky being greeted with the strains of a waltz from one of his ballets. The wheel had turned full circle. Upon arrival in New York, he kept off the subject of new compositions and of his new home with reporters. Instead, he extolled Grofé and said he would be attending a concert with the Paul Whiteman band on 4 November at which Grofé's *Grand Canyon Suite* would be played for the first time. Grofé, the jazz orchestrator, was a long-time associate of Paul Whiteman's and can be credited with a good part of the success of Gershwin's *Rhapsody in Blue*.

On 11 December in an interview in *The New York Times*, he talks about how he disliked the recording process and how necessary it was for him to play before a live audience:

> I cannot conceive of playing without one. If I were shut up in a little cigar-box of a room and were told that my audience was listening somewhere outside I could not play well. The most precious thing for me when I play is the feeling of contact established with my audience. Anticipation of this contact, on days when I play, gives me the utmost pleasure. An artist's performance depends so much on his audience that I cannot imagine playing without one. If I should broadcast, it would have to be under the same conditions that exist when I appear in Carnegie Hall. In order to play well inside a radio studio I should find it necessary to think only of my visible audience, rather than of the millions listening outside.[39]

In fact, Rachmaninoff did not permit broadcasts of his performances. This was not for fear that they might be recorded, since at that time home-recorders were virtually unknown, but that he might play below par. With the wider public over the air, who could concentrate solely on his playing, he did not choose to risk revealing any defect in his music-making. If he were

announced to play one of his concertos in a broadcast then the
radio would be obliged to make do using the recording of his
Second Piano Concerto. Undoubtedly, records have assisted in
the over-familiarisation of the classics which has inevitably contributed to a greater concern with accuracy of execution. By the
1930s, the kind of mistakes Anton Rubinstein made would have
been intolerable. Unfortunately Rachmaninoff was not able, as
was Horowitz in later years, to play live in front of an audience
and have his performance recorded, and then re-record whatever
changes he wished before allowing publication. Such sophis-
ticated tampering was not possible in the days of the 78 rpm
record; a whole side (four minutes of music) would have had to
be remade. His sister-in-law, Sophia Satina, tells:

> [how] nervous he would become at a recording, despite the
> most courteous attention shown him by technicians, engi-
> neers and everyone involved ... [H]e missed the contact with
> the public he always felt so keenly in concerts. He was always
> demanding of himself. When he listened to a recording, he
> would veto and destroy tests mercilessly ... He would often
> say that the records he had made served as the best example of
> what to avoid in performance.[40]

1932–1936

Celebrations: Fortieth anniversary of first public appearance as pianist, birth of grandson, sixtieth birthday: Senar complete: Composes Rhapsody on a Theme of Paganini, which reinforces his reputation as composer: Starts work on Third Symphony: Adds Beethoven's First Piano Concerto to his concert repertory.

The 1932/33 season was the occasion of three Rachmaninoff celebrations. The first, the fortieth anniversary of his first appearance in concert on 30 January 1892, was celebrated eleven months late on 22 December 1932 at Carnegie Hall. He played a concert with the New York Philharmonic and at the end 'a delegation of his transplanted compatriots [led by Somov and Ostromislensky] took the stage and presented him with an emblazoned scroll and a wreath.'[1] The second celebration was the birth of his grandson, Alexander Conus, and the third, his sixtieth birthday. This was commemorated in Paris on 5 May by his recital at Salle Pleyel and he was greeted with 'innumerable addresses; [including] Alfred Cortot [who] spoke for the Conservatoire.'[2] Afterwards, he wrote to Somov: 'I received at the jubilee some fifteen hundred testimonials, it would be worth your while to travel here just to read them. Now a few words about the concerts: In London – full. Played very well. In Brussels, half-empty – played middling. In Paris, almost full – played well, but with a minus.'[3] Medtner summed up his Jubilee season:

> The unbroken contact of his entire being with art itself can be sensed each time his touch produces sound. It is never impersonal or empty. It is [as] individual a sound as a bell is. His effect resides in his perception of the original musical image. He seems to be improvising, even when it is not his own music it is as if the composer were playing it the first time.[4]

That November, the United States at last recognised the Soviet Union. No sooner had the liner that the Rachmaninoffs were travelling on docked than reporters from *New York Evening Post* questioned him on his attitude to the news. His riposte was oblique: 'You cannot understand the hopeless homesickness of us older Russians. Even the air in your country is different.' When the reporter demanded to know in what precise way it was different, he replied: 'No, I cannot say in what way.'[5] Whatever he may have meant did not seem to upset anyone in the Soviet Union and a letter came from the conductor Coates[6] bearing good news: his compositions were once again being played regularly. Forgotten was the effect of *The New York Times* Tagore letter he had written – or more likely only signed, for the fluent English suggests it would have been the work of one of the other signatories.[7]

After a recital in London he wrote to the Somovs: 'Nowhere does it seem am I received with such pomp as here. Before the concert I didn't feel well and came on to the platform wearing a rather sour expression. But the welcome so touched me that I at once decided to play well.'[8] During that month, confirmation came of Coates' report from the Soviet Union in the form of a letter from Wilshaw, about the Russian premiere of his *Three Russian Songs* at the Bolshoi:

I was sitting in the front row, the programme included Scriabin's *Prometheus* and *Poème d'extase*, Moussorgsky's choruses on Jewish themes (which, by the way, I do not much care for) and then your choruses. Golvanov's baton moved almost imperceptibly, and suddenly, very loudly, came the voices of *Over the River* – which ended far too soon for me. When the women's voices of the second chorus began, *Eh! Vanka*, my heart began to pound so much that my attention was distracted. In the third, *Powder and Paint*, what with the increasing speed of the pizzicato, I simply grew numb. I could take no more, tears began to flow. I can't tell you how deeply moved I was.[9]

His concert season came to an end with recitals in Paris and Liège after which, on 9 April, the Rachmaninoffs left for their new retreat in Switzerland. They arrived at Senar at sunset. Leaving his wife in the lodge he took a walk alone round the estate. The impression he gained greatly impressed him. The spring gardens were all spruce, with everything in bud. Although it was too dark to go into the house, still he ventured to look at it. Interestingly for a composer whose music was so much out of his time, Senar was built in the latest modern style – certainly nowhere could have looked less like Ivanovka. At length, he went back to the lodge and he and his wife retired. The next morning they woke early. They were dressed and ready in a trice and had hardly time for a quick coffee before the builder came to take them around the house. They were not disappointed. He wrote to the Somovs: 'Stupendous! Our chauffeur, Natasha took him around later, was right when he said, "You can charge just for looking." I walk through the house and feel like a millionaire – though not every millionaire has such a house.' In the next few days he wrote to Wilshaw calling Senar 'a small place' where he would be able to concentrate on landscaping and gardening. This understatement was perhaps less his sense of humour than a sense of modesty, when he remembered the indigence of his old Russian friend.

He had hardly been in the house a few days when a new grand piano arrived from Steinway's in New York. He was touched and delighted, and upset that his 'vile ignorance of English' obliged him to cable a thank you via Paris and his daughters, who translated it. He determined at once to write a new work to celebrate his arrival at his new home and wrote to Somov asking that he forward some music to, as it were, retune him. He wanted a copy of his *All-Night Vigil* and two of Rimsky-Korsakov's operas: *Le Coq d'or* and *The Legend of the Invisible City of Kitezh*. 'Whenever I feel depressed or restless,' he would say, 'I know that just to read a Rimsky-Korsakov score will restore my good humour.' First, however, he had a minor operation in the same clinic where his granddaughter, Sophie, then aged eight, was recovering from appendicitis. When he was well enough to return home, his wife persuaded him that to fully recuperate he should first have a holiday, so they spent the rest of the month at Monte Carlo and Lake Como. He wrote to Sophia Satina on the 25th, 'after returning home I shall begin to work seriously'.

Not until 1 July was Rachmaninoff finally able to settle down and compose his most successful post-revolutionary work: Rhapsody on a Theme of Paganini. Although it was essential that he should have no distractions and his privacy be scrupulously respected, he liked to know friends were nearby only just out of earshot. That summer Horowitz, once again, was at the Palace Hotel, Lake Lucerne. Rachmaninoff would telephone him almost daily with news of the progress of his work: 'I have a new variation to play for you.'[10] About the eighteenth variation he observed: 'I have composed this for my manager – well, maybe that will save the piece.' On 19 August, he wrote to his sister-in-law apologising for his long silence:

I finished it only yesterday late in the evening, but I've been hard at work for seven weeks from morning to night. The work is rather large. It is written for piano and orchestra, and takes about twenty to twenty-five minutes to play. But it is not a concerto. It is called Symphonic Variations on a Theme of Paganini. I'll tell Foley to arrange for me to play it this season. If he does, and I don't doubt he will, then you'll hear it. I am glad I managed to finish it in the first year of living at my new home. It will hopefully compensate me for the many follies I let myself in for building Senar. At least, that's how I like to think of it.[11]

And so it did. However much he may have spent on Senar was as a grain of sand in the Sahara when compared with what the Rhapsody earned, and is still earning, for his estate – it is the last great popular work in the concert repertory.

The theme of Paganini's is that from the last of his 24 Caprices for violin in A minor. It had already been used as a source of variations by many composers, including Liszt and Brahms, whose works Rachmaninoff knew but did not copy. More recently, the theme was also used by Lutoslawski, Johnny Dankworth and Andrew Lloyd Webber. Because of its infinite flexibility it is, Wadham Sutton explains, an ideal source of variations. It is made up of a basic musical idea: a perfect cadence in the first half, and in the second a harmonic progression expressing itself in a musical aphorism. The melodic line is characterised by a four-note semi-quaver pattern. Rachmaninoff uses it to open and close the Rhapsody; it divides in two with the second developing the first and then returns once again to the original. As Seroff states:

the striking feature of this composition is that he shows in it a new style. It has no song-like seemingly Russian themes. Laconic in its statements, with a scarcity of pedal and with rather dry, martellato colouring of short episodes, it sounds like a contemporary composition [or as near to contemporary as Rachmaninoff could get]. The few variations written in his old style only emphasize further its new approach.[12]

Indeed, no one knew this better than Rachmaninoff, which seems borne out by Horowitz's memory of his remark about the eighteenth variation. Although he was much taken up with the Paganini Variations, it was by no means the only work he added to his concert repertory that summer. He also played the Bach/ Tausig Toccata and Fugue in D minor, Brahms's Ballade in G minor (Op. 118 No. 3), two Scarlatti sonatas and two mazurkas and the Impromptu in F sharp by Chopin.

The Rachmaninoffs left Switzerland on 15 September for Paris and on the 27th they travelled on to New York. His American season began on 12 October. On 3 November he gave a recital at Carnegie Hall, on which occasion his playing was at its best, to judge by reviews. Chotzinoff, in *New York Evening Post*, acclaimed him. 'When Rachmaninoff plays as magnificently as he did at his recital on Saturday afternoon the listener cannot help wondering when the composer of the piano concertos, the études, the preludes etc., had found the time to become one of the world's greatest pianists.'[13] In *The Sun*, Henderson expatiated:

What other pianist could have played the Mazurka [in A minor, Op. 68 No. 2] more exquisitely? Yet Rachmaninoff is not registered among Chopin specialists. Then came a reading of the C sharp minor scherzo delivered as only a giant of the keyboard could. The last group consisted of Liszt's *Funerailles* and Eleventh Rhapsody. One does not hear Liszt played this way often, with a fastidious regard for every musical quality in each work. And the artist showed not the slightest sign of weariness as he neared the end of the recital. His fingers were as supple, his tone as full of colour and variety, his revelation of form as clear and his enthusiasm as warm as at the beginning.[14]

Leonard Liebling, another critic, rushed home and immediately put pen to paper, not for his newspaper, but simply to congratulate:

Dear Mr Rachmaninoff. I have just come from your recital and I feel impelled to do something which has never occurred before in my career as a critic; that is, to write a private letter of admiration for an artist. You gave performances of such loftiness, fancy, and fire, that you altogether captured my mind, heart and imagination. I pride myself on knowing the piano and its eminent players intimately almost from the days of my babyhood, but I have rarely been so stirred, so completely, as by your art this afternoon. It was superb, soulful, and supreme. I wish to thank you as warmly as I feel at this moment. My gratitude, too, for giving generous place to the too much neglected Liszt.[15]

Rachmaninoff introduced Rhapsody on a Theme of Paganini for the first time at Baltimore on 7 November with the Philadelphia Orchestra under Stokowski. One critic wrote: 'Not an important opus, in all probability, but one eminently worth hearing.'[16] He must have left before the end, perhaps in order to meet the newspaper's deadline, otherwise he would at least have taken note of the audience's reception. Even Rachmaninoff was surprised by the furore it created. 'It looks suspicious that it had such an immediate success with everybody,'[17] he wrote to the Somovs. Its reception was no less warm when he introduced it in its first season at Philadelphia, Chicago, Washington and St Louis. Robert Simon, in *The New Yorker*, greeted it in New York on 12 January 1935, at a concert with the Philharmonic: 'The Rhapsody is something for audiences and what our orchestras need at the moment is more music for audiences. More music for audiences means more audiences for music, and with this sage apothegm, I conclude with another salute to Rachmaninoff.'[18]

Abram Chasins addressed his enthusiasm directly to the composer:

Liszt and Brahms both having used it before, it seemed to me that there was not very much left to do with this theme, the possibilities had been exhausted, but you have conclusively proven the contrary. The marvellous orchestral colour, the ingenuity of your invention and complete mastery of form are all overwhelmingly beautiful. Although these comments are as unnecessary as the statement that you played the piano as only Rachmaninoff can.[19]

The previous month he recorded it with the Philadelphia Orchestra under Stokowski at Camden, New Jersey. It is interesting how he plays the famous melody. As Robert Philips writes:

Variation eighteen ... makes a striking comparison with later pianists ... Rachmaninoff ... keeps the music moving all the time ... [H]e plays [the first upbeat group] irregularly, with tenuti on the first three semiquavers (sixteenth notes), then a shortened final semiquaver which gives an impulse onto the first beat of the next bar. He does the same with the upbeats over the next three bars, in subtly varying ways. [He] also arpeggiates chords, and, at the seventh bar of the theme, brings out an internal melodic counterpoint by playing notes early. ... [It] gives [his] playing a unique 'speaking' quality.[20]

His European tour that season included twenty-seven performances. It began at the end of January with engagements in Copenhagen, Oslo and Stockholm. By the beginning of March, he was in Great Britain appearing in a number of cities including Manchester, London and Edinburgh. From there he crossed into continental Europe giving concerts in Paris and Zurich. It was at the suggestion of his wife that he agreed to undertake some performances in Spain, but he was shocked; concerts he found more like night-club engagements, not beginning until eleven at night and with audiences chattering away even whilst he was playing. He vowed never to go again. The effect of the length of his European season that year had him once again determining to cut the number of concerts he would give in future. After his medical problems of the previous summer he expressed his relief when a famous doctor in Zurich assured him that all was in order, 'including his fifty francs!'[21] he observed wryly. Better news, he noted, was that of Foley's abortive attempt to arrange a South American tour; memories of his Hispanic tour must still have been fresh.

By the middle of May, carried away by the success of the rhapsody, he was writing to Sophia Satina that he had begun work on another new composition (his Third Symphony), although he didn't tell what it was. On 3 July, he went to Baden-Baden Spa but was back at Senar after three weeks and by 22 August had finished the first movement. He then wrote to Somov that his doctor insisted he take another break of twelve days with 'pine-electrical baths, rest and massage'.[22] Although he did manage to get a little work done on the second movement during the mornings, it was not until after he had returned to Senar, on 18 September, that he had the opportunity to continue it. On the 26th, he wrote to Satina:

> I have finished two-thirds but the last third is still in rough. If you take into account that the first two-thirds took seventy days intensive work, and the last third, thirty-five days, there is insufficient time. Travels will soon begin again, on the 30th, and I must settle down to practising the piano. So it looks as if completing the work will be held over until next year.[23]

On the same day he wrote to Wilshaw, 'When I had health – I possessed extraordinary laziness, as that begins to disappear all I can think of is work. This proves that I don't belong among the genuine talents, for I consider that real talent, real ability, is the result of efficient work from the first day you realize you are talented.'[24] This became a sort of *idée fixe* for him, and he would say something similar in another interview he gave the following season: 'I consider that a capacity for hard work is in itself a talent, and only a few artists who have inherited both musical gifts and working talents attain the highest peaks of their professions.'[25] By this time, the disturbance created by the Russian Revolution in his creative life had spent itself. All he could now think of, as he regained the courage to look forward, was how little time he had left.

He returned to America to resume his concert schedule on 25 October. In New York, he played a recital on 2 November, at which the Soviet humorists Ilf (Ilya Androvich) and Petrov (Evgeny Katayev) were present. They describe him as:

> tall, bent, and thin, with a long sad face, his hair closely cropped. He sat down at the piano, separated the folds of his cuffs with his large hand, and turned to the audience. His expression seemed to say: 'Yes, I am an unfortunate exile and am pleased to play before you for your contemptible dollars, and for this humiliation I ask very little – silence!'[26]

He appeared thirty-six times that season. In Minneapolis, on the 29th, Sherman in *The Star* wrote:

> From the moment he steps on to the platform, he is the same crafty sorcerer, the gaunt, wise ogre in evening dress who shambles to the piano to draw from it the blazing fires of eloquence and the slow flame of poetry. What may have surprised many was that from the man who looks like an oracle of remote and superior wisdom should have come the brilliance, the Lisztian pyrotechnics, the sheer mischief of his Rhapsody.[27]

On 13 January 1936, at the end of the season and after playing the Rhapsody under Stokowski in New York, he departed for Europe. After playing the Rhapsody again in Paris, this time under Cortot, he went to Senar to gather up the score of his Third Symphony for further work and to write in bowings with the assistance of his old friend Julius Conus. That year he went as near to Russia as he had been for eighteen years, playing the Rhapsody in Warsaw. Poland was then an independent state, whereas when he last appeared there it had been a province of imperial Russia.

After a recital in Vienna on 26 February, the Swans joined him for dinner at the Hotel Bristol. When he had unwound sufficiently, they asked him why he did not manage to relax sooner.

> He gave a sly look and said: 'You see; I am like an old grisette. She is skinny and worn, but the urge to walk the streets is so strong that in spite of her years she goes out every night. So it is with me, I am old and wrinkled, and I still have to play. I could not play any less, I want to play all I can.'[28]

On 30 March he played the Third Concerto with Malcolm Sargent in London. *The Times* complained of his never including in orchestral concerts anyone else's works but his own. Though he may have played them wonderfully, he would be the first to admit that there were other finer concertos than his own. 'It was a pity that the rest of the programme was made up of a Borodin Symphony when he might have played a classic.'[29] Rachmaninoff kept this review and in the 1937/38 season he would add to his repertory Beethoven's First Piano Concerto (Op. 15). On 15 April he sent it to Wilshaw lamenting: 'How strange life is. When one is young and strong, one has to wait for engagements. Now I am weak, I do not know how to protect myself from them. I cannot satisfy even half of them.'[30]

Back at Senar on the 16th after finishing his concert season, he found a pile of unopened correspondence awaiting him, including offers to present his new symphony, although he had not yet completed it. From Philadelphia, Ormandy wrote asking for the score of *The Bells* and suggesting that he might like to conduct it himself. Rachmaninoff sent it to him telling him he was remodelling the choral parts for a performance in

Sheffield that October with Henry Wood. Ormandy went on
to propose an all-Rachmaninoff festival and wondered whether
he might have the opportunity to premiere his Third Symphony
with the Philadelphia Orchestra. Rachmaninoff recommended
that he should ask Foley first 'because I am not sure whether he
has made any promise to Stokowski'.[31] In such fashion he neatly
side-stepped getting involved in the struggle going on between
the orchestra's management and Stokowski. For Rachmaninoff,
Stokowski and the Philadelphia Orchestra were special. As
he said himself: 'Stokowski had created a living thing. He
knows what you want, puts it in, and he infuses vitality into
every phrase.'

On 20 May, Stokowski wrote Rachmaninoff a letter address-
ing another matter:

> I have been thinking of our performance of your new
> Variations. I feel more and more convinced that we ought
> to broadcast this work some time so as to give millions of
> people who live in remote places the opportunity of hear-
> ing this remarkable music. Of course this could only be well
> done if we have exceptionally good transmission equipment.
> Although this will be difficult to obtain, I feel confident we
> can obtain it. I am not going to try in any way to persuade
> you to do this because I know your intense dislike of the
> distortion which in radio so often ruins music. But there are
> ways of broadcasting so that the music is not spoiled but can
> give pleasure to literally millions of people. This cannot be
> done by the wholesale method in which radio is now being
> carried on, but for a special occasion like the one I am dream-
> ing of such a high quality broadcasting is possible.[32]

We do not know whether Rachmaninoff ever replied to
Stokowski but we do know that he never permitted broadcasts
to be made of his concerts. Whether this was, as Stokowski
conjectures, because of the sound quality of broadcasts at that

time, is questionable. RCA Victor's artistic director, Charles
O'Connell, suggests otherwise:

> I realized that Rachmaninoff was not in the least concerned
> with technicalities of recording, and would take my word
> that a given record was good because he was quite indifferent
> to its quality as a recording. He was concerned only with his
> own performance, and would rarely permit the publication
> of any record in which his playing was not flawless.[33]

At the end of June, Rachmaninoff was able to write to his
sister-in-law Sophia that he had at last finished his symphony:
'Yesterday morning I completed my work, and you are the first
to be informed. The first performance is promised Stokowski
– probably in November. I thank almighty God I was able to
complete it. No need to be secretive about it. Tell everyone you
wish.'[34] On 1 July, he motored to Aix-les-Bains with his wife to
take the waters for the arthritic problem he had been suffering
from for nearly a decade: the knuckle of the little finger on his
right hand had become swollen and made it difficult to play the
piano. Nothing about the place seems to have much appealed
to him: 'the regimen can be defined in two words – boring and
perspiring,'[35] he told the Somovs. He was, he claimed, contemp-
tuous of doctors, and he seemed to have made them aware of
his dislike. They told him he should rest; unnecessary advice,
he thought, since the only thing he could be sure of doing
every day was to go to the baths, warm his hands in the vapours
and drink glasses of water. Although he was careful to whom
he said it, he was sure the waters were only the sort one found
everywhere. He did, however, manage to smuggle in proofs of
parts of the symphony so that he had something to read. He was
counting the minutes off until they could leave Aix, which they
did finally on the morning of 25 July. Back at Senar he practised the works that were new to his repertory for the following
season: the Bach/Liszt Fantasia and Fugue in G minor, Chopin's

Mazurka in F minor (Op. 7 No. 3), two Field nocturnes and Liszt's Paganini Etude No. 2 and Valse *oubliée* No. 3.

His first engagement that autumn was in London in October where he played the Rhapsody with the London Symphony Orchestra. From there he went to Sheffield for a performance of his Second Concerto with the Hallé Orchestra and to supervise *The Bells*, which Henry Wood was conducting. Wood had originally planned to introduce it in October 1914, but the First World War obliged its postponement and it was not until 1921 that he conducted its British premiere in Liverpool. As Rachmaninoff had not returned to Europe by then, Wood had to manage without him. On that occasion, Wood tells, 'I had the utmost difficulty in getting the chorus to keep up the speed and maintain clarity, amongst the great mass of chromatic passages, and certainly vocal power was out of the question.' [36] *The Bells* is one of Rachmaninoff's most demanding works. Wood spent four hours rehearsing chorus and orchestra, yet the work takes less than forty minutes to perform. Something of its surpassing difficulty is confirmed by an incident Wood recalls when Rachmaninoff himself was present at a rehearsal in Sheffield. Seating himself at the piano, ready to play it, he leafed quickly through Goldenweiser's reduction, announcing he would do his best but it looked much too difficult. By this time he seems to have become aware of the importance of allowing singers sufficient opportunity to make their own effect, as he told Wood: 'There are too many notes and words for it to be chorally effective'.

Rachmaninoff arrived in America that year in time for the first performance of his Third Symphony on 6 November. It was conducted by Stokowski at the Academy of Music, Philadelphia. But there was no repetition of the success of the Rhapsody on a Theme of Paganini. Schloss in *The Philadelphia Record* wrote that 'the symphony was a disappointment at least to one member of yesterday's audience. There are echoes of the composer's earlier lyric spaciousness of style, but sterility seems largely written in the pages of the new score.'[37] When it was repeated in New York four days later, Haggin in *Brooklyn Daily Eagle* was dismissive: 'a chewing over again of something that had never had importance to start with.'[38] Downes in *The New York Times* was more polite but hardly enthusiastic:

> The prevailing characteristics of Rachmaninoff's style are evident. These are the broad, curving Slavic melodies, which can say so much with a simple instrumentation confined principally to the strings. There are the throbbing rhythms; the relapses, at one moment, to a point when the whole orchestra seems to lie supine without strength, only to rise with fresh accumulation of force and to shake with fury. There is the impression of frustrated strength, which gathers to crash helplessly against some obstacle. It cannot be said, however, that in these pages Rachmaninoff says things that are new; even though his idiom is more his own than ever before ... Nor is it easy to avoid the impression at first hearing of a certain diffuseness. There is a tendency to over-elaboration of detail, and to unnecessary extensions, so that the last movement, in particular appears too long. Would not a pair of shears benefit the proportions of the work?[39]

Although *The New York Times*[40] reported that at the Philadelphia premiere the audience persisting in applauding even after the orchestra had gone off and Rachmaninoff had come out to take a bow, the work was not a success to compare with the Rhapsody. Whereas he made no post-premier alterations to the Rhapsody, with the symphony he felt obliged to make a number of amendments and cuts before it was published. The critical reception offended him; particularly a reviewer who claimed that he did not have a Third Symphony in him. 'Personally,' he sniffed to Wilshaw, 'I am firmly convinced that it is a good work. Sometimes I know composers may be mistaken, but I am holding to my opinion.'[41] 'It's quite possible that in fifty years time it will be rediscovered like Schumann's lost Violin Concerto, and become a sensational success.'[42] A later performance in the UK under Beecham was described as abominable by Medtner, though whether he was referring to the work or the performance is unclear. In London in 1937 Rachmaninoff offered to pay for rehearsals if a recording was made, but this did not take place until 1939 when it was included in The Rachmaninoff Cycle in Philadelphia.

In a letter to Aslanov, he denies that the work was what he would have called Russian, yet we may doubt whether Rachmaninoff was aware by this time just how Russian-sounding his music was. He may not have been associated with 'The Five', but like Tchaikovsky's, his music was still inextricably Russian. At its Moscow premiere, which took place on 11 July 1943, three months after his death when Hitler's troops were deep in Russia, the critic in *Pravda* hailed it as 'a lyric poem about Russia and praises the melodious sweeping themes with their clearly marked Russian character.'[43]

1937–1939

*Importance to him of piano playing: Makes his first flight from
London, Northolt to Paris, Le Bourget: Adapts Rhapsody for ballet
on the Paganini legend: Henry Wood introduces Third Symphony
in Great Britain: Death of Chaliapin: Plays revised First Piano
Concerto: Imminence of Second World War in Europe causes him to
move from Switzerland to the United States.*

During the 1936/37 season, Rachmaninoff went on his usual
American concert tour making a total of thirty-nine appearances in sixteen weeks. By this time he had been giving them
for almost twenty years. Such was his pace that in many cities
he would arrive in the morning, play in the evening, and leave
the next day. Notwithstanding the Depression, the plethora
of offers he received each season made it necessary for him
to turn some down. For the first years of his career as a travelling virtuoso he was often beset by neuralgia, but by now,
indicatively, it had disappeared and the tedium of travel became
meat and drink to him. That year he appeared as a soloist in
St Louis and Pittsburgh in one of his piano concertos, while
the orchestra played his Third Symphony. He gave recitals
across the country proceeding via Denver and Kansas, making

a detour to Canada and then stopping at Washington, Boston, New York, Philadelphia, Baltimore and Columbus. At each city, Foley arranged for journalists to meet him at the station. '[Rachmaninoff's] eyes actually filled as he described the man who had guided his career since 1923 and had become a close and trusted friend.'[1]

The tour not only provided him with funds, but was also a necessary ego fillip. At one stop, when he arrived at a very early hour, he was subjected to journalists who demanded to know what he thought of modern music. He replied, 'I am very pessimistic about modern music – as I always am before breakfast.'[2] At another, when asked where he found the best audiences, he side-stepped the question. 'No audience is bad,' he said: 'There are only bad artists.'[3] At Portland, one journalist wanted to know where he was now living – he was a Russian, was he not? 'On the train,' he replied, 'in the Pullman car.'[4] It was difficult to say whether this was his idea of a joke, or simply that he did not quite understand. The same thing might be said of a response to a question put to him upon arrival in Minneapolis – whether he was planning his retirement. 'Certainly I will retire,' he replied. 'This trip has made me especially tired.'[5] Maybe all he could think of was the sleepless night he had spent on the train. His humour may not have been very subtle but that he was capable of it is apparent from another occasion when he came out for an encore and, announcing a new composition, sat down and began the opening chords of the Prelude in C sharp minor, 'flinging it at the audience like a bone to a dog'.[6]

When he left town, as often as not the train was delayed and he would find something to do: writing letters or bringing out the score of his symphony to correct. He sent Somov alterations he made in the cello parts, observing ruefully: 'today I played like a hack. Occasionally there's no one who plays worse than I do.'[7] Then he would be back again hitting the trail. At the end of February, he barely had time to get to the portside in New York before the boat embarked for Europe. He began a recital tour in the UK starting in Birmingham on 10 March. Two weeks later he played his last afternoon concert in London, departing the same day from Northolt to Le Bourget airport, Paris (part of his annual trip he was now making by air). With his European tour behind him, back at Senar on 24 April he told Somov how the weather was unseasonable, cold and blustery. He was planting some more trees and apprehensive whether the wind might blow them down on the house. For the next two weeks he was determined to rest, although his arthritic finger was still making it necessary to practise an hour a day. He was feeling much better, reading and walking, and getting a lot of regular sleep. The Medtners were already at Senar on 4 May and Horowitz, who had recently recovered from an illness, arrived with his wife. Rachmaninoff wrote to Somov asking him to send over an album of Godowsky pieces for four hands, so that Horowitz and he could play them. At the beginning of June he wrote to Wilshaw in Moscow again complaining how sick, tired and old he felt. He was still preoccupied with his Third Symphony, 'convinced that it is a good work. But, sometimes the composer is wrong, yet I maintain my opinion.'[8] Wilshaw reminded him how much Tchaikovsky had suffered as a result of critics: 'although he may have been grieved by their attitude, yet he went on composing,'[9] he endeavoured to cheer him.

That summer he thought of revising his Fourth Concerto but didn't need much persuading to put it aside. In company with his wife, younger daughter, her son and their dogs, they drove to the Adriatic coast resort of Riccione at the beginning of July, where they rented a villa. The day before leaving he wrote to Sophia Satina, 'my mood could change for the better if I wrote something. That would help my state of mind. But I cannot begin anything, so I've begun practising early.'[10] New additions to his concert repertory for the following season included: Bach's Italian Concerto in F, Chopin's Mazurka in F minor (Op. 63 No. 2), Debussy's *Suite Bergamasque*, Liszt's *Weinen, Klagen, Sorgen, Zagen* and most interestingly Beethoven's First

Piano Concerto. He wrote to Wilshaw with regard to the latter: 'there's divine music.'[11] This would be the first work with orchestra that was not his own that he would play in concert for sixteen years.

At Senar in August, the choreographer Fokine and his wife came on a visit. Fokine wanted him to compose a ballet score, but he was evasive and they parted without coming to a decision. On the 23rd, Fokine wrote him a lengthy letter,[12] going through the many ideas they had discussed. From the myths of Ovid ('there is rich material for both composer and choreographer. Although I remember your rather indifferent look') to Pushkin, Lermontov, Byron, Shelley, Zhukovsky, Wilde, Poe, *A Thousand and One Nights*, The Decameron – 'indeed, almost anything that would make a suitable subject.' Then Rachmaninoff had a brainwave: although he was not in the right mood to consider composing new music (the discouraging reception of his Third Symphony being uppermost in his mind), why not adapt a work he had already written for a ballet? Rhapsody on a Theme of Paganini came to mind. After several fruitless attempts to telephone Fokine, he finally wrote him a letter detailing the idea:

Have you ever thought of the Paganini legend—how he sells his soul to the Evil Spirit in exchange for perfection of art and a beautiful woman? All the variations on *Dies irae* represent the Evil Spirit. Those in the middle, from variation eleven to eighteen, are the love episodes. Paganini appears the first time in the Theme and for the last time in the twenty-third variation. After which, until the end, it is the triumph of his conquerors. The first appearance of the Evil Spirit is in the seventh variation, where at figure nineteen there can be a dialogue with Paganini, when his theme appears alongside *Dies irae*. Variations eight, nine and ten represent the progress of the Evil Spirit. The eleventh is a transition to the world of love. Variation twelve, the minuet, is the first appearance of the woman, through to the eighteenth. The thirteenth is the first appearance of the woman with Paganini. The nineteenth is the triumph of Paganini's art, his diabolical pizzicato. It would be good to show Paganini with a violin – not, of course, a real one, but some kind of fabricated, fantastic one. I also think that at the end of the action the characters representing the Evil Spirit in the struggle for the woman and art should look like caricatures of Paganini himself. And their violins should be even more monstrous – please don't laugh![13]

But Fokine did not. He enthusiastically accepted the idea. In 1939, the following year, Fokine would introduce a ballet entitled *Paganini* with Rachmaninoff's music, at Covent Garden.

It might seem surprising that Rachmaninoff should have thought up such a story after, and not before, he had written the music. The scenario was a rationalisation of something he had always had at the back of his mind, a way of representing what we may call a musical *idée fixe*. The *Dies irae* theme by this time had become almost his signature tune. From London on 9 September, Fokine wrote asking 'what is this *Dies irae*?'[14] Fokine's query was not so extraordinary, as the *Dies irae* is part of the Catholic Liturgy and not the Orthodox.

When Rachmaninoff arrived in New York on 12 October, a reporter from *The Sun* was at the dockside wanting to know whether he would be introducing any new works that season:

No nothing new, only in the summer do I have time to compose, but this year I was lazy. One grows older. Now, I can play only concerts. You may remember they gave my Third Symphony here last season. Only critics understand everything after a single hearing. Sometimes such quick understanding is a dangerous thing, I should not be brave enough to say whether a work is good or bad after hearing it only once.[15]

On the 27th he gave a recital in New York. A few days later, Chasins wrote congratulating him and apologising for not coming backstage on the night because there were 'so many others'.[16] When they met at Steinway's Christmas reception, Chasins' forthcoming concert appearance had been announced. Chasins was to play his new Second Piano Concerto with John Barbirolli and the New York Philharmonic. Rachmaninoff asked him who he was practising it with. Chasins told him that no piano reduction had yet been made so he was obliged to practise it alone. 'But that is impossible,' Rachmaninoff replied. 'Send me the score, I will look it over and practice it with you.'[17] Chasins was amazed, but sure enough, a couple of weeks later Rachmaninoff came to his studio and worked with him some four hours.

> His meticulous workmanship was demonstrated in the perfection with which he knew and played the orchestra part. Over and over and over again we practised some thorny passage, crawling along at a painfully slow pace, he was unsparingly generous with suggestions both compositional and pianistic, all with supreme tact and humour.[18]

Chasins goes on to say how unlike his popular image – as a cold and distant person – he was. He recalls how Rachmaniniov had showed him a photograph of himself out of *Life* magazine: 'He looked at it. "Hm!" he said "very dramatic!" then autographed it "To Abram Chasins ... Bravo!"'[19]

That year Rachmaninoff gave thirty-nine performances in America, appearing for the last time on 20 December. After Christmas he returned to Europe and spent January 1938 at Senar. In February, he resumed his European programme with eighteen concerts in the UK, Scandinavia, Holland, Austria, Hungary and France. On 10 March at Manchester he played Beethoven's First Concerto and the Paganini Rhapsody with the Hallé orchestra. On the 12th in London he gave a recital at Queen's Hall. On this occasion he included the Bach/Liszt *Weinen, Klagen, Sorgen, Zagen Variations*; the shorter version, not that anticipated in the programme notes, as Gray-Fiske was quick to note in *Hampstead News and Advertiser*:

> One cannot blame the audience for not knowing obscure works, but our great critics subsequently treated us to a fine exhibition of ignorance and inanity. The next day we read: 'Bach/Liszt Variations Abandoned' [*The Times*]. 'Rachmaninoff began in unusual style by stopping halfway through Liszt Variations, etc., etc. But even if they did not realize that Rachmaninoff was playing an entirely different piece, their commonsense should have told them that an artist of such eminence would never stop playing as a result of mere caprice, irritation or memory lapse – so much – or, so little – for critical infallibility.[20]

In London on 22 March Henry Wood conducted the first UK performance of the Third Symphony. Wood commented: 'it scored a real success – what a lovely work it is'.[21] In his autobiography he remembers how:

> It impresses me as being of the true Russian romantic school; one cannot get away from the beauty and melodic line of the themes and their logical development. As did Tchaikovsky Rachmaninoff uses the instruments of the orchestra to their fullest effect. I go so far as to predict that it will prove as popular as Tchaikovsky's Fifth.[22]

On 2 April, at a morning rehearsal with the BBC Symphony Orchestra, Wood tells how, 'Rachmaninoff attended and expressed his unbounded satisfaction both with the playing and reading of his work'.[23] Rachmaninoff must have been pleased that Wood thought so highly of it. Indeed, it was probably Wood's enthusiasm – which time has justified even if the Third

Symphony has not proved as popular as Tchaikovsky's Fifth –
that kept Rachmaninoff from voicing any reservations he may
have had about his conducting. The next year, when he heard
a performance broadcast from London with Wood conducting,
he wrote to Sophia Satina that 'it did not on the whole satisfy
me (especially the first movement).'[24] His British tour ended
that season when he played his First Concerto with the London
Philharmonic Orchestra conducted by Thomas Beecham.

On 10 April he was to have been in Vienna, for a second
visit that season, to conduct his Third Symphony and *The Bells*.
However, with the Anschluss having taken place the previous
month, he reported to the Somovs: 'I have, of course, cancelled.
We live as on a volcano.'[25] He was continuing his European tour
when news reached him of the grave illness of Chaliapin, and he
rushed to Paris to see him.

> As often in the past, I managed to distract him a little, just
> before my departure, he started to tell me that he wanted to
> write another book for artists on the subject of the art of the
> stage. He spoke, of course, very, very slowly. He was panting
> and his heart barely working! I let him finish and said, stand-
> ing up, that I also had plans; that as soon as my performances
> were over I was going to write a book too, and the subject
> of it would be Chaliapin. He gave me a smile and patted my
> hand. And so we parted – Forever![26]

When Rachmaninoff returned the next day, Chaliapin was in
a coma. For a Russian newspaper in Paris, *Posledniye Novosti*,
Rachmaninoff wrote an obituary for his long-time friend:
'"Dead only is he who is forgotten." I once read such an inscription on a grave in a cemetery. If that is true, then Chaliapin will
never die. He cannot die.'[27] 'It is impossible to describe how he
sang. He sang as Tolstoy wrote.'[28]

It took Rachmaninoff some time to recover from Chaliapin's
death. Chaliapin was a part of his Russian life, which although

then receding fast, seemed to him somehow to become ever closer as he grew older. That he was still feeling its effect is apparent in a letter he wrote on the 29th to Somov. He complained how he could no longer drive straight and was forever scraping the car against the garage wall. He had begun to forget basic Russian words and needed time to remember business affairs, his eyesight was deteriorating and he was growing deaf. Three months later, however, he seemed to have been at least partially restored to health. Once again to the Somovs he was writing of the Third Symphony, enumerating its admirers, among them the conductor Fritz Busch and 'Henry Wood [who] is fascinated by it, as I am, myself!'[29] Though not yet of a mind to concentrate on any new composition, he began working on changes he had been planning to make to the Fourth Concerto. He also spent three hours a day practising for the 1938/39 season, in which he would make fifty-nine concert appearances, adding to his repertory: Rameau's Variations in A minor, Beethoven's Sonata in C minor (Op. 111), three of Chopin's Etudes (Op. 25) and 12 Preludes. Although physically tired, it was mental fatigue that he was really suffering from, for he was as much the workaholic as ever. Having finally completed revisions to the Third Symphony, he forwarded them to Somov to send to Foley for publication with the following peremptory inscription: 'The parts I am sending you have been attentively checked by me, which means THEY MUST BE BLINDLY FOLLOWED.'[30]

He began the concert season in England again that year before departing for America. He appeared at the Albert Hall, London, on 5 October as part of Wood's Jubilee benefit concert in aid of musicians. The first part of the evening was devoted to a new work, *Serenade to Music* by Vaughan Williams, performed by sixteen leading British singers, and after the interval he played his Second Concerto. He went on to America and began his annual schedule of performances. This time he played his First Piano Concerto on a number of occasions in a short tour beginning in Philadelphia, with the orchestra conducted by Ormandy. In San

Francisco on 18 November he appeared in recital at the opera house. Alfred Frankenstein in *The Chronicle* wrote:

> How privileged we are to witness a kind of pianistic king-ship that in future years will be enshrined in the mythology of music as one of the colossal and incredible achievements of the grand old times, much as performances of Liszt are now regarded. For Rachmaninoff is one of the four or five great lords of the interpretative realm. He has held that enviable position for long but, if recollection of past recitals can be relied on, his art has ripened even further and more gloriously in recent years.[31]

On the 30th, Rachmaninoff wrote to Somov from Seattle agreeing to his giving up working for him so that he could take up full-time employment. 'I have grown old and it's hard for me to part from people I love. Nevertheless I say, go, go! Financially it will be better for you, and more interesting too from the business point of view.'[32] During the two-week Christmas break, he went to a performance of Humperdinck's *Hansel and Gretel* at Brearley School to see his thirteen-year-old granddaughter in the role of Gretel. He wrote to Medtner telling him how grateful he was to have received his new sonata and used a round of Christmas engagements as his excuse for not having had time to play it, although he wanted to, he assured him. He suggested Medtner might play it to him when they met in London. Upon arrival in the UK, as was his normal practice, he undertook provincial engagements: first at Glasgow and Sheffield and then, although unwell, not following doctor's advice, at Middlesborough. However, he had recovered sufficiently to appear at Queen's Hall, London on 11 March at an afternoon recital. That evening, he was made an honorary member of the Savage Club. Afterwards at dinner he was the guest of the pianist Moiseiwitsch. James Agate, the drama critic, was also there and remembers:

I had plenty of opportunity to study in Rachmaninoff that
visual magnificence which comes naturally to great men like
Irving and Chaliapin, to whose type this major artist belongs.
It is an extraordinary mask, at once gentle and farouche,
noble, melancholy and sardonic ... When the lean figure rose
to leave, everybody in the room stood up. Apart from royalty,
this has happened at the Savage only in the cases of Irving and
Lord Roberts.[33]

On 2 April, he wrote to the Somovs from Paris saying that
although he had finished that season's concerts, he was being
pestered to take part in a benefit recital. Eventually, his daughter Tatiana persuaded him he should, as it would not take place
until the 25th and there was at least time for a couple of weeks'
rest at Senar. After leaving Paris with Tatiana and her young son,
he took a car trip round the nearby countryside in the hope of
finding a villa or farm for her to rent; her husband was in the
French army and she needed somewhere safe to live if war did
break out. Although he thought it should not be too difficult to
find, he wrote to Somov afterwards that everyone else seemed to
have the same idea.

Meanwhile, Fokine had been writing about preparations for
the Paganini ballet, scheduled for its first performance at the end
of June. He wondered whether Rachmaninoff would permit
him to repeat part of the eighteenth variation; the conductor,
Antal Dorati, was against doing so without first securing his
permission. Rachmaninoff raised no objections and promised he
would himself come over to London for the premiere. *Paganini*
was first performed at Covent Garden on 30 June. *The Times*
critic wrote: 'Rachmaninoff's Rhapsody makes an unexpectedly good score for dancing as it stands without modification,
except for a new quiet ending provided by the composer.'[34]
Fokine observed, with some amusement, 'this new quiet ending
is an exact repeat of music heard seven minutes before!'[35] This
critic was presumably the same one who did not seem to know

that Liszt had written two versions of his Bach arrangement *Weinen, Klagen, Sorgen, Zagen*. Fokine finished by expressing the hope that this would not be their last collaboration.

A month and a half before the premiere of Paganini, on 15 May, Rachmaninoff slipped on the parquet flooring at Senar momentarily stunning himself, although he did not break any bones. On 22 June, he wrote to Fokine that he had to walk with a stick and that doctors warned him that he might be lame for another two weeks. He offered to come for a later performance instead, but in the end he did not. Although he was able to undertake engagements again before the end of the summer, he was unable to walk without pain for nearly two years. Bertensson wonders whether the accident may not have had even more of a profound effect. Perhaps he remembered Tolstoy's macabre novella, *The Death of Ivan Ilych*, about the man who falls injuring his side, apparently only slightly, but eventually dies agonisingly from protracted cancer. Indeed, melanoma, from which Rachmaninoff died, is a type of cancer. Meanwhile Rachmaninoff, like everyone else in Europe in the summer of 1939, was apprehensive about the imminence of war. He wrote to the Somovs: 'I am a weak man! I love Senar very much. Whenever the sun comes out, I walk in the garden and think – "God, how good – if only war doesn't come." But we have little sun now. Very little – one could say it was Hitler weather!'[36] If the international situation made him apprehensive, his own situation – the slow recuperation from his fall – made him gloomy. 'As far as I am concerned ... I cannot improve now. I am unlikely to be able to compose again. I've grown too old; I cannot say I feel the better for realizing it.'[37]

With Austria now occupied by Germany, the Salzburg Festival had been moved to Lucerne. That year Horowitz, Toscanini, Casals, Adrian Boult, Bronislav Huberman and Rachmaninoff were all taking part in concerts. On 11 August, Rachmaninoff appeared for the last time in Europe making what transpired to be his farewell. He played Beethoven's First Piano Concerto and the Paganini Rhapsody with the Suisse Romande

Orchestra conducted by Ansermet. After which he wrote, 'I shall consider myself justified in taking to my heels.'[38] At the last minute, however, the Maharajah of Mysore came round to congratulate him and expressed a desire to visit Senar. So a few days later the Maharajah visited with a convoy of visitors, some before him and others after him. Rachmaninoff had to grin and bear it. Although he secured bookings to leave Europe on the *Queen Mary* on the 16th, the Maharajah insisted on reciprocating their hospitality – they were to come to his Lucerne hotel to take breakfast with him and hear his daughter play the piano. Rachmaninoff felt obliged to do so. When he heard the girl at least he was agreeably surprised. Only then could he and his family depart for Paris. They reached Le Havre two weeks later than planned, and took the *Aquitania* for New York on August 30, four days before the outbreak of the Second World War in Europe.

1939–1943

Appears in New York and Philadelphia in The Rachmaninoff Cycle conducting and playing on the piano his own music: Composes his last work, Symphonic Dances (Op. 45): Settles in Los Angeles and makes last recordings: Meets Stravinsky: By this time the demand for his music was such that it was more frequently performed, notwithstanding some critics not finding it to their taste.

As we saw from Rachmaninoff's first visit to the USA in 1910, he may not have cared much for it but there was nowhere else he could earn as much money. After the Russian Revolution in 1918 and with the war still going on in Europe, it seemed like the preferable place to establish himself as a concert pianist. Throughout the 1920s and 1930s he remained based there, becoming the world's highest paid pianist. But his attitude to the country remained ambiguous and he never felt at home there. As soon as he was financially established he began to spend an ever-increasing part of each year back in Europe, appearing in concerts and spending the summers in France and later Switzerland. But the outbreak of the Second World War made it impossible for him to continue cooped up and he was obliged to leave Europe once again. This time, determining to accept the inevitable, he took out American citizenship.

After arriving in New York, the family went out to Orchard Point, an estate they rented near Huntington in New Jersey. This included seventeen acres and a mile-long stretch of beach. Here, just as Rachmaninoff had delighted in fast cars, he was now able to continue his new-found enthusiasm for speedboats which he so much enjoyed on Lake Lucerne, with a new boat which he named, inevitably, 'Senar'. Some distance from the house was a studio where he was able to practise the piano without being overheard. At once he set to work adding to his repertory: Bach's French Suite No. 6, one of Poulenc's novelettes, Liszt's *Totentanz* and transcription of Schubert's *Die Forelle*. That season he would make forty-three appearances as pianist. He appeared in concert on 3 November with the Minneapolis Symphony Orchestra for the first time, under its young Greek conductor Dmitri Mitropoulos. His programme included Beethoven's First Concerto and Liszt's *Totentanz*. This was the only occasion since leaving Russia that he would play two works with orchestra, neither of which was his own. It was also the only occasion he ever played the Liszt piece, though he had conducted it on three occasions nearly forty years before in Russia with Siloti playing the piano. The reason he chose it may have been because he wished to make a recording of it, or perhaps because it contains a reference to his 'house' theme: *Dies irae*.

Later that month, on the 24th, he appeared in Philadelphia in the first of three concerts styled The Rachmaninoff Cycle at the Academy of Music, with Ormandy and the Philadelphia Orchestra. It began with Ormandy conducting the Second Symphony, after which he played his First Piano Concerto and Rhapsody on a Theme of Paganini. A week later, on 1 December, the second concert began with him playing his Second Concerto, followed by Ormandy conducting *The Isle of the Dead* and ended with him playing his Third Concerto. On the 8th, he conducted his Third Symphony and *The Bells* (in the English translation) with Susanne Fisher, Jan Peerce, Mack Harrell and the Westminster Choir. His style as conductor impressed the reviewer from *The Philadelphia Inquirer*: 'grave,

scholarly, earnest utterly devoid of ostentation or excesses on
the podium, the tall intense Russian gave his cues yesterday in
clear-cut fashion, using his score throughout in his own music'.[1]
It may have surprised some, but it calls to mind Beecham's mis-
chievous riposte when a reporter asked why he used a score and
Toscanini didn't: 'because I can read one!'

The Rachmaninoff Cycle was then repeated at Carnegie Hall,
New York. It came in a busy period musically – Koussevitzky
was conducting the Boston Symphony in an all-American programme and Toscanini, with the NBC orchestra, broadcasted
the fifth concert in its Beethoven cycle. After the first evening
Downes, in *The New York Times*, wrote:

> When Rachmaninoff appeared for the first time on the stage
> to play his concerto most of the audience rose in his honour,
> from those on the floor to those near the roof. Their admi-
> ration for him and their enjoyment of his music were more
> evident than words can make them here. The occasion was a
> memorable tribute to a great artist.[2]

On the 10th, the final evening, he conducted for the first time in
New York since 1910. Downes went on in the same vein:

> Rachmaninoff, on the rare occasions when this writer has
> heard him lead an orchestra, has proved as masterly in his
> control, musicianship and projective power as he is when he
> plays the piano. And the styles of the pianist and conductor
> are of a piece. There is the same complete lack of ostentation,
> the same artistry and apparent reserve, the same command-
> ing evocative power. From the first down-beat last night his
> mastery was obvious, as also the response he secures from the
> singers and players. The Philadelphia Orchestra is famous
> for the quick sensitiveness of the players as to the wishes
> of the functioning leader, whoever he may be. But what
> Rachmaninoff secured is only obtained when the players

know and obey instinctively the wishes of a master whose presence and power are indisputable.[3]

Afterwards John Williamson, director of the Choir, told Rachmaninoff what a privilege it had been singing under his direction and how the choir had fallen in love with him:

> This sounds rather absurd, I know, but they all say you are the sweetest man they have ever met. Perhaps you have never had young people use that adjective before but they so fell in love with your absolute sincerity, with your simplicity and your great honesty that they used the word 'sweet' in its literal unsentimental meaning.[4]

In those weeks Rachmaninoff's schedule was full: on 4 February he recorded his First and Third Concertos and a week later, the day following the Carnegie Hall concert, his Third Symphony. At the time, America was not yet at war but the effect of the New Deal had already begun to revivify the recording industry; indeed, this was the largest group he had made since 1930. By the 21st, in a letter to Hirst, he spends only a few words on The Rachmaninoff Cycle, but was more preoccupied with his daughters. The elder had arrived in New York with her daughter, as well as four dogs, which he thought far too many. He was more fearful of the fate of the younger, as she was still in France. She had managed to find a home about forty miles from Paris and her husband had not been sent to the front but was an instructor somewhere in France. He admired her strength of character but was worried, not so much on account of the war as of her not managing to obtain a driving licence.

In the 1939/40 season, his tour took him right across the United States. In Los Angeles he appeared playing his Second Concerto with Stokowski. Afterwards, although that much further from their old home, he was greeted by a Russian contingent from the film colony including the actors Gregory

Ratoff, Akim Tamiroff and the artist Feodor Chaliapin, Jr
(the son of the singer). In January the weather had been warm
enough for him to bathe in the Pacific and he had not wanted to
leave, but there was only a short respite before he had to be off
again making his usual round of appearances. After his concert
schedule was completed in March, he recorded a selection of his
own solo piano works: four preludes, two *Etudes-tableaux*, the
Oriental Sketch and his transcription of his song *Daisies*. He also
revised three works from his early years: *Mélodie* (Op. 3 No. 3),
Humoresque (Op. 10 No. 5) and Moment Musical in E flat minor
(Op. 16 No. 2). By this time he had inevitably simplified some of
the originally more complex piano writing.

That year, with the war going on in Europe, there was no
question of his returning and so in May, after undergoing
another minor operation, he retired once again to Orchard
Point. Here working conditions were ideal. The Somovs,
Greiners, Chekhovs, Horowitzs and Fokines all lived nearby,
and when he felt like it he could motor round to see them or take
'Senar' across the sound. At the beginning of July, he composed
what would prove to be his last new work, Symphonic Dances
(Op. 45). Notwithstanding some unpleasant post-operative
treatment, his wife recalls the rigorous regime he set himself
to finish it and at the same time prepare his forthcoming concert season. Every day, after coffee, he would start composing
from half past eight in the morning. At ten he would practise
the piano for a couple of hours, and then from twelve to one
be back composing again. After lunch he would lie down for a
rest, and then from three, with only a short break for dinner,
resume composing until ten in the evening. Whilst orchestrating the dances he contacted his old acquaintance, the Broadway
composer Robert Russell Bennett. He wanted to write a saxophone part and needed to know which member of the family he
should use. When Bennett called, he went to the keyboard and
played a reduction of the orchestral writing. Bennett recalled his
delight 'when Rachmaninoff sang, whistled, stomped, rolled

his chords, and otherwise conducted himself not as one would expect of so great and impeccable a virtuoso'.[5]

He wrote to Ormandy on 21 August: 'I have finished a new symphonic piece, which I naturally want to give first to you and your orchestra. It is called *Fantastic Dances*; I shall now begin the orchestration. Unfortunately I still have a great deal of practice to do and don't know whether I shall be able to finish it before November.'[6] It had originally been his intention, Sophia Satina remembers,[7] to call the three movements, 'Noon, Twilight and Midnight'. From the beginning he had endeavoured to interest Fokine in turning it into a ballet. In September he invited him over and played it through. To judge from Fokine's response, which he wrote on the 23rd, he seems to have been less enthusiastic about it than he was with the Rhapsody; he urged him not to inhibit his natural musical fecundity with too strongly marked rhythms, like the waltz, 'the thought of dancing should be a side issue'.[8] Satina states that he thought the Dances one of his best compositions[9] and knowing how sensitive he was it seems likely that it was Fokine's criticism that caused him to drop the idea of a ballet. At any rate, by 17 October he had removed 'Fantastic' from the title. He told *New York World-Telegram*: 'It should have been called just Dances but I was afraid people would think I had written dance music for jazz orchestras.'[10]

That year his concert tour included thirty-one recitals and twelve appearances with orchestra. His first recital was on 14 October. McLauchlin, in *The Evening News*, wrote: 'It actually appears that Rachmaninoff is pursuing an upward curve; that his facility is easily as great as it was twenty years ago and that the mind and heart of him employ that unimpaired facility to speak more movingly every season'.[11] At each station when he left town, as his wife recounts, he would follow his usual practice; whenever he had a few minutes waiting for a train, he would bring out the proofs of the Symphonic Dances and start correcting them, as he had been doing since 1935 with the Third Symphony. That season, an engagement took him to Havana,

Cuba, where he had not appeared for seventeen years. To the critic Vance in *Havana PM* he spoke wisely in an interview: 'Taken individually the people of an audience may be poor critics of music, but as a complete body, the audience never errs.'[12]

Back in New York, after a two-week break over Christmas when he played the role of Santa Claus for his granddaughter, he went again to Philadelphia at the beginning of 1941. On 3 January at the Academy of Music, Ormandy conducted the Philadelphia Orchestra in the world premiere of the Symphonic Dances. At the dress rehearsal Rachmaninoff told the orchestra: 'When I was a young man, Chaliapin was my great idol. Now he is dead. Since then, everything I write is with the Philadelphia sound in my ears.'[13] He dedicated the Dances to Ormandy and the orchestra. On the 7th they repeated the work in New York. The Dances may not have scored an immediate unequivocal success like the Paganini Rhapsody, nevertheless, Downes, in *The New York Times*, was not uncomplimentary:

> They are simple in outline, symphonic in texture and proportion. The first one, vigorously rhythmed and somewhat in a pastoral vein, is festive in the first part and more lyrical and tranquil in the middle section. The second Dance begins with a muted summons, or evocation, of the brass, a motto repeated in certain places, and for the rest there are sensuous melodies, sometimes bitter-sweet, sometimes to a Viennese lilt – and Vienna is gone. In the last Dance, the shortest and most energetic and fantastical of the three, an idea obtrudes which has obsessed the musical thinking of Rachmaninoff these many years – the apparition, in the rhythmical maze, of the terrible old plain chant, the *Dies irae*.[14]

At the end of the month he gave concerts in the south near the Mexican border, at Harlingen and Corpus Christi, Texas. He then went north-west to California and, after a rest seeing friends in Hollywood, was back in Chicago on 13 March to conduct the

Symphony Orchestra on the occasion of its fiftieth anniversary celebrations. He conducted his Third Symphony and *The Bells* (the English version) with the Apollo Musical Club. Although Pollak, in *Chicago Daily Times*:

> thought as a composer he may be too conservative for our tastes a quarter of a century hence, yet as a composer, pianist or conductor he is unfailingly impressive. His technical genius in a variety of fields, his absolute musical integrity, the spell of his own person, all these lead to the spontaneous tribute: 'What a wonderful old man.'[15]

Nevertheless, Rachmaninoff found the effort of conducting strained his arms and he determined to make just one last appearance recording the Symphonic Dances with the Philadelphia Orchestra for Victor records, but for some reason it was not made. O'Connell of RCA Victor offers an explanation:

> I never felt that the Dances added a great degree of lustre to the composer's name, but what was more important, the work was not notably a success with the public. I discreetly postponed the matter until it was not only impracticable but impossible. A little later we engaged the Chicago Symphony Orchestra to make 'Red Seal' records, and one of the first things on their programme that season was Rachmaninoff's Symphonic Dances, whereupon, conditions being quite different from those existing in Philadelphia, I proposed that they record the Dances. Rachmaninoff was not at all enthusiastic and when it transpired that Dr Stock would conduct, he became actively resentful and things became rather uncomfortable between us. When I was in a position to tell him the whole story, however, I was restored to his good graces.[16]

But this explanation raises more questions than it answers. If, as O'Connell states, RCA Victor did not want to record the

Symphonic Dances with Rachmaninoff and the Philadelphia
Orchestra, why should it have toyed with the idea of doing
so with Stock and the Chicago Symphony? In fact, it did not
make a recording with either. We can well understand that
Rachmaninoff should have become resentful, and one can
hardly believe that O'Connell's telling him the whole story
would have, as he states, restored him to his good graces.

For some while the Rachmaninoffs had heard nothing of their
daughter, Tatiana, who was then in France. News from Europe
was bad and they needed something to distract them. The Nazi
menace was at its most terrifying; on 22 June Hitler swept into
the Soviet Union and in only weeks the Germans had reached
the purlieus of Moscow. That summer Rachmaninoff became
preoccupied with work he had been shelving for years: another
revision of his Fourth Piano Concerto. As he told Somov in July
1938 he regarded its failure as being principally due to faults in
the construction of the last movement, accordingly he set to
work revising it. For the following season he would add to his
repertory the Schumann piano concerto, his new transcription
of Tchaikovsky's Lullaby and a couple of Chopin's mazurkas.
After recitals in Syracuse and Utica, on 17 October he played
the Fourth Concerto in Philadelphia with Ormandy. Even a fan
like Schloss, in *The Philadelphia Record*, although describing his
playing as 'increasingly miraculous for all his sixty-eight years,
Rachmaninoff is still one of the most virile and brilliant pianists
before the public today, yet with all due respect to the great
artist who wrote it his Fourth Concerto is a trifle dull.'[17]

The initial success of the German divisions in Russia
delighted many 'White Russians', but not Rachmaninoff; he
would listen attentively to the short-wave radio in the hope that
some way might be found of stopping them. His Carnegie Hall
recital, on 1 November, raised 4000 dollars for Russian charities to help assist with relief shipments of medical, surgical and
food supplies, but since the United States was not yet at war he
was discouraged from advertising its beneficiaries. On the 6th

and 7th he appeared in Chicago playing the Fourth Concerto, and Stock conducted the Symphony Orchestra in an all-Rachmaninoff programme which also included *Vocalise*, *The Isle of the Dead* and his Third Symphony. Typically, notwithstanding the size of the audience and his own tumultuous reception, Pollak in *Chicago Daily Times* was harsh:

> To listen to such a programme is like sitting down to a seven-course dinner with Beluga caviar for each course, Rachmaninoff no more deserves a concentrated evening than do Reger, Franck or Saint-Saëns and, in twenty years, he won't get one. The Third Symphony is magnificently plush, full of those overstuffed melodies, the drugged lyricism, the brief military passages marcato and those familiar rising chords of the ninth. As for the Fourth Concerto it is an unbelievably empty piece with a slow movement that sounds like an Alec Templeton improvisation on 'Three Blind Mice' and a finale devoid of anything but decoration.[18]

After playing it in five other cities, where its reception was no more enthusiastic, Rachmaninoff dropped it, only performing it once again at the recording session in December.

By 9 December, when he gave a recital in St Louis, President Roosevelt had declared war; there was no further need for equivocation. Although Rachmaninoff once declared that 'music can only succeed where there is peace and quiet', that did not stop him giving concerts. To continue his schedule however it was necessary for him to find a more fitting climate, and the result of his recent visits to California persuaded him to settle there. The Rachmaninoffs rented a Beverly Hills estate on Tower Road; a property with a pool, garden and a music room of sufficient size to be able to accommodate two grand pianos. The house was situated high up and enjoyed a magnificent view looking out across to the Pacific. It was here that Chasins arrived a little early for a visit one day:

as I approached I stood outside the door, unable to believe my ears. Rachmaninoff was practising Chopin's Etude in thirds [G sharp minor, Op. 25 No. 6], but at such a snail's pace that it took me a while to recognize it because so much time elapsed between each finger stroke and the next. Fascinated, I clocked this remarkable exhibition; twenty seconds per bar was his pace for almost an hour while I waited riveted to the spot, quite unable to ring the bell. Perhaps this way of developing and maintaining an unerring mechanism accounted for his later sarcasm towards colleagues who practised their programmes once over lightly between concerts.[19]

As we saw earlier, his technique of practising so very slowly had also made Arthur Hirst unable to recognise Liszt's *Waldesrauchen* when he heard him practising that. It accounts for the remarkable finish of his playing we hear in the movement from the Mozart sonata he recorded for Edison, and no doubt for Evgenia Somov's enthusiasm for his playing of the Czerny Sonata which she heard him practising.

At the end of February 1942 he went out to Victor's Hollywood studios and made his last recordings. On these, the quality is shallow and sounds cooped-up – as if he were playing an upright. One might call the selection *Pièces brèves*. It included his own transcriptions of: the Prelude, Gavotte and Gigue from Bach's Third Violin Partita;Tchaikovsky's Lullaby (the last transcription he would write); Kreisler's *Liebesfreud* and *Lilacs*. He also recorded transcriptions by Liszt of Schubert's Standchen and Chopin's *Madchens Wunsch* and *Die Heimkehr*; and by Tausig of Schumann's *Der Kontrabandiste*. The Horowitzs lived nearby and Vladimir would come round to play recitals of duets with Rachmaninoff. On one such occasion, on 15 June, they included Mozart's Sonata for two pianos (K. 447), Piano Concerto in D (K. 537) and Rachmaninoff's Second Suite for two pianos. Bertensson was one of those present: 'It is impossible to word my impression of this event. "Power" and "joy" are the two words that come to mind – expressive power, and joy experienced by the two players, each fully aware of the other's greatness. After the last note no one spoke – time seemed to have stopped.'[20] At another, they repeated the Mozart works, played Rachmaninoff's two piano transcription of the Symphonic Dances (after which there was some talk of their recording it, though they never did) and finished with *Polka Italienne*. One day that July they went together to Walt Disney's Studios; after sitting through the film *Mickey's Opry House*, in which Mickey Mouse plays the Prelude in C sharp minor, Rachmaninoff told its creator. 'I have heard my inescapable piece done marvellously by some of the best pianists, and murdered cruelly by amateurs, but never was I more stirred than by the great Maestro mouse!'[21]

By the end of July the Rachmaninoffs, finding that Beverly Hills suited them, decided to purchase a home of their own. They bought one in a residential neighbourhood, 610 Elm Drive, with a garden full of trees and flowers, though they did not move in until the following month. It was the fifth property Rachmaninoff had bought, and the only one he had managed to sell was in New York; Ivanovka had gone, Moscow had gone, Dresden had gone, and so too had Senar – at least as far as he was concerned. The only worry about the present political situation was, he joked, whether the Japanese might get to California. There seemed not much likelihood of that, but only a few nights later when the Rachmaninoffs were at a friend's house for dinner, the lights suddenly went out and an air-raid warning sounded. He was reassured when his host announced that it was only a test. In the darkness another of the guests, Julia Fatova, who had been in the Music Studio of the Moscow Arts Theatre, began to sing softly. When she had finished, in the hush, Rachmaninoff begged her not to interrupt the mood and, finding his way to the piano, accompanied her until the lights came back on.

Although he had come all the way to California, it was still not far enough: war news to the fore and the troublesome time permitted him no escape. In the pro-Soviet temper of the day, the radio broadcast Chaliapin in *Boris Godounov*, Rimsky-Korsakov's Russian Easter Overture and Stravinsky's *Firebird*. It must have been amazing to see how moved Rachmaninoff was even listening to Stravinsky – 'his eyes filled with tears, and he exclaimed – "Lord, how much genius there is in this – it is real Russia!"'[22] It was when Rachmaninoff told his neighbour Nicolai Mandrovsky how worried he was not hearing anything from his daughter in France that Mandrovsky told him about Stravinsky, living nearby in a similar situation, with his children in Paris. It was then that Rachmaninoff thought to invite Stravinsky to his house. No two composers, in spite of the fact that less than ten years separated them, could have written music more radically different. Stravinsky could not but respect Rachmaninoff as a pianist, but his scorn of his composition was no secret. Rachmaninoff, on the other hand, felt he had always admired *Firebird*; he seems to have forgotten his conversations with Bauer and Yasser only a few years previously and his scarcely concealed antipathy even to the music of Debussy and Scriabin, never mind Stravinsky.

When Stravinsky came to dine at the Rachmaninoffs', the pianist Arthur Rubinstein was also among the invited. There is something of the irrepressible Rubinstein in his telling of the tale, and when we consider that he was recalling this nearly forty years later it is surprising how accurate some of the details are. Rubinstein tells how Rachmaninoff was suffering from stomach ache, but more likely it was a symptom of his final illness:

> Swallowing a morsel of pressed caviar, Rachmaninoff addressed Stravinsky with a sardonic laugh. 'Ha-ha-ha your *Petrushka*, your *Firebird*, ha-ha, never gave you a cent of royalties – eh?' 'What about your C sharp Prelude and all those concertos of yours, all you published in Russia, eh? You had to play concertos to make a living, uh?' The ladies and I were terrified lest it might lead to a nasty scene between the two composers but, lo and behold, quite the contrary happened.

Both great masters began to count out the sums they could
have earned and became so involved in this important matter
that when we got up they retired to a small table and continued happily daydreaming of the immense fortunes they
might have earned. When we were leaving, they exchanged a
hearty handshake at the door and promised each other to find
more sums to think of.[23]

No doubt it was because of their isolation on the west coast of
the USA during the Second World War, that subjects born in
Imperial Russia – like Rachmaninoff, Stravinsky, Horowitz and
Rubinstein – were united by the political circumstances of the
day, despite their musical differences.

At the Hollywood Bowl concerts on 17 and 18 July
Rachmaninoff played in the open-air arena. Although consoled
by the large fee he earned, he was suffering from severe lum-
bago: 'While playing I had the unpleasant sensation that the cold
wind was blowing right through me.'[24] 'I could hardly stand up
and when I walked I looked like a comma.'[25] These were probably other symptoms of the illness he was already suffering from.
In a letter to Somov, he writes how difficult it had been securing
keys to the Elm Drive house from the previous owners. He also
suggests that for a house-warming they should send him fifty
glass cigarette-holders. No doubt this was his idea of a joke, but
it is surprising that he was still smoking considering his general
health. Three weeks later he went to the Hollywood Bowl again
to hear Horowitz play his Third Concerto. Although he seated
himself as far from the front as he could, afterwards he came all
the way down to the stage to tell Horowitz: 'This is the way I
have always dreamed that my concerto should be played, but I
never expected to hear it that way on earth.'[26]

On 23 August, he wrote to Mandrovsky: 'Yesterday I
received a telegram about Fokine's death. What a great sorrow!
Chaliapin, Stanislavsky, Fokine – there's an epoch in art!'[27] At
that time a quarter of a century had passed since the Russian

Revolution and deaths were coming fast. He was still some months from being seventy when he began his final concert season in Detroit on 12 October. Gentry in *The Evening News* jumped the gun:

> Although we know the number of opportunities left to hear this Titan of the keyboard are growing fewer – he is seventy-years-old now – yet there seems to be no faltering of his fingers, no weakening of his attack, no waning of his powers. The facility with which he can encompass the technical demands of the lightening passages in a Liszt bravura piece, for example, is something you can hardly bring your ear to believe.[28]

On 20 November, he played the Second Concerto at a Minneapolis concert under Mitropoulos. A month later, on 17 December, he appeared in New York, with Mitropoulos conducting the New York Philharmonic; he played the Rhapsody and the orchestra played the Symphonic Dances for the first time. 'The triumph of the evening was the fresh critical consideration given to the Dances in Mitropoulos's interpretation,' declared a critic.

Afterwards, a group of friends sought to improvise a party for Rachmaninoff to celebrate his jubilee. He expressed his pleasure when Steinway commemorated the occasion by sending him a new piano. For the next six weeks over Christmas, he interrupted his concert schedule and rested with his wife and daughter in New York. During that time *Life* photographer Eric Schall took a number of portraits of him, which confirm the disturbing pallor his complexion seems to have taken on. By the middle of January, he was complaining of fatigue and had a severe pain in his left side. For some time the Rachmaninoffs had heard nothing from Tatiana in France and news from Russia was at its most grim; German troops had plunged deep in Russia reaching Leningrad in the north and Stalingrad in the south. Unlike Napoleon, however, they never did manage to get to Moscow. Rachmaninoff resumed his concerts on 3 February at State College, Pennsylvania. Elena Somov wrote that she and her husband would be coming to the next concert at Columbus, Ohio on the 5th and notwithstanding Rachmaninoff's prevaricatory reply, so they did. Afterwards she wrote to him how shocked she had been by his general appearance. She advised him to give up concerts and devote himself to composition, but he told her he was too tired to write music. When she reminded him of the fire and inspiration he had shown in the Symphonic Dances, he replied that he did not know how that had happened – it must have been his last flicker.

In Chicago, he appeared with Hans Lange at Orchestra Hall playing Beethoven's First Concerto and his own Rhapsody – the last concerted music he wrote and the last he played in public. In Chicago he saw a doctor but was diagnosed with only slight pleurisy and neuralgia. He resumed his travels appearing at Louisville, Kentucky on the 15th. By this time, he felt so poorly that he was willing to cancel his next appearance (Knoxville, Tennessee) except that he had already postponed a concert there the previous season. So it was that he played his last recital at the Alumni Memorial Auditorium on the 17th at quarter past eight in the evening. The programme was as follows:

English Suite No. 2	Bach
Papillons (Op. 2)	Schumann
Second Sonata in B flat minor (Op. 35)	Chopin
Etudes-Tableaux:	Rachmaninoff
No. 4 in B minor (Op. 39)	
No. 2 in A minor (Op. 39)	
Etudes:	Chopin
No. 3 in E (Op. 3)	
No. 5 in E minor (Op. 25)	

| 'Magic Fire Music' (*Die Walküre*) | Wagner-Brassin |
| 'Spinning Chorus' (*Fliegende Holländer*) | Wagner-Liszt |

Encores:
Etudes: Liszt
No. 3 in D flat
Gnomenreigen

The next day, the Rachmaninoffs departed for Florida but only got as far as Atlanta when they were obliged to give up the effort. Instead they went to New Orleans where he could take a couple of days' respite before resuming their journey to Texas. When he arrived in New Orleans, however, he felt much worse and they decided it would be better to go straight to Los Angeles, where he could consult a Russian doctor. He had to wait three days in the Roosevelt Hotel before seats could be found on a train, war conditions being what they were. On the 22nd, he dictated letters to Seroff and to Rashevsky: 'I am very run down, the pains in my side seem stronger and I feel extremely weak,'[29] he told them. Eventually they departed but it took the train sixty hours before they finally reached Los Angeles, at nine in the evening on the 26th. It was necessary to send a telegram to advise the hospital when they would arrive. They were met by, he told Somov, 'two fellows who grabbed me under the arms and brought me here'.[30]

For the next three days Alexander Golizin, a Russian doctor from Moscow University, carried out tests but in the end he let Rachmaninoff return to Elm Drive, so depressed was he by the hospital surroundings. On 2 March, a Russian-speaking nurse having been found, he seemed to be at least calmer, although he continued to complain of increasing pains in his arms. In the course of the next few weeks his appetite decreased rapidly and swellings began to appear on his body. At length, in the middle of the month, a surgeon undertook a minor operation and carried out a thorough examination. It was soon discovered that he was suffering from a rapid type of cancer, known as melanoma, by this stage far too advanced for any surgery to be efficacious. His elder daughter, Irina, and his sister-in-law, Sophia, were summoned to California. News of his condition was kept from him although he deteriorated rapidly. For a time he could read but eventually his wife and daughter had to read to him, and he could only listen to the radio. He would worry about his younger daughter: 'I am afraid I shall not see her again'.[31] News from Russia had been better at least; the Red Army had retaken several towns and the German retreat had begun: 'Praise the Lord! God grant them strength,'[32] he murmured. He became increasingly weak and morphine was administered. Dr Golitzin believed that by this time he must have realised he was dying. Three days before his death he began to lose consciousness. He knew nothing of a telegram that arrived on the 22nd, signed by leading Soviet musicians, congratulating him on his birthday.[33] He died at half past one on the morning of 28 March 1943, four days before his seventieth birthday.

In the issue of *Musical Courier* on 5 April, eight days after his death, Rachmaninoff contributed to a symposium on the state of music conducted by Leonard Liebling. By so doing, as it were posthumously, he wrote his own valediction:

I feel like a ghost wandering in a world grown alien. I cannot cast out the old way of writing, and I cannot acquire the new. I have made intense efforts to feel the musical manner of today, but it will not come to me. I cannot cast out my musical gods in a moment and bend the knee to new ones. The new kind of music seems to me to come, not from the heart, but from the head. Its composers think rather than feel. They have not the capacity to make their music 'exult' as Hans von Bulow called it. They meditate, protest, analyze, reason, calculate, and brood – but they do not exult. It may be that they compose in the manner of the times, but it may be, too, that the spirit of the times does not call for expression in music.[34]

Born in pre-revolutionary Russia, Rachmaninoff was an unashamed romantic: cosseted from his youth, believing implicitly in the rightness of his views, brought up in a society long-since vanished. By the time of his death he had grown completely out of step with the world. This is reflected in the critical attitude to him when classical music was still thought a progressive art, but his could hardly be made to fit such a mould. As Eric Blom writes of Rachmaninoff in the fifth edition of *Grove's Dictionary of Music*, published in 1954:

> As a composer he can hardly be said to have belonged to his time at all ... Technically he was highly gifted, but also severely limited. His music is well constructed and effective, but monotonous in texture, which consists in essence mainly of artificial and gushing tunes accompanied by a variety of figures derived from arpeggios. The enormous popular success some few of Rachmaninoff's works had in his lifetime is not likely to last, and musicians never regarded it with much favour. The Third Piano Concerto was on the whole liked by the public only because of its close resemblance to the second.[35]

It took until long after the Second World War, by which time electric recording had had time to facilitate a more complete picture of the music of the past, for the idea to be questioned that although the passage of time causes music to change, it does not necessarily improve it. Today, the enormous popularity of many of Rachmaninoff's works is greater than ever – it is not so much the music that is severely limited but Blom's criticism. Blom should have remembered that prophecies are not for critics, but for seers and soothsayers.

Notes

Preface

1. *After* 1921, by which time he had established himself as a pianist, only at the end of his career did he give a few performances of *beethoven's* concerto in C (Op. 15), and one each of Liszt's *Totentanz* and Schumann's Concerto in A minor.
2. Samaroff, Olga in *New York Evening Post*, 20 Feb. 1927.
3. Chasins, Abram, *Speaking of Pianists*, p.45.
4. Cardus, Neville in *The Manchester Guardian*, 23 Nov. 1929.
5. The Complete Rachmaninoff: RCA 09026-61265-2.

Chapter 1: 1873–1885

1. This date is from the pre-revolutionary or the Julian calendar, which was used in Russia until 1918. By the nineteenth century, 'Old Style' [O.S.] as it is called, had fallen twelve days behind 'New Style' [N.S.].
2. Riesemann, Oscar von, *Rachmaninoff's Recollections*, p.4.
3. Ibid., p.11.
4. Bertensson, Sergei and Leyda, Jay. *Sergei Rachmaninoff: A Lifetime in Music*, p.4.
5. Apetyan, Z.A. (ed.), *Reminiscences about Rachmaninoff*, vol.1, p.41.
6. Riesemann, *Recollections*, p.5.
7. Olga Trubnikova to Varvara Satina, 1930.
8. Swan, Alfred and Katherine, 'Rachmaninoff: Personal Reminiscences' in *The Musical Quarterly*.

9.   L. Defert to Rachmaninoff, 5 Sep. 1934.

10. Apetyan, *Reminiscences*, vol.1, p.15.

11. Riesemann, p.12.

Chapter 2: 1885–1889

1.   Seroff, Victor, *Rachmaninoff*, p.14.

2   Walker, Bettina, *My Musical Experiences*, p.87.

3.   Ibid., p.88.

4.   Apetyan, Z.A. (ed.), *Literary Legacy*, vol.1, p.151.

5.   Riesemann, Oscar von, *Rachmaninoff's Recollections*, p.41.

6.   Apetyan, *Literary Legacy*, vol.1, p.150.

7.   Riesemann, *Recollections*, p.43.

8.   Ibid., pp 44–5.

9.   Ibid., p.47.

10. Seroff, *Rachmaninoff*, p.17.

11. Apetyan, vol.1, p.194.

12. Riesemann, p.50.

13. Ibid., p.49.

14. Ibid., p.51

15. Cooke, James Francis, *Great Pianists on Piano Playing*, pp 218–19.

16. Philip, Robert, *Performing Music in the Age of Recording*, p.172.

17. Although Sergei and Natalia Rachmaninoff did record live at a party his Italian Polka. Josef Hoffmann's many live recordings include: Golden Jubilee Concert, Carnegie Hall (28 Nov. 1937); Academy of Music, Philadelphia (4 Apr. 1938); Casimir Hall, Curtis Institute of Music, Philadelphia (7 Apr. 1938).

18. Hoffmann plays the orchestral version of the Andante Spianato (Op. 22) in the concert of 28 Nov. and the solo version in the recital of 4 Apr.

19. Riesemann, p.53.

20. Bertensson, Sergei and Leyda, Jay, *Sergei Rachmaninoff: A Lifetime in Music*, p.13.

21. Ibid., p.14.

22. Tchaikovsky's Diary, 8 Dec. 1886.

23. Ibid.

24. Bertensson and Leyda, *Sergei Rachmaninoff*, p.15.

25. Ibid., p.16.

26. Martyn, Barrie, *Rachmaninoff: Composer, Pianist, Conductor*, p.37.

27. This concert took place on 20 Oct. 1912.

28. Rimsky-Korsakov, Nikolay, *My Musical Life*, p.418.

29. Ibid., p.382.
30. Ibid., p.384.
31. Riesemann, pp 60–1.
32. Martyn, *Rachmaninoff*, p.40.
33. Bertensson and Leyda, p. 20.
34. Seroff, pp 30–1.
35. Bertensson and Leyda, p.27.

Chapter 3: 1889–1893

1. Rachmaninoff to Natalya Skalon, 10 Jan.1891.
2. Dictated reminiscences.
3. Not only Bertensson and Leyda, but also Martyn acknowledges her assistance.
4. Bertensson, Sergei and Leyda, Jay, *Sergei Rachmaninoff: A Lifetime in Music*, p.26.
5. Ibid., p.39.
6. Bukinik, Mikhail, 'Reminiscences of Young Rachmaninoff' in *Local 802*, May 1943.
7. Tzitovich (ed.), *Goldenweiser's reminiscences of S.V Rachmaninoff* (Moscow 1947).
8. Rachmaninoff to the Skalon sisters, 5 Feb. 1891.
9. Riesemann, Oscar von, *Rachmaninoff's Recollections*, p.31.
10. Rachmaninoff to Natalya Skalon, 26 Mar. 1891.
11. Ibid.
12. Rachmaninoff to the Skalon sisters, 31 May 1891.
13. Martyn, Barrie, *Rachmaninoff: Composer, Pianist, Conductor*, p.89.
14. Rachmaninoff to the Skalon sisters, 11 July 1891.
15. Rachmaninoff to Slonov, 20 July 1891.
16. Martyn, *Rachmaninoff*, p.49.
17. Seroff, Victor, *Rachmaninoff*, p.26.
18. Rachmaninoff to Natalya Skalon, 31 Oct. 1891.
19. Ibid., 7 Dec. 1891.
20. Apetyan, Z.A. (ed.), *Reminiscences about Rachmaninoff*, vol.1, p.23.
21. Rachmaninoff to Natalya Skalon, 18 Feb. 1892.
22. Ibid.
23. Dobuzhinsky M.V. (ed.), *Pamyati Rakhmaninova* (N.Y., 1946).
24. Martyn, p.48.
25. Apetyan, *Reminiscences*, vol.1, p.180.
26. Bertensson and Leyda, *Sergei Rachmaninoff*, pp 45–6
27. Apetyan, *Reminiscences*, vol.2, pp 405–6.

28. A.N.S. in *Dnevnik Artista*, Apr. 1892.
29. Avierino, N.K., 'Iz vospominanii o S.V. Rakhmaninov' in *Novyi Zhurnal*, XVIII, 1948.
30. Rachmaninoff to Slonov, 7 June 1892.
31. Rachmaninoff to Natalya Skalon, 10 June 1892.
32. Ibid., 2 Aug. 1892.
33. Ibid., 13 Oct. 1892.
34. *Artiste*, Nov. 1892.
35. Dobuzhinsky, *Pamyati Rakhmaninova*
36. Rachmaninoff to Slonov, 14 Dec. 1892.
37. Rachmaninoff to Natalya Skalon, 7 Feb. 1893.
38. S. Kruglikov in *Artiste*, May 1893.
39. Riesemann, *Recollections*, p.41.
40. Quoted in an article on Rachmaninoff by Fred Gaisberg in *Gramophone*, Aug. 1943.

Chapter 4: 1892–1897

1. Tchaikovsky to Modest Tchaikovsky, 17 Apr. 1893.
2. Rachmaninoff to Modest Tchaikovsky, 14 Oct. 1893.
3. Rachmaninoff to Chekhov, 9 Nov. 1898.
4. Bertensson, Sergei and Leyda, Jay, *Sergei Rachmaninoff: A Lifetime in Music*, p.60.
5. Ippolitov-Ivanov, *Russkoi Muzyki*, 50.
6. Rachmaninoff to Slonov, 3 Sep. 1894.
7. Rachmaninoff to the Skalon sisters, 3 Oct. 1893.
8. Bertensson and Leyda, *Sergei Rachmaninoff*, p.62.
9. Martyn, Barrie, *Rachmaninoff: Composer, Pianist, Conductor*, p.85.
10. Rachmaninoff to Natalya Skalon, 17 Dec. 1893.
11. Tanayev's Diary
12. Martyn, *Rachmaninoff*, 93.
13. Rachmaninoff to Zatayevich, 7 Dec. 1896.
14. Rachmaninoff to Slonov, 24 July 1894.
15. Rachmaninoff to Slonov, 17 July 1895.
16. Rachmaninoff to Slonov, 9 Nov. 1895
17. Riesemann, Oscar von, *Rachmaninoff's Recollections*, p.96.
18. Swan, Alfred J. and Katherine, 'Rachmaninoff: Personal Reminiscences' in *The Musical Quarterly*.
19. Ibid.
20. Riesemann, *Recollections*, p.106
21. Cui in *St Petersburg News*, 22 Jan. 1896.

22. Taneyev's Journal, Mar. 1896.
23. Sabaneyeff, 'Moi vstrechi: Rachmaninoff' in *Novoye Russkoye Slovo*, 28 Sep. 1952.
24. Martyn, p.111.
25. Taneyev's Diary, March 1896.
26. Taneyev to Belayev, 26 Oct. 1896.
27. Riesemann, p.98.
28. Ibid., p.99
29. Ibid.
30. Ibid.
31. Cui in *St Petersburg News*, 17 Mar. 1897.
32. Apetyan, Z.A. (ed.), *Reminiscences about Rachmaninoff*, vol.1, p.429.
33. Ibid., p.352.
34. Rachmaninoff to Zateyevich, 6 May 1897.
35. Riesemann, p.98.
36. Rachmaninoff to Asafiev, 13 Apr. 1917.

Chapter 5: 1897–1902

1. Seroff, Victor, *Rachmaninoff*, p.58.
2. Bortnikova, *Autographs of Rachmaninoff* in the archives of State Central Museum of Music Culture, Moscow.
3. *The Musical Times*, May 1899.
4. Swan, Alfred and Katherine, 'Rachmaninoff: Personal Reminiscences' in *The Musical Quarterly*.
5. Chaliapin, Feodor, *Man and Mask: Forty Years in the Life of a Singer*, p.186.
6. Swan, 'Rachmaninoff: Personal Reminiscences'.
7. Apetyan, Z.A. (ed.), *Reminiscences about Rachmaninoff*, vol.1, p.242.
8. Seroff, Victor, *Rachmaninoff*, p.59.
9. Riesemann, Oscar von, *Rachmaninoff's Recollections*, pp 106–7.
10. Ibid., p.108.
11. RCA 09026-61265-2-3.
12. Lipayev in *Russkaya Muzykalnaya Gazeta*, Jan. 1898.
13. The Headman in Rimsky-Korsakov's *May Night* and the Miller in Dargomizhsky's *Russalka*.
14. Dictated reminiscences by Rachmaninoff.
15. Chaliapin, Feodor, *Pages from My Life*, p.141.
16. Riesemann, *Recollections*, pp 111–12
17. Chaliapin, Feodor, *Man and Mask: Forty Years in the Life of a Singer*, p.114.
18. Dobuzhinsky M.V. (ed.), *Pamyati Rakhmaninova* (N.Y., 1946).

19. *The Times* (London), 21 Apr. 1899.
20. Rachmaninoff to Goldenweiser, 18 June 1898.
21. Martyn, Barrie, *Rachmaninoff: Composer, Pianist, Conductor*, p.122.
22. Riesemann, p.112.
23. Rachmaninoff to Morozov, 22 June [O.S.] or 5 July [N.S.] 1900.
24. Chaliapin, *Pages*, p.155.
25. Rachmaninoff to Morozov, 9/22 July 1900.
26. Martyn, *Rachmaninoff*, p.121.
27 Lipayev in *Russkaya Muzykalnaya Gazeta*, No. 55, 1900.

Chapter 6: 1902–1906

1. Anna Trubnikova in *Ogonyok*, No. 4, 1946.
2. Rachmaninoff to Morozov, 4 June 1902.
3. Ibid., 17 June 1902.
4. Engel in *Russkiye Vedomosti*, 10 Feb. 1903.
5. Schorr to Rachmaninoff, 29 July 1929.
6. Ibid.
7. Rachmaninoff to Morozov, 18 Aug. 1903.
8. Riesemann, Oscar von, *Rachmaninoff's Recollections*, p.130.
9. Chaliapin, Feodor, *Pages from My Life*, p.130.
10. Ibid., pp 210–11.
11. Seroff, Victor, *Rachmaninoff*, p.72.
12. Martens, Frederick H., *Little Biographies: Rachmaninoff*.
13. Kruglikov, Semyon, 'Bolshoi Theatre' in *Novosti Dnya*, 5 Sep. 1904.
14. Apetyan, Z.A. (ed.), *Reminiscences about Rachmaninoff*, vol.2, p.350.
15. Ibid., vol.1, p.423.
16. Rachmaninoff to Morozov, 4 Aug. 1904.
17. Riesemann, *Recollections*, pp 131–2.
18. Swan, Alfred J. and Katherine, 'Rachmaninoff: Personal Reminiscences' in *The Musical Quarterly*.
19. Riesemann, pp 127–8.
20. Rimsky-Korsakov, Nikolay, *My Musical Life*, p.415.
21. Engel in *Russkiye Vedomosti*, 14 Jan. 1906.
22. Riesemann, p.131.
23. Apetyan, *Reminiscences*, vol.1, p.359.
24. Ibid., vol.2, p.35.
25. Telyakovsky, Imperatorsky Teatri, 1905.
26. Rachmaninoff to Morozov, 27 Apr. 1906.
27. Ibid., 17 May 1906.
28. Trubnikova in *Ogonyok*, No. 4, 1946

29. Rachmaninoff to Morozov, 18 Aug. 1903.
30. Rachmaninoff to Kerzin, 2 Aug. 1906.
31. Rachmaninoff to Morozov, 22 Aug. 1906.

Chapter 7: 1906–1909

1. Rachmaninoff to Morozov, 9 Nov. 1906 [N.S.].
2. Ibid.
3. Ibid.
4. Ibid.
5. Ibid., 11 Feb. 1907 [N.S.]
6. Martyn, Barrie, *Rachmaninoff: Composer, Pianist, Conductor*, p.181.
7. Kuznetsov, Constantin, 'Rakhmaninov's Creative Life' in *Sovyetskaya Muzyka*, No 4, 41, 1945.
8. Rachmaninoff to Morozov, 13 Apr. 1907.
9. Ibid.
10. Ibid., 5 May 1907.
11. Haskell, Arnold, *Serge Diaghileff*, p.174.
12. Riesemann, Oscar von, *Rachmaninoff's Recollections*, p.146.
13. Ibid.
14. Swan, Alfred J. and Katherine, 'Rachmaninoff: Personal Reminiscences' in *The Musical Quarterly*.
15. Riesemann, *Recollections*, p.151.
16. Engel in *Russkiye Vedomosti*, 3 Feb. 1908.
17. Rachmaninoff to Morozov, 12 Apr. 1908.
18. *The Times* (London), 28 May 1908.
19. Rachmaninoff to Stanislavsky, 14 Oct. 1908.
20. Engel in *Russkiye Vedomosti*, 19 Oct. 1908.
21. Rachmaninoff to Morozov, 26 Nov. 1908.
22. Ibid., 2 Dec. 1908.
23. Ibid., 11 Dec. 1908.
24. Ibid.
25. Ibid., 6 June 1909.
26. Rachmaninoff to Slonov, 1 Jan. 1909.
27. Rachmaninoff to Morozov, 21 Mar. 1909.
28. Chereshev in *Moscovskiye vedomosti*, 16 Apr. 1909.
29. Basanta Roy in *Musical Observer*, May 1927.
30. Martyn, Barrie, *Rachmaninoff: Composer, Pianist, Conductor*, p.206.
31. Details of Toscanini's relations with Puccini can be found in many different biographies. Those with Strauss are highlighted in the dispute over the

Italian premiere of *Salome*. Toscanini was originally to have conducted it in
the 1905/06 season at the Regio, Turin (the theatre had secured the rights)
but by that time Toscanini had moved to La Scala, Milan. He insisted that
wherever he went, so too would *Salome*. However, the Regio was not
prepared to relinquish it and Toscanini was obliged to wait another four
days, so Strauss himself conducted the premiere in Turin on 22 December.
Strauss went to the Milan performance and wrote to his wife: 'In Milan
the *Kappelmeister* performed a symphony without singers; at Turin, on
the contrary, the orchestra accompanies and one understands the singers'
every word.' Strauss's Salome was Gemma Bellincioni, who by that time
had only a shred of voice, whereas Toscanini had Salomea Kruczelnicka,
a singer of noted vocal worth. Although Toscanini continued to conduct Strauss's tone poems, this was the only time he ever conducted a
Strauss opera.

32. O'Connell, Charles, *The Other Side of the Record*, p.168.
33. Rachmaninoff to Morozov, 6 June 1909.
34. Yasser, J., 'Progressive Tendencies in Rachmaninoff's music' in *Tempo*,
    winter 1951/2.
35. Rachmaninoff to Yasser, 30 Apr. 1935.
36. 'Vladimir Horowitz introduced by Phillip Ramey' in *The Chicago Sun-
    Times*, 29 Nov. 1977.
37. Culshaw, John, *Sergei Rachmaninov*, p.75.

Chapter 8: 1909–1911

1. Bertensson, Sergei and Leyda, Jay, *Sergei Rachmaninoff: A Lifetime in Music*,
   p.161.
2. Aldrich, Richard in *The New York Times*, 4 Nov. 1909.
3. Hale, Philip, *The Boston Symphony Orchestra Notes*, 1909/10.
4. Aldrich, Richard in *The New York Times*, 21 Nov. 1909.
5. *The New York Times*, 6 Jan. 1929
6. Henderson, W.J. in *The Sun* (New York), 1 Dec. 1909.
7. Rachmaninoff to Zoya Pribitkova, 12 Dec. 1909.
8. Riesemann, Oscar von, *Rachmaninoff's Recollections*, pp 159–60.
9. Aldrich, Richard in *The New York Times*, 28 Jan. 1910.
10. Bertensson and Leyda, *Sergei Rachmaninoff*, p.165 and Seroff, Victor,
    Rachmaninoff, p.114.
11. Prokofiev, Grigori in *Russkiye Vedomosti*, 6 Apr. 1910.
12. Rachmaninoff to Morozov, 4 June 1910.
13. Ibid., 31 July 1910.

14. Apetyan, Z.A. (ed.), *Reminiscences about Rachmaninoff*, vol.1, p.133.
15. *Russkaya Muzykalnaya Gazeta*, 3 Apr. 1911
16. Rachmaninoff to Morozov, 31 July 1910.
17. Martyn, Barrie, *Rachmaninoff: Composer, Pianist, Conductor*, p.227.
18. Ibid., p.228.
19. Rachmaninoff in *Russkiye Vedomosti*, 21 Nov. 1911.
20. Avierino, N.K., 'Iz vospominanii o S.V. Rakhmaninove' in *Novyi Zhurnal*, XVIII, 1948.
21. Rachmaninoff to Provitkova, 9 Aug. 1911.
22. Riesemann, *Recollections*, p.237. (As Martyn notes, Riesemann confuses the opus numbers).
23. Martyn, *Rachmaninoff*, p.232.
24. *The Times* (London), 14 Oct. 1911.
25. Engel in *Russkiye Vedomosti*, 15 Dec. 1911.

Chapter 9: 1912–1914

1. Bertensson, Sergei and Leyda, Jay, *Sergei Rachmaninoff: A Lifetime in Music*, p.165 and Seroff, Victor, *Rachmaninoff*, p.176.
2. Shaginyan in *Novy Mir*, IV, 1943.
3. Rachmaninoff to Shaginyan, 15 Mar. 1912.
4. Ibid., 29 Mar. 1912.
5. Ibid., 28 Apr. 1912.
6. Ibid., 8 May 1912.
7. Prokofiev, Grigory in *Russkiye Vedomosti*, 21 Oct. 1912.
8. Sabaneyeff, Leonid in *Golos Moskvi*, 21 Oct. 1912.
9. Apetyan, Z.A. (ed.), *Reminiscences about Rachmaninoff*, vol.2, p.300.
10. Engel in *Russkiye Vedomosti*, 24 Oct. 1912.
11. Rachmaninoff to Shaginyan, 12 Nov. 1912.
12. Busoni, Ferrucio, Letters to his Wife, 19 Nov. 1912.
13. Bauer, Harold, *His Book*, p.213.
14. Riesemann, Oscar von, *Rachmaninoff's Recollections*, pp 170–1.
15. Martyn, Barrie, *Rachmaninoff: Composer, Pianist, Conductor*, p.242.
16. The only opera Mengelberg conducted was a concert performance of Strauss's *Der Rosenkavalier*.
17. Rachmaninoff to Shaginyan, 29 June 1913.
18. Tyuneyev, Boris in *Russkaya Muzykalnaya Gazeta*, Dec. 1915.
19. Rachmaninoff to Shaginyan, 29 June 1913.
20 Ibid., 30 Aug. 1913.
21. Linitzki in *Russkaya Muzykalnaya Gazeta*, Jan. 1914.

22. Karatygin in *Rech*, 24 Nov. 1913.
23. Tyuneyev in *Russkaya Muzikalnaya Gazeta*, Dec. 1914.
24. Rachmaninoff, *Autobiographical Sketches*.

Chapter 10: 1914–1917

1. After the outbreak of the First World War St Petersburg was renamed Petrograd.
2. Rachmaninoff to Yasser, 30 Apr. 1935.
3. Riesemann, Oscar von, *Rachmaninoff's Recollections*, p.177.
4. Martyn, Barrie, *Rachmaninoff: Composer, Pianist, Conductor*, p.261.
5. Rachmaninoff to Siloti, 1 Nov. 1914.
6. Goleyzovsky to Rachmaninoff, 22 Apr. 1915.
7. Apetyan, Z.A. (ed.), *Reminiscences about Rachmaninoff*, vol.2, pp 148–9.
8. Ibid., p.304.
9. Ibid., p.305
10. Riesemann, *Recollections*, p.182.
11. Ibid., pp 180–1.
12. Apetyan, *Reminiscences*, vol.2, p.411.
13. Ibid., p.157.
14. Prokofiev, Grigori in *Russkaya Muzykalnaya Gazeta*, 6 Dec. 1915.
15. Yasser, Josef in *Novoya Russkoye Slovo* (New York), 22 Feb. 1931
16. Martyn, *Rachmaninoff*, p.182.
17. Avierino, N.K., 'Iz vospominanii o S.V. Rakhmaninov' in *Novyi Zhurnal*, XVIII, 1948.
18. Rachmaninoff to the Editor of *Russikiye Vedomosti*, 7/16 June 1915
19. Ibid., pp 151–2.
20. Rachmaninoff to Shaginyan, 20 Sep. 1916.
21. Scott, Michael, *The Record of Singing*, vol 2, p.25.
22. Rachmaninoff to Koshetz, 1 Sep. 1916.
23. Engel in *Russkiye Vedomosti*, 25 Oct. 1916.
24. Rachmaninoff to Koshetz, 22 Dec. 1916.
25. Apetyan, vol.2, p.155.
26. Engel in *Russkiye Vedomosti*, 5 Dec. 1916.
27. Sabaneyev in *Muzykalni Sovremennik*, 23 Dec. 1916.
28. Riesemann, pp 182–3.
29. Culshaw, John, *Sergei Rachmaninov*, pp 39–40.
30. Riesemann, pp 184–5.
31. Rachmaninoff to Siloti, 1 June 1917.
32. Riesemann, p.187.

33. Seroff, Victor, *Rachmaninoff*, p.161.
34. Ibid., p.162.

Chapter 11 : 1917–1920

1. All dates now are given in N.S.
2. Rachmaninoff, Autobiographical sketches.
3. Martyn, Barrie, *Rachmaninoff: Composer, Pianist, Conductor*, p.292.
4. Seroff, Victor, *Rachmaninoff*, p.165.
5. Searle, Humphrey, *Franz Liszt*, p.442.
6. Huneker in *The New York Times*, 21 Nov. 1919.
7. Dobuzhinsky M.V. (ed.), *Pamyati Rakhmaninova* (N.Y., 1946).
8. Hale, Philip in *The Boston Herald*, 16 Dec. 1918.
9. Parker, H.T. in *Boston Evening Transcript*, 16 Dec. 1918.
10. Huneker in *The New York Times*, 22 Dec. 1918.
11. Hale, Philip in *The Boston Herald*, 23 Feb. 1919.
12. Huneker in *The World* (New York), 30 Jan. 1919.
13. Rosenfeld in *The New Republic*, 15 Mar. 1919.
14. Bertensson, Sergei and Leyda, Jay, *Sergei Rachmaninoff: A Lifetime in Music*, pp 219–20.
15. Downes, Olin in *The Boston Post*, 26 Nov. 1939.
16. Sanborn, Pitts in *The Evening Telegram* (New York), 11 Feb. 1920.
17. Bertensson and Leyda, *Sergei Rachmaninoff*, p.221.
18. Philip, Robert, *Performing Music in the Age of Recording*, p.33.
19. The dates of birth of Chaliapin and Rachmaninoff are also given in N.S.

Chapter 12 : 1920–1924

1. Bertensson, Sergei and Leyda, Jay, *Sergei Rachmaninoff: A Lifetime in Music*, p.222.
2. Riesemann, Oscar von, *Rachmaninoff's Recollections*, p.198.
3. Martyn, Barrie, *Rachmaninoff: Composer, Pianist, Conductor*, p.294.
4. Rachmaninoff to Avierino, 1 Nov. 1920.
5. Rachmaninoff to Medtner, 29 Oct. 1921.
6. Ibid., 15 Nov. 1921.
7. Martyn, *Rachmaninoff*, p.295.
8. Hale in *The Boston Herald*, 8 Dec. 1921.
9. *Lincoln State Journal*, 24 Jan. 1922.
10. H.T. Parker in *Boston Evening Transcript*, 20 Feb. 1922.
11. *The Observer* (London), 7 May 1922.

12. Rachmaninoff to Dagmar Rybner, May 1922.
13. Rachmaninoff to Medtner, 25 Aug. 1922.
14. Rachmaninoff to Wilshaw, 9 Sep. 1922.
15. Stanislavsky to Rachmaninoff, 26 May 1922.
16. Rachmaninoff to Evgeni Somov, 27 Jan. 1923.
17. Bertensson, 'Rachmaninoff as I knew him' in *The Etude*, March 1948.
18. Gliere-Wilshaw cantata, Rachmaninoff Archive, Library of Congress.
19. Morozov to Rachmaninoff, 1 Dec. 1922 and 4 Mar. 1923, Rachmaninoff to Morozov, 15 Apr. 1923.
20. Ostromislensky in *Novoye Russkoye Slovo* (New York), 18 Dec. 1932.
21. Rachmaninoff to Morozov, 18 Nov. 1923.
22. Ibid., 15 Dec. 1923.
23. Rachmaninoff to the Somovs, 12 May 1924.
24. Culshaw, John, *Sergei Rachmaninov*, p.161.
25. Martyn, p.299.

Chapter 13: 1924–1927

1. Rachmaninoff to Wilshaw, 21 Aug. 1924.
2. *New Orleans Item*, 21 Jan. 1925.
3. Flower, Elsie in *The Stockton Evening Record*, 23 Feb. 1925.
4. Rachmaninoff to Wilshaw, 16 May 1925.
5. Rachmaninoff to Evgeni Somov, 24 Jan. 1925.
6. Rachmaninoff to Wilshaw, 16 May 1925.
7. Ibid., 2 July 1925.
8. Rachmaninoff to Dagmar Rybner, 8 Sep. 1925.
9. Parker, H.T. in *Boston Evening Transcript*, 9 Nov. 1925.
10. Dobuzhinsky M.V. (ed.), *Pamyati Rakhmaninova* (N.Y., 1946).
11. Martyn, Barrie, *Rachmaninoff: Composer, Pianist, Conductor*, p.63.
12. Rachmaninoff to Medtner, 14 Jan. 1926.
13. Ibid., 9 Sep. 1926.
14. Medtner to Rachmaninoff, 13 Sep. 1926
15. Samaroff, Olga in *New York Evening Post*, 20 Feb. 1927.
16. Stokes, Richard in *The Evening World* (Philadelphia), 23 Mar. 1927.
17. Martyn, *Rachmaninoff*, p.309.
18. Gilman, Lawrence in *The New York Herald Tribune*, 23 Mar. 1927.
19. Sanborn, Pitts in *The Evening Telegram* (New York), 23 Mar. 1927.
20. Chotzinoff in *The World* (New York), 23 Mar. 1927.
21. Rachmaninoff to Julius Conus, 28 Jul. 1927.

Chapter 14: 1927–1930

1. Blumenfeld to Rachmaninoff, 28 Dec. 1921
2. Vladimir Horowitz, interview by Phillip Ramey in *The New York Times*, 29 Nov. 1977.
3. Ibid.
4. Chasins, Abram, *Speaking of Pianists*, p.137.
5. Sleeve note by Charles Foley, RCA LVT 1009.
6. Rachmaninoff, 'The Artist and the Gramophone' in *Gramophone*, Apr. 1931.
7. Lochner, Louis P., *Fritz Kreisler*, pp 265–6.
8. Rachmaninoff to Kreisler, 11 Jan. 1929.
9. Sleeve note, Scott, HMV HLM 7062.
10. Newman, Ernest in *The Sunday Times* (London), 27 May 1928.
11. Bertensson, Sergei and Leyda, Jay, *Sergei Rachmaninoff: A Lifetime in Music*, p.253.
12. Rachmaninoff to the Somovs, 17 June 1928.
13. Olga Conus, 'Memories of a Personal Friend' in *Clavier*, Oct. 1973.
14. *8 Uhr Abendblatt*, 10 Nov. 1928.
15. Paul Zschorlich in *Deutsche Zeitung*, 23 Nov. 1928.
16. Walter Damrosch in *The New York Times*, 23 Dec. 1928.
17. Holmes in *The Evening News* (Detroit), 6 Feb. 1929.
18. Rachmaninoff to Evgeni Somov, 7 Feb. 1928.
19. Memorandum of Alexander Greiner, 29 Mar. 1929.
20. Rachmaninoff to Somov, 30 May 1929.
21. Riesemann, Oscar von, *Rachmaninoff's Recollections*, p.5.
22. Rachmaninoff to the Somovs, 3 Nov. 1929.
23. Neville Cardus in *The Manchester Guardian*, 25 Nov. 1929.
24. Rachmaninoff to Respighi, 2 Jan. 1930.
25. Rachmaninoff to Hoffmann, 14 Jan. 1930.
26. Hoffmann to Rachmaninoff, 4 Apr. 1930.
27. Swan, Alfred J. and Katherine, 'Rachmaninoff: Personal Reminiscences' in *The Musical Quarterly*.

Chapter 15: 1930–1932

1. Henderson in *The Sun* (New York), 16 Feb. 1930.
2. Swan, Alfred J. and Katherine, 'Rachmaninoff: Personal Reminiscences' in *The Musical Quarterly*.

3. Martyn, Barrie, *Rachmaninoff: Composer, Pianist, Conductor*, p.404.
4. Rachmaninoff to Evgeni Somov, 24 Mar. 1930.
5. Hoffmann to Rachmaninoff, 4 Apr. 1930.
6. Rachmaninoff to Evgeni Somov, 25 Apr. 1930.
7. Ibid., 13 June 1930.
8. Swan, 'Rachmaninoff: Personal Reminiscences'.
9. Ibid.
10. Bertensson, Sergei and Leyda, Jay, *Sergei Rachmaninoff: A Lifetime in Music*, pp 299–300.
11. Bertensson and Leyda, *Sergei* Rachmaninoff, pp vi–vii.
12. Seroff, Victor, *Rachmaninoff*, p.194.
13. Bertensson and Leyda, p.300.
14. Ibid.
15. Riesemann, Oscar von, *Rachmaninoff's Recollections*, p.10.
16. *The New York Times*, 15 Jan. 1931.
17. *Vechernaya Moskva*, 9 Mar. 1931.
18. *Pravda*, Mar.(?) 1931.
19. Cushing, Edward in *Brooklyn Daily Eagle*, 29 Mar. 1931.
20. *The New York Times*, 8 Apr. 1931.
21. Yasser, Joseph in *Novoye Russkoye Slovo* (New York), 10 Nov. 1931.
22. Ibid.
23. Martyn, *Rachmaninoff*, p.317.
24. Prokofiev, Materiali dokumenti, vospominaniya, p.287.
25. Howell, Ruth in *Washington Daily News*, 6 Nov. 1931.
26. Rachmaninoff to Medtner, 21 Dec. 1931.
27. Swan, 'Rachmaninoff: Personal Reminiscences'.
28. Horowitz interview by Phillip Ramey in *The New York Times*, 29 Nov. 1977.
29. *Horowitz plays Rachmaninoff*: CBS 72940 (UK); *Horowitz Concerts 1979/80*: RCA RL 13775 (Germany).
30. Rachmaninoff to Sophia Satina, 8 Aug. 1931.
31. Swan, 'Rachmaninoff: Personal Reminiscences'.
32. Dobuzhinsky M.V. (ed.), *Pamyati Rakhmaninova* (N.Y., 1946).
33. Gunn in *Chicago Herald and Examiner*, 15 Jan. 1932.
34. Rachmaninoff to Evgeni Somov, 5 Apr. 1932.
35. Swan, 'Rachmaninoff: Personal Reminiscences'.
36. De Geynst in *La Nation Belge*, 6 May 1933.
37. Rachmaninoff to the Somovs, 15 Aug. 1932.
38. *The Star* (London), 1 May 1933.
39. *The New York Times*, 11 Dec. 1932.
40. Apetyan, Z.A. (ed.), *Reminiscences about Rachmaninoff*, vol.1, pp 108–9.

Chapter 16: 1932–1936

1. Thompson in *New York Evening Post*, 23 Dec. 1932.
2. Bertensson, Sergei and Leyda, Jay, *Sergei Rachmaninoff: A Lifetime in Music*, p.298.
3. Rachmaninoff to Evgeni Somov, 9 May 1933.
4. Medtner in *Rossiya Slavyanstvo*, 1 May 1933.
5. *New York Evening Post*, 26 Dec. 1933.
6. *The New York Times*, 31 Mar. 1934.
7. Ibid.
8. Rachmaninoff to the Somovs, 14 Mar. 1934.
9. Wilshaw to Rachmaninoff, 8 May 1934.
10. Horowitz interview by David Dubal WNCN, New York, February 1980.
11. Rachmaninoff to Sophia Satina, 19 Aug. 1934.
12. Seroff, Victor, *Rachmaninoff*, pp 187–8.
13. Chotzinoff in *New York Evening Post*, 5 Nov. 1934.
14. Henderson in *The Sun* (New York), 3 Nov. 1934.
15. Liebling to Rachmaninoff, 3 Nov. 1934.
16. *Musical Courier*, 17 Nov. 1934.
17. Rachmaninoff to the Somovs, 14 Nov. 1934.
18. Simon, Robert in *The New Yorker*, 12 Jan. 1935.
19. Abram Chasins to Rachmaninoff, 28 Dec. 1934.
20. Philip, Robert, *Performing Music in the Age of Recording*, pp 172–3
21. Rachmaninoff to Rybner-Barclay, 4 May 1935.
22. Rachmaninoff to Evgeni Somov, 22 Aug. 1935.
23. Rachmaninoff to Sophia Satina, 26 Sep. 1935.
24. Rachmaninoff to Wilshaw, 27 Sep. 1935.
25. Rachmaninoff to Amram Scheinfeld, Dec. 1937.
26. Ilf and Petrov, *Little Golden America*, trans. Malamuth, 1937.
27. Sherman in *The Star* (Minnealopis), 30 Nov. 1935.
28. Swan, Alfred J. and Katherine, 'Rachmaninoff: Personal Reminiscences' in *The Musical Quarterly*.
29. *The Times* (London), 31 Mar. 1936.
30. Rachmaninoff to Wilshaw, 15 Apr. 1936.
31. Rachmaninoff to Ormandy, 11 May 1936.
32. Stokowski to Rachmaninoff, 20 May 1936.
33. O'Connell, Charles, *The Other Side of the Record*, p.167.
34. Rachmaninoff to Sophia Satina, 30 June 1936.
35. Rachmaninoff to the Somovs, 5 July 1936.
36. Wood in *Sheffield Festival Programme*, 1936.
37. Schloss in *The Philadelphia Record*, 7 Nov. 1936.

38. Haggin in *Brooklyn Daily Eagle*, 11 Nov. 1936.

39. Downes in *The New York Times*, 11 Nov. 1936.

40. *The New York Times*, 8 Nov. 1936.

41. Rachmaninoff to Wilshaw, 7 June 1937.

42. Newton, Ivor, *At the Piano*, p.156.

43. Khubov in *Pravda*, 26 July 1943.

Chapter 17: 1937–1939

1. Chasins, Abram, *Speaking of Pianists*, p.77.

2. Frankenstein in *The San Francisco Chronicle*, 6 Feb. 1937.

3. *Dublin Evening Mail*, 26 Mar. 1938.

4. Hazen in *The Morning Oregonian*, 23 Jan. 1937.

5. *The Minneapolis Star*, 30 Nov. 1935.

6. *The Evening News* (Detroit), 5 Feb. 1937.

7. Rachmaninoff to Evgeni Somov, 19 Jan. 1936.

8. Rachmaninoff to Wilshaw, 7 June 1937.

9. Wilshaw to Rachmaninoff, 18 June 1937.

10. Rachmaninoff to Sophia Satina, 30 June 1937.

11. Rachmaninoff to Wilshaw, 7 June 1937.

12. Fokine to Rachmaninoff, 30 June 1937.

13. Rachmaninoff to Fokine, 29 Aug. 1937.

14. Fokine to Rachmaninoff, 9 Sep. 1937.

15. King in *The Sun* (New York), 13 Oct. 1937.

16. Abram Chasins to Rachmaninoff, 2 Dec. 1937.

17. Sleeve notes by Abram Chasins, *The Four Rachmaninoff Concertos*: RCA Victor: LM-6123.

18. Ibid.

19. Chasins to Satina, 27 Oct. 1948.

20. Gray-Fiske in *Hampstead News and Advertiser*, 12 Mar. 1938.

21. Wood to Rachmaninoff, 26 Nov. 1937.

22. Wood, Henry, *My Life of Music*, p.350.

23. Ibid., p.349.

24. Rachmaninoff to Sophia Satina, 3 Aug. 1939.

25. Rachmaninoff to the Somovs, 27 Mar. 1938.

26. Rachmaninoff to Sophia Satina, 20 Apr. 1938.

27. Rachmaninoff in *Posledniye Novosti* (Paris), 17 Apr. 1938.

28. Swan, Alfred J. and Katherine, 'Rachmaninoff: Personal Reminiscences' in *The Musical Quarterly*.

29. Rachmaninoff to Somov, 29 July 1938.

30. Rachmaninoff to the Somovs, 31 July 1938.

31. Frankenstein in *The San Francisco Chronicle*, 19 Nov. 1938.

32. Rachmaninoff to Somov, 30 Nov. 1938.

33. Agate, James in *Ego 4*, 11 Mar. 1939.

34. *The Times* (London), 1 July 1939.

35. Fokine to Rachmaninoff, 30 June 1939.

36. Rachmaninoff to the Somovs, 2 Apr. 1939.

37. Ibid., 5 July 1939.

38. Rachmaninoff to Somov, 3 Aug. 1939

Chapter 18 : 1939–1943

1. *The Philadelphia Inquirer*, 9 Dec. 1939.

2. Downes in *The New York Times*, 27 Nov. 1939.

3. Ibid., 11 Dec. 1939.

4. J.F. Williamson to Rachmaninoff, 20 Dec. 1939.

5. R.R. Bennett to Sergei Bertensson and Jay Leyda, 29 Oct. 1949.

6. Rachmaninoff to Ormandy, 21 Aug. 1940.

7. Apetyan, Z.A. (ed.), *Reminiscences about Rachmaninoff*, vol.1, p.103.

8. Fokine to Rachmaninoff, 23 Sep. 1940.

9. Apetyan, *Reminiscences*, vol.1, p.103.

10. E. Arnold in *New York World-Telegram*, 17 Oct. 1940.

11. McLauchlin, R. in *The Evening News* (Detroit), 15 Oct. 1940.

12. V. Spence in *Havana PM*, 8 Jan. 1941.

13. Bertensson, Sergei and Leyda, Jay, *Sergei Rachmaninoff: A Lifetime in Music*, p.363.

14. Downes in *The New York Times*, 8 Jan. 1941.

15. Pollak in *Chicago Daily Times*, 14 Mar. 1941.

16. O'Connell, Charles, *The Other Side of the Record*, p.168.

17. Schloss in *The Philadelphia Record*, 18 Oct. 1941.

18. Pollak in *Chicago Daily Times*, 7 Nov. 1941.

19. Sleeve notes by Abram Chasins, *The Four Rachmaninoff Concertos*: RCA Victor: LM-6123.

20. Bertensson and Leyda, *Sergei Rachmaninoff*, pp 370–1.

21. *Musical Courier*, July 1942.

22. Bertensson and Leyda, p.373.

23 Rubinstein, Arthur, *My Many Years*, p.490.

24. Rachmaninoff to Evgeni Somov, 24 July 1942

25. Rachmaninoff to Mandrovsky, 29 June 1942.

26. *The Milwaukee Journal*, 13 Apr. 1943.

27. Rachmaninoff to Mandrovsky, 23 Aug. 1942.

28. Gentry in *The Evening News* (Detroit), 13 Oct. 1942.

29. Rachmaninoff to Rashevsky, 22 Feb. 1943.

30. Rachmaninoff to Evgeni Somov, 27 Feb. 1943.

31. Seroff, Victor, *Rachmaninoff*, p.205.

32. Bertensson and Leyda, p.383.

33. Which suggests that it had been forgotten that Soviet Russia had by then moved over to the Gregorian calendar, for his birthday was not until 1 April [N.S.].

34. Rachmaninoff (ed. Leonard Liebling) in *Musical Courier*, 5 Apr. 1943.

35 *Grove's Dictionary of Music and Musicians,* 10 vols (London, 1954).

Bibliography

This list includes the works that I have most often referred to. The main sources for quotations from Rachmaninoff's correspondence are the five volumes edited by Apetyan and documentary evidence included in The Rachmaninoff Archive in the Library of Congress. Further bibliographic information is to be found in Palmieri's research guide, and Threfall and Norris give a complete listing of his compositions. I should particularly like to express my gratitude to Barrie Martyn for his generous assistance to me personally, as well as for his *Rachmaninoff: Composer, Pianist and Conductor,* a work of encyclopædic length, depth and detail.

Apetyan, Z.A. (ed.), *Literary Legacy*, 3 vols. (Moscow, 1978/80).
Apetyan, Z.A. (ed.), *Reminiscences about Rachmaninoff*, 2 vols. (Moscow, 1988).
Asafyev, Boris, *Selected Works*, vol. 2. (Moscow, 1954).
Bauer, Harold, *His Book* (New York, 1948).
Bazhanov, Nikolai, *Rachmaninov* (Moscow, 1983).
Bertensson, Sergei and Leyda, Jay, *Sergei Rachmaninoff: A Lifetime in Music* (New York, 1956).
Busoni, Feruccio, *Feruccio Busoni* (Oxford, 1932).
Chaliapin, Feodor and Gorky, Maxim, *An Autobiography as Told to Maxim Gorky*, trans. and ed. by Nina Froud and James Hanley (London, 1968).
Chaliapin, Feodor, *Man and Mask: Forty Years in the Life of a Singer* (London, 1935).
Chaliapin, Feodor, *Pages from My Life* (London, 1937).
Chasins, Abram, *Speaking of Pianists* (New York, 1957).
Cooke, James Francis, *Great Pianists on Piano Playing* (Philadelphia, 1913).

Culshaw, John, *Sergei Rachmaninov* (London, 1949).

Gaisberg, Fred, *Music on Record* (London, 1946).

Haskell, Arnold, *Serge Diaghileff* (London, 1957).

Horowitz, Joseph, *Understanding Toscanini* (New York, 1987).

Keldish, Y.V., *Rachmaninoff and His Times* (Moscow, 1973).

Lambert, Constant, *Music Ho!* (London, 1937).

Lochner, Louis P., *Fritz Kreisler* (London, 1951).

Martyn, Barrie, *Rachmaninoff: Composer, Pianist, Conductor* (London, 1990).

Medtner, Nicolai, *The Muse and the Fashion, being a defence of the foundations of the art of music*, trans. Alfred J. Swan (Haverford, PA, 1951).

Montagu-Nathan, M., *Contemporary Russian Composers* (London, 1917).

Newton, Ivor, *At the Piano* (London, 1966).

O'Connell, Charles, *The Other Side of the Record* (New York, 1927).

Palmieri, Robert, *Sergei Vasil'evich Rachmaninoff: A Guide to Research* (New York, 1985).

Piggott, Patrick, *Rachmaninoff's Orchestral Music* (London, 1974).

Plaskin, Glenn, *Horowitz: A Biography* (New York, 1983).

Riesemann, Oskar von, *Rachmaninoff's Recollections* (London, 1934).

Rimsky-Korsakov, Nikolay, *My Musical Life*, trans. J.A. Joffe (New York, 1923).

Rubinstein, Anton, Autobiography, trans. A. Delano (Boston, 1890).

Rubinstein, Arthur, *My Many Years* (New York, 1980).

Sabaneyev, Leonid R. in *Modern Russian Composers*, trans. J.A. Joffe (London, 1927).

Schonberg, Harold C., *The Virtuosi: Classical Music's Legendary Performers from Paganini to Pavarotti* (New York, 1985).

Scott, Michael, *The Record of Singing*, vols. 1 and 2 (London, 1977 and 1979).

Scott, Michael, *The Great Caruso* (New York, 1988).

Searle, Humphrey, *The Music of Liszt* (London, 1954 and 1966).

Seroff, Victor, *Rachmaninoff* (London, 1951).

Sorabji, Kaikhosru, *Around Music* (London, 1932).

Stanislavski, Constantin, *My Life in Art* (London, 1924).

Swan, Alfred J., *Russian Music* (London, 1973).

Swan, Alfred J. and Katherine, 'Rachmaninoff: Personal Reminiscences' in *The Musical Quarterly*, vol.30, January 1944, pp 1–19; May 1944, pp 174–91.

Threlfall, Robert and Norris, Geoffrey, *A Catalogue of the Compositions of S. Rachmaninoff* (London, 1982).

Tierney, Neil, *The Unknown Country: A Life of Igor Stravinsky* (London, 1977).

Walker, Robert, *Rachmaninov: His Life and Times* (New York, 1978).

Wood, Henry, *My Life of Music* (London, 1938).

Index